Mind Bugs

Learning, Development, and Conceptual Change
Lila Gleitman, Susan Carey, Elissa Newport, and Elizabeth Spelke, editors

Names for Things: A Study in Human Learning, John Macnamara, 1982

Conceptual Change in Childhood, Susan Carey, 1985

"Gavagai!" or the Future History of the Animal Language Controversy, David Premack, 1986

Systems That Learn: An Introduction to Learning Theory for Cognitive and Computer Scientists, Daniel N. Osherson, 1986

From Simple Input to Complex Grammar, James L. Morgan, 1986

Concepts, Kinds, and Cognitive Development, Frank C. Keil, 1989

Learnability and Cognition: The Acquisition of Argument Structure, Steven Pinker, 1989

Mind Bugs: The Origins of Procedural Misconceptions, Kurt VanLehn, 1990

Mind Bugs

The Origins of Procedural Misconceptions

Kurt VanLehn

A Bradford Book
The MIT Press
Cambridge, Massachusetts
London, England

This book was typeset by Asco Trade Typesetting Ltd. Hong Kong
and printed and bound in the United States by Halliday Lithograph.

Library of Congress Cataloging-in-Publication Data

VanLehn, Kurt.
  Mind bugs : the origins of procedural misconceptions / Kurt VanLehn.
    p. cm.—(Learning, development, and conceptual change)
  Includes index.
  ISBN 0-262-22036-9
  1. Learning, Psychology of. 2. Cognition in children.
3. Subtraction. 4. Machine learning. 5. Artificial intelligence.
I. Title. II. Series.
FB318.V36 1989
153.1'5—dc20   89-12493
                                                     CIP

For JSB

Contents

Series Foreword

This series in learning, development, and conceptual change includes state-of-the-art reference works, seminal book-length monographs, and texts on the development of concepts and mental structures. It spans learning in all domains of knowledge, from syntax to geometry to the social world, and is concerned with all phases of development, from infancy through adulthood.

The series engages such fundamental questions as

The nature and limits of learning and maturation: the influence of the environment, of initial structures, and of maturational changes in the nervous system on human development; learnability theory; the problem of induction; domain specific constraints on development.

The nature of conceptual change: conceptual organization and conceptual change in child development, in the acquisition of expertise, and in the history of science.

Lila Gleitman
Susan Carey
Elissa Newport
Elizabeth Spelke

Preface

This book owes much to my mentor, John Seely Brown, who launched me on this line of research and supported me while I pursued it. The book itself was substantially improved by close readings from Alan Collins and Jeff Shrager. Many people read early drafts of it, including Hal Abelson, Peter Andrea, Richard Burton, Stu Card, Johan de Kleer, Andy DiSessa, Steve Purcell, and Patrick Winston. I deeply appreciate all this excellent help.

The nucleus of this work was my Ph.D. dissertation, which was submitted to MIT in 1983 (Xerox Palo Alto Research Center technical report CIS-21). The data base used in that research, which consists of error data from several thousand subjects, has been retained, but the theory developed there has been completely overhauled, with new hypotheses that rest more firmly on empirical evidence.

Thanks are due to the Cognitive Sciences Program of the Office of Naval Research for funding this research and to Xerox Corporation for providing the research facilities. Jamesine Friend organized the field study whose data plays a central role in supporting the theory. Richard Burton is the author of Debuggy, a data analysis program that was absolutely essential to the research. Most of all I would like to thank my wife, Micki Chi, for her advice and encouragement. Quite literally this book would not have been written without it.

Mind Bugs

Chapter 1
Introduction

Most theories in the physical sciences are *nomological*. They state laws, often in the form of equations or constraints, from which testable assertions are derived deductively. Classical mechanics is a prototypical example of a nomological theory. On the other hand most theories in cognitive psychology are *systematic* (Haugeland 1978). They state a system of representations and procedures whose execution yields testable behaviors. Anderson's Act* theory is a prototypical example (Anderson 1983). Both systematic and nomological theories have general, abstract assumptions from which concrete, testable predictions are derived. For nomological theories the derivation is a kind of deduction. For systematic theories it is a kind of computation. However, systematic theories hold that the derivation process itself models a process occurring in the real world. Nomological theories make no such claim about their derivations.

The theory presented herein is *generative*. A generative theory is like a systematic theory in that it has a system of representations and procedures whose execution yields testable behaviors. This derivational process, however, is *not* claimed to be a model of any process occurring in the real world. In this respect a generative theory is like a nomological theory because neither of them claims that their derivational processes model real-world processes.

The prototypical generative theories are theories of natural-language syntax of the kind pioneered by Noam Chomsky (Chomsky 1965). A Chomskyan theory typically has three parts: a representation language for grammars, an acquisition function, and an interpretation function. The acquisition function should be able to take a large sample of the sentences in any natural language and output a grammar. The grammar is a formal expression in the representation language posited by the theory. When the interpretation function is given the grammar, it should be able to generate (or parse) any sentence in the natural language. Thus far it sounds as if the theory were systematic: it has two "processes" and a representation of knowledge.

However, the acquisition function is not really viewed as describing the actual mental processes of learning a language, and the interpretation function is taken as bearing only a dim resemblance, if any, to the psychological processes of generating or understanding natural language. Strictly speaking, the whole ensemble is properly viewed in the same way as the mathematical equations of a nomological theory are viewed: they deductively imply some testable assertions about the syntax of sentences. Sometimes generative theories even use lawlike constraints to define their acquisition and interpretation functions (for examples a noun phrase can move anywhere subject to the following constraints . . .). As in standard nomological theorizing, linguists try to find a small set of general laws/constraints. It is considered an advance to find a new law from which several older laws can be derived deductively.

The theory to be presented is a generative theory of mathematical skills. In form it is analogous to a Chomskyan theory of syntax. In place of a natural language, this theory has an algorithm, such as subtracting two multidigit numbers. The algorithm is not thought of as a single object, however, but rather as an infinite set of problem-solution pairs, just as a natural language is viewed as an infinite set of sentences. In place of a grammar this theory has a procedure, which is an expression in a theoretically posited representation language. There is an acquisition function that takes in a formalized version of the training given to the students and outputs a procedure. (Actually, because students often do not acquire the same procedure even when they are given the same training, the acquisition function produces a variety of procedures.) There is an interpretation function that takes a procedure and a problem as input and produces a solution to the problem.

As in linguistic theories, the internal machinations of the acquisition function are not taken as describing the psychological process of learning a procedure. Similarly the interpretation function is related to the psychological processes of problem solving only in that it generates the same solution paths as subjects do. The internal parts of the interpretation function (for examples, its working memory) are not viewed as models of cognitive structures or processes.

Insofar as possible the functions and representation language posited by this theory are specified by lawlike statements, which are labeled *assumptions* in the sequel (although *hypotheses* is sometimes used just to break the monotony). The relationships between the theory's assumptions and its predictions are worked out by embedding the assumptions in a computer program, named Sierra, and executing the program. The data structures produced by Sierra are the theory's predictions about the given situation; the processes used by Sierra to produce those predictions are psychologically meaningless.

In short this theory is a generative theory that is quite similar in form to a Chomskyan theory of syntax. This type of theory is, I believe, a novelty in the problem-solving and skill-acquisition literature, where almost all theories since at least Newell and Simon's (1972) have been systematic.

Although there has been a great deal of discussion about the merits of the generative approach (see, for instance, Chomsky 1965, Pylyshyn 1973, Marr 1977, Anderson 1990), the majority opinion seems to be that generative theories are simply a tool in the cognitive scientist's arsenal. Although generative theories often yield insights into cognition, they are certainly not the only means of obtaining insights. Of course the only way to find out if an investigative tool will yield new insights is simply to try it. That is exactly what this research sets out to do: to apply the tool of generative theorizing to a novel domain of inquiry, the learning of mathematical skills.

Having introduced the form of the theory, it is time to introduce its content.

It has often been assumed that knowledge for solving arithmetic problems, such as $837 - 129$, is extremely simple to acquire and use. A common assumption is that such knowledge is represented as a mental program—an expression in some mental language whose syntactic form determines its application. A second assumption is that such mental programs are learned by memorization[1] and practice-driven compilation. A third assumption is that mental programs for an algorithm are distinct from the logical justification, design, or teleology of the algorithm; students often know the program, but do not understand its design or justification. Newell and Simon (1972, p. 822) summarized these common beliefs when they made the following claim about the acquisition of algorithms:

> (1) At the outset the algorithm is followed by reference, step by step, to a recipe stored in external memory. (2) The recipe is memorized (stored internally), but still has to be executed by step-by-step interpretation. (3) The memorized recipe is "mechanized"—that is to say, compiled in the internal language of programs, so that it can now be executed directly and without interpretation. (4) More or less independently of the previous sequence, an understanding may be acquired of the logical justification for the algorithm—of why it works. Observe that a high level of mechanization can be achieved in executing the algorithm, without any evidences of understanding; and a high level

of understanding can be achieved at a stage where the algorithm still has to be followed from an externally stored recipe (The latter is likely to be true only of relatively elaborate algorithms—e.g., the simplex algorithm for linear programming.)

For arithmetic algorithms the general finding is that few students learn the justification of the algorithm, even if they master the procedural components (this finding is discussed in the next chapter). This has led to two lines of research. One line, associated with education, seeks ways to help students learn the justifications. The other line, associated with psychology, seeks a theory of how students learn procedures. The research I present is along the psychological line. Its aim is a theory of how procedures are actually acquired, rather than a method for teaching a deep, meaningful understanding of algorithms.

Until recently the leading theory of procedure acquisition was the memorize-compile theory outlined in the first three steps of the Newell and Simon quote. Several formal models of this theory were developed and tested in the task domains of arithmetic algorithms (Badre 1972), puzzles (Hayes and Simon 1974), and geometry (Anderson 1982).

In the late 1970s a phenomenon was uncovered that could not be easily explained by the memorize-compile theory. Brown, Burton, and their colleagues showed that many students have buggy procedures, where a buggy procedure is a correct procedure with one or more small perturbations, or *bugs*, installed in it (Brown and Burton 1978, Burton 1982, VanLehn 1982). In a sample of 1,325 subjects, the Brown group found 75 distinct primitive bugs occurring in hundreds of combinations. Similar studies have uncovered 68 bugs in the fraction arithmetic (Tatsuoka 1984), 57 bugs in integer arithmetic (Tatsuoka and Baillie 1982), and dozens of bugs in linear equation solving (Sleeman 1982, Sleeman 1984a) and in writing Lisp programs (Anderson 1988).

What made these findings surprising is not the mere fact that bugs existed. Educators have always assumed that some errors, the "systematic" ones, come from defective knowledge, whereas others come from unintended actions during execution, or *slips* as Norman (1981) calls them. There was a tendency to assume, however, that sloppy execution often cooccurred with defective knowledge and that defective knowledge might even be the result of practice-driven compilation of slips. This view of bugs is consistent with the memorize-compile theory of procedure acquisition.

The bug data showed conclusively that the supposed cooccurrence of bugs and slips did not actually exist. Many students were found who executed their buggy procedures meticulously—some would even give the same wrong answers, digit for digit, when tested at one-week intervals using the same twenty-problem test (VanLehn 1982). However, many of these performances *appear* random because (1) there are many rare bugs, which occur only in the performance of one or two subjects out of a thousand, and (2) most bugs depend on idiosyncratic features of the problems (for example, omit a borrow if the column to be borrowed from has two zeros in it). Thus educators often overlooked students' bugs and wrongly attributed their errors to slips. It was only when computer-based diagnostic programs, such as Burton's Debuggy program (Burton 1982) or Sleeman's LMS (Sleeman 1982), were applied to the data that these rare and idiosyncratic bugs were detected. The investigators, aware that they were challenging time-honored traditions in education, always applied conservative criteria for systematicity, and only classified a behavior as buggy when the null hypothesis (slips) was extremely improbable.

The memorize-compile theory is not supported by the lack of correlation between bugs and slips, but it is not refuted by it either. It could be that students who flawlessly execute buggy procedures have simply practiced their buggy procedures so much that slips, which were once plentiful and caused the bugs, have now virtually disappeared from the students' performance. The real difficulty presented by the bug data, however, is not the lack of cooccurrence of bugs and slips. The real difficulty lies deeper, in the characteristics of the individual bugs themselves.

Initially it appeared that the memorize-compile theory could explain the characteristics of individual bugs. If bugs are just compiled slips, then the kinds of slips students make should correspond exactly to the kinds of bugs they have. Suppose that students' slips are due to imperfect memorization of the list of steps that constitute the procedure. If memorizing a list of steps is similar to memorizing a list of words, one would expect bugs to correspond to the types of errors seen in experiments on verbal learning, that is, omissions, permutations, or intrusions. That is, one would expect to see students omitting a step, permuting the orders of adjacent steps, blending the components of steps, or including steps from other similar procedures. A model along thses lines was proposed by Young and O'Shea (1981). They used productions to represent steps. Imperfect memorization was simulated by deleting productions, permuting the components of a production (for example, changing the production for $N - 0 = N$ into $0 - N = N$), and adding productions from addition. The model was partly successful in that it could explain some of the most common bugs in subtraction. Later analysis using improved bug data, however, showed that it could account for only 13 percent of the 75 known subtraction bugs (see chapter 7).

Simple models of memory failure are based on information loss of various kinds. Sometimes parts of the target information are lost (for example, steps are omitted from a procedure). Other times information is lost that is needed for unambiguous access to the target information, leading to retrieval of the wrong information (for example, when steps for addition appear in a subtraction procedure) or inability to retrieve anything at all. The inadequacies of Young and O'Shea's model are due to the basic assumption that information loss is the cause of bugs. The problem is that many bugs have conditions and actions that simply do not appear in *any* arithmetic algorithm, so a model based on loss of information due to imperfect memorization cannot explain these bugs.

Perhaps it is not the memorization process that is causing the bugs, but some other process of the memorize-compile theory. According to that theory, there were four processes involved in procedure acquisition and execution:

1. *Memorization* of external recipes, which produces a declarative version of the procedure
2. Problem solving by *interpretation* of the declarative version of the procedure
3. *Compilation* of the declarative version into a procedural version
4. Problem solving by *direct execution* of the procedural version.

It is usually assumed that interpretation and direct execution only read the procedure; they do not change it. Compilation is assumed to be correctness preserving. So the only process that can cause bugs appears to be the memorization process, and the foregoing analysis of Young and O'Shea'a work has already ruled out memorization as the sole source of bugs because it is not powerful enough to explain all bugs (although it does a fair job of predicting the most common ones). It appears that the memorize-compile theory is incomplete.

The theory presented in this book is based on several modifications to the four-process model. The first modification is merely to simplify the model by ignoring the procedural-declarative distinction. Thus there will be no model of compilation in this theory, nor will the interpretation and direct execution processes be distinguished. Instead there is simply an acquisition function that creates a procedure, and an interpretation function that solves problems using the procedure. To put it in terms of the four processes, the memorization process (1) has been relabeled "acquisition" to accommodate some different assumptions about its character. The interpretation process (2) and the direct execution process (4) have been merged and labeled "interpretation." The compilation process (3) has been omitted. The resulting model is simpler because it has only two parts: an acquisition function and an interpretation function. This modification to the four-process model is intended only as a simplification, not as a denial of the reality of the procedural-declarative distinction. This simplification is needed to allow a clearer focus on the important modifications to the memorize-compile theory, which are presented next.

The first important modification is to assume that the execution of cognitive procedures is not exactly like the execution of computer procedures. When people reach an impasse, perhaps because their procedure directs that they perform an impossible action, they do not simply halt and issue an error message, as a computer would. Rather they consider the impasse itself to be a problem and try to solve that. In a test-taking situation they use simple strategies, such as deciding to skip the goal or action being attempted at the time of the impasse. These operations are called *repairs*. Since the original proposal of impasses and repairs (Brown and VanLehn 1980), Newell, Laird, Rosenbloom, and their colleagues have demonstrated that the basic idea of treating an impasse as a "metalevel" problem has extraordinary generality (Laird, Newell, and Rosenbloom 1987, Newell 1990). This modification to the memorize-compile theory is discussed further in chapter 2.

The second modification to the memorize-compile theory is the assumption that learning of subtraction procedures (and perhaps other procedures as well) is driven not by natural-language recipes but instead by examples of the execution of the to-be-acquired procedure. For instance, an example might consist of a problem whose solution is printed in the textbook or the sequence of writing actions of a teacher or peer, perhaps annotated with comments like "I'm taking the 5 from the 7" that explain some of the primitive computations. Other recent theories of skill acquisition also assume that examples, rather than natural-language recipes, drive the learning process (e.g., Anzai and Simon 1979, Anderson, Farrell, and Saurers 1984). Chapter 4 is devoted to the examples-versus-recipes issue.

When subjects learn from examples of a procedure's execution, they face two challenges. The first is that an example is only an instance of the procedure's execution, so the learner must generalize in order to form a procedure. For instance, one can see that a borrow was performed for $34 - 17$ and that $4 < 7$ in the units column. But is $<$ the right test, or is $\leq$ a better generalization? Is it always the units column that should be tested, or does it have something to do with the position of the borrow's actions?

The second challenge stems from the fact that an example can only demonstrate parts of a procedure that happen to be relevant to the example's problem. For instance, if a procedure has an "if-then-else" statement, the "then" part might be used on one example, and the "else" part might be used on another, but never can both be used at exactly the same time. Thus to obtain a complete procedure, a learner must integrate parts of the procedures that have been extracted from several examples. For instance, if two examples seem to have distinct solution paths, then the learner has to figure out what kind of condition branch is required and where to place it in the procedure's structure. In short the two challenges, that face someone learning from examples are *generalization* and *integration*.

The theory's account of how people solve the generalization and integration problems has the characteristic form of explanations from generative theories. In this case the formal explanation consists of specifying a representation language for procedures then describing the acquisition function as all possible expressions in the language that are consistent with the training examples and obey certain constraints. Although the acquisition function is introduced more fully in a few pages, a gloss of its main assumptions follows:

1. The representation language is a specially crafted production system language.
2. "Consistency with an example" means that the given production system's solution path for the example's problem is the same as the example's solution path.
3. The main constraint on generalization is that the conditions of productions are as specific as possible—if they were made any more specific, the production system would fail to be consistent with the examples. Specificity is determined by a certain measure based on the syntax of the production system language.
4. The main constraint on integration is that the acquired production system has as few productions as possible or equivalently, given the types of training used, that the production system has at most one production per lesson. (This is a particularly coarse and inaccurate rendition of the actual assumption made by the theory.)

These assumptions are, with one exception, roughly similar to those made by other theories of skill acquisition. Assumption 1 is common to Soar (Laird, Newell, and Rosenbloom 1987), Act* (Anderson 1983, Anderson, Farrell, and Saurers 1984, Anderson and Thompson 1986), and many other cognitive models (Klahr, Langley, and Neches 1987). The particular production system proposed in this theory however, has some unusually tight restrictions on the use of working memory. Chapter 3 presents the representation and the motivations for its various features.

The assumptions that people learn from examples (assumption 2) and tend to generalize the examples as little as possible (assumption 3) are implicit in several models of skill acquisition. For instance, when Soar learns, it includes in the acquired productions all the information to which it referred in generating a solution to that part of the example (Laird, Rosenbloom, and Newell 1986). Contextual information that is present but not referenced is not included in the acquired productions. Like Soar this model includes all the referenced information, but unlike Soar it includes contextual information whenever that information is constant across all the the examples (but there are some caveats to this—see chapter 6). Act* has a complicated generalization-discrimination-strengthening mechanism whose tendencies to generalize or specialize cannot be easily estimated without running the model (Anderson 1983, Anderson, Kline, and Beasley 1979). Chapter 6 is devoted to the generalization problem.

The treatment of the integration problem (assumption 4) is perhaps the most novel part of the acquisition theory. In fact most contemporary theories of skill acquisition duck the integration problem entirely. They do not specify in any simple way how subprocedures learned at distinct times are integrated. Instead integration occurs as a by-product of compilation. In Soar, Act*, and most other contemporary models of skill acquisition, productions (or their equivalents) are created by automatic "compilation" processes as the production system runs. Exactly how training that is presented at different times is integrated depends on exactly when and how productions are compiled, and that depends in turn on details of the cognitive architecture and the way the training is presented. So these theories make no simple statement about how subskills are integrated when learning a complex, multipart skill. Thus the fact that this theory explicitly addresses the integration problem makes its treatment of acquisition novel. The integration problem is discussed in depth in chapter 5.

This theory's typical explanation for a bug differs significantly from the typical explanation used in the memorize-compile model. In this theory the prototypical "bug story" has the acquisition function generating a procedure that either lacks productions or has overly specific productions. For instance, the procedure may have no code for borrowing, or its borrowing code may be so specific that it works properly only on certain types of borrows. This imperfection causes an impasse. A variety of bugs may be generated, differing only in how the impasse was repaired. This type of explanation is very different from the forgetting-based explanations offered by the memorize-compile theory.

The impetus behind revising the memorize-compile theory is explaining the surprising variety of bugs found in the bug data. As mentioned previously, a model based on imperfect memory generates 13 percent of the known bugs. In one particularly rigidly controlled demonstration, presented in chapter 7, it is shown that this theory can explain 33 percent of the known bugs, including almost all of the most common bugs. Hand simulation indicates that a more liberal use of parameters would allow the model to explain up to 85 percent of the observed bugs. In addition to explaining more bugs than the memorize-compile theory, this theory successfully predicts that specific patterns of bugs will appear. For instance, it predicts that some students will have the same underlying procedure, but may repair its impasses differently at different times. This would make it appear as if they were shifting among several different bugs. Such *bug migrations* have been found.[2]

On balance the most novel prediction that this theory has to offer concerns the causal relationships between training and bugs. These relationships are large-scale phenomena in that the causes for a particular bug may be distributed over a several-year interval. The generative theory used here, which substitutes nomologically defined functions for mechanistic-process models, is the key to making this direct connection. When the theory is freed from the constraint of mentioning only psychologically plausible processes, it can capture regularities in large-scale behavior much more easily.

Unfortunately there are not many data on large-scale learning behavior, other than bugs, that are appropriate for testing this theory. For instance, to predict the power law of practice (Rosenbloom and Newell 1981), wherein the speed of performance increases as the power of the number of trials of practice, would require a fine-grained model of execution whose speed could be measured, and the theory does not specify such a model. To predict the retention of procedures over long periods of time, the theory would need a model of memory. Although it might seem that transfer data could be used to test the theory's predictions, closer examination indicates that they are not all that useful either.[3]

As it currently stands, the empirical test of the theory consists only of its prediction of bug data. However, the bug data are extraordinarily rich and difficult to explain. The analogy with linguistics is quite apt here. It might seem as if predicting the set of syntactic structures that occurs in English is so easy that it offers little constraint on a theory of grammar. Indeed simple models, such as the one taught in high-school grammar courses, suffice for analyzing a large number of syntactic structures, including most of the commonly occurring ones. But accounting for the remaining ones is extremely difficult. Those residual syntactic structures have been used successfully for years in differentiating and testing linguistic theories. Similarly it is easy to explain many of the most common bugs, but difficult to explain the others. Thus as in linguistics the bug data are often sufficient to settle important theoretical issues, as demonstrated in the arguments that run throughout this book.

Sometimes it may seem that this theory is a viable alternative to Act*, Soar, or other theories of the cognitive architecture. Although it omits specifying most of the essential components of a cognitive architecture, such long-term memory, working memory, and compilation, it does use many of the same technical constructions, such as productions, goals, and so on. However, many of the similarities are only superficial. For instance, it will turn out that the interpretation function of this theory has a stack as its working memory. Act* and Soar also have stacks. Their stacks, however, are intended to represent the contents of the subject's working memory; questions of retrieval and capacity are germane. The stack used in this theory is a formal entity, whose relationship to the contents of human memory is unknown and unimportant. Because this theory has rather different objectives from its predecessors (that is, it is a generative theory, and its predecessors are systematic theories), it does not make sense to compare them point by point.

More to the point I do not think that such a comparison could be done. Architectural theories, as Newell (1990) points out, are good at explaining medium-scale phenomena, which last from 100 ms to 10 s. For phenomena larger than that, such as problem solving or procedure acquisition, the explanation tends to fall increasingly on the structure of the task domain rather than on the idiosyncrasies of the particular architecture that is performing the task. If we were to try Act*, Soar, and other architectural theories as explanations of bug acquisition, we would have to specify the task domain to them, then let them run for thousands of cycles. Depending on how we specify that task domain, we could probably cause them to fail or succeed at predicting the bug data. Thus the bug data are not a fair test of their power, and, as already noted, this theory makes no contact with the medium-scale phenomena that are appropriate tests for architectural theories. So the theories are simply incommensurate.

There is one detail left, and that is to name this theory. The earliest investigations into the origins of bugs yielded a theory of procedural problem solving called *Repair Theory* (Brown and VanLehn 1980). Subsequently a learning theory was added to Repair Theory, yielding an integrated explanation for the *acquisition* of correct and buggy procedures (VanLehn 1983a). Although the learning theory once had its own name, Step Theory, the two theories have become so intertwined that I now just consider them two aspects of the same theory. Following the tradition in systematic theorizing, the combined theory is named after the computer program associated with it, Sierra. When necessary to distinguish them, I refer to "Sierra's theory" or "the Sierra program."

In summary the goal of this research is to understand how people acquire procedural skills in instructional settings and in particular how they acquire bugs and bug migrations. The method used to obtain this goal is imported from linguistics, which makes it a novelty in the literature on cognitive skill acquisition. Another novel aspect of the theory is its treatment of the integration problem. The notion of impasse-driven problem solving was once novel, but has become quite widespread recently.

The remainder of this chapter completes the introduction of the theory. Section 1.1 describes the task domain in general terms and the bugs that are found among students of that task domain. Section 1.2 describes the theory's methodological objectives and introduces Sierra, the computer program that is used to generate the theory's predictions. Following that is a section that sketches the theory's assumptions and their support. The last section brings this esoteric rendition of the theory's claims down to earth with an example of how the theory explains the acquisition of a few specific bugs.

1.1 Learning Elementary Arithmetic Skills

The ultimate goal of this research is to understand how people learn cognitive skills in instructional settings. The long-term research strategy is to begin by studying a particular skill, then if all goes well, to test the theory's generality on other skills. The initial studies focused on how elementary-school students learn ordinary, written arithmetic calculations.

The main advantage of arithmetic procedures, from a methodological point of view, is that they are virtually meaningless to most students. They seem as isolated from commonsense intuitions as the nonsense syllables used in the Ebbinghaus paradigm for studying verbal learning. In the case of the subtraction algorithm, for example, most elementary-school students have only a dim conception of its underlying semantics, which is rooted in the base-ten representation of numbers (Resnick 1982, VanLehn and Brown 1980, VanLehn 1986). When compared with the procedures students use to make change or play games, arithmetic procedures are as dry, formal, and isolated from everyday interests as nonsense syllables are different from real words. This isolation is the bane of teachers, but a boon to psychologists. It allows psychologists to study a skill that is much more complex than recalling nonsense syllables, and yet it avoids bringing in a whole world's worth of associations. Other skills, such as algebra equation solving, programming, and college physics, are also quite isolated from common sense. The methodological advantages of these task domains are so great that all the major computational theories of skill acquisition address formal, common-sense-free task domains, even though they risk lack of generality by doing so.

This section introduces the arithmetic task domain. First it presents the instruction that students receive then the behavior they produce. The theory's main job is to explain what kinds of mental structures are acquired by that instruction and how those structures guide the production of the observed behavior.

1.1.1 Learning Procedures from Lesson Sequences of Examples and Exercises
In a typical American school, arithmetic procedures are taught incrementally via a lesson sequence that extends over several years. In the case of subtraction there are about ten lessons that introduce new material. These lessons introduce the procedure incrementally, one step per lesson, so to speak. For instance, the first lesson of the multicolumn curriculum might show how to do subtraction of two-column problems. The second lesson demonstrates three-column problem solving. The third introduces borrowing, and so on. The ten lessons are spread over about three years, starting in the late second grade (that is, at about age seven). These lessons are interwoven with lessons on other topics, as well as many lessons for reviewing and practicing the material introduced by the ten lessons.

In the classroom a typical lesson lasts about an hour. The teacher solves some problems on the board with the class, then the students solve problems on their own. If they need help, they ask the teacher, or they refer to worked examples in the textbook. A textbook example consists of a sequence of captioned "snapshots" of a problem being solved (see 1.1). Textbooks have very little text explaining the procedure, perhaps because some young children do not read well. Textbooks contain mostly examples and exercises.

Take a ten to make 10 ones.	Subtract the ones.	Subtract the tens.
$\overset{2\ 15}{\cancel{3}\cancel{5}}$	$\overset{2\ 15}{\cancel{3}\cancel{5}}$	$\overset{2\ 15}{\cancel{3}\cancel{5}}$
-19	-19	-19
	6	16

1.1
A typical textbook example

When students learn arithmetic, they learn more than just an algorithm for solving problems. In particular, students who have mastered arithmetic calculation must know the number facts (for example, that $3 + 5 = 8$) and the syntax of arithmetic notation. Arithmetic syntax is not particularly complex. It amounts to knowing that digits should be grouped into columns and rows, but not, say, into diagonals. For algebra and other mathematical calculi, the notational syntax is more complicated. It is assumed that each kind of knowledge has its own distinctive structure (format) and is learned in its own distinct way.

The theory's goal is to describe the structure and acquisition of just one of the types: knowledge of the problem-solving algorithm. For the other types—number facts and notational syntax—the structure and even the content will simply be stipulated.

1.1.2 Describing Systematic Errors with Bugs

All of the many empirical studies of arithmetic errors separate systematic errors from slips (Buswell 1926, Brueckner 1930, Brownell, 1941, Roberts 1968, Lankford 1972, Cox 1975, Ashlock 1976, Brown and Burton 1978, VanLehn 1982). Systematic errors appear to stem from consistent application of a faulty method, algorithm, or rule. Slips are unsystematic "careless" errors (for example, fact errors, such as $7 - 3 = 5$). Because slips occur in expert performance as well as student behavior, the common view is that they are due to inherent "noise" in the human information processor. Systematic errors on the other hand are taken as stemming from mistaken or missing knowledge, the product of incomplete or misguided learning. Only systematic errors are used in testing the present theory.

The distinction between errors that are based on flawed knowledge (bugs) and errors that are caused by "random noise" (slips) is fundamental to everything that follows. Although all investigators of arithmetic errors endorse the distinction and provide a variety of ways to distinguish between the two types of errors, there persists a widespread sentiment that all mistakes are the virtually random responses of children who do not yet understand the place-value system. It is worth a moment to review some data that show unequivocally that knowledge-based errors (bugs) are common. In one study, reported in chapter 7, third-grade students were tested twice, several days apart, using tests with the same 20 subtraction problems. (The order of the problems was permuted to disguise the similarity of the test.) Of these students 53 made a nontrivial number of errors (three or more). They missed a mean of 8.75 problems out of 20. For each student I calculated a score equal to the percentage of wrongly answered problems on the first test that received exactly the same answer on the second test. For instance, suppose a student missed four problems on the first test, and the answers were 3405, 2607, 34, and 17192. Suppose that on the second test the subject's answers for those problems were 3406, 2607, 34, and 16192. Because two of the four answers are identical, the student's score is 50 percent. For the 53 students in the sample, the mean score was 34 percent. If students are guessing randomly whenever they do not know how to calculate answer correctly, and p is the probability that they guess the same answer on two trials with the same problem, then the expected number of problems answered identically is 8.75p (because Np is the expected mean number of success over N trials with a probability of p of success on any one trial). Thus the observed result would equal the expected one if $p = 0.34$. It would take a rather elaborate model of random guessing to arrive at the prediction that two guesses, each consisting of a multidigit string of numbers, would come out the same 34 percent of the time.

This is only one demonstration among many that show that some errors are so systematic and stable that one simply must assume that they are caused by flaws in the students' knowledge rather than careless mistakes or random reactions to lack of knowledge. Thus if we want to understand how students acquire knowledge and flawed knowledge in particular, then it makes sense to examine as closely as possible the types of systematic errors that students exhibit, because these errors will reveal the students' knowledge structures, which will in turn tell us something about their learning processes.

Brown and Burton (1978) used the metaphor of bugs in computer programs in developing a formalism for describing systematic errors. Their basic idea was that a student's errors can be accurately reproduced by taking some formal representation of a correct procedure and making one or more small perturbations to it, such as deleting a rule. The perturbations are called bugs. A systematic error is represented as a correct algorithm for the skill plus a list of one or

306	80	183	702	3005	7002	34	251
− 138	− 4	− 95	− 11	− 28	− 239	− 14	− 47
78	76	88	691	1087	4873	24	244

1.2
Problems solved with the two bugs Borrow-Across-Zero and Diff-N− N = N. The first bug corresponds to omitting the step in borrowing across zero wherein the zero is changed to a nine. The second bug, which shows up only in the last two problems, substitutes the rule N − N = N for the rule N − N = 0.

more bugs (see 1.2 for an example). Bugs describe systematic errors with unprecedented precision. If a student makes no slips, then his or her answers on a test exactly match the buggy algorithm's answers, digit for digit. Bug data are the main data for testing this theory.

Burton (1982) developed an automated data-analysis program, *Debuggy*. Data from thousands of students learning subtraction were analyzed with Debuggy, and 75 different kinds of bugs were observed (VanLehn 1982). Similar studies discovered 68 bugs in addition of fractions (Shaw et al. 1982), several dozen bugs in simple linear equation solving (Sleeman 1984a), and 57 bugs in addition and subtraction of signed numbers (Tatsuoka and Baillie 1982). Chapter 7 presents one such bug study in detail and uses its results to measure the accuracy of the theory's predictions. The chapters 9 and 10 list all known subtraction bugs, with an explanation and example of each.

The connotations of bugs in the computer-programming sense do not necessarily apply to bugs in cognitive procedures. In particular, bugs in human procedures are not always stable. They may appear and disappear over short periods of time, often with no intervening instruction, and sometimes even in the middle of a testing session (VanLehn 1982). Often one bug is replaced by another, a phenomenon called *bug migration*. Bugs and bug migrations are quite common among students who are in the middle of learning subtraction. The proportions range from 10 to 50 percent, depending on the way students are tested and where they are in the lesson sequence.

Mysteries abound in the bug data. Why are there so many different bugs? What causes them? What causes them to migrate or disappear? Why do certain bugs migrate only into certain other bugs? Often a student has more than one bug at a time—why do certain bugs almost always occur together? Do cooccurring bugs have the same cause? Most important, how is the educational process involved in the development of bugs? One objective of the theory is to explain some of these bug mysteries.

1.2 *Methodological Objectives*

Although the methodological concerns that drive this research were in fact adopted from the Chomskyan paradigm of linguistic inquiry, that is somewhat irrelevant to whether or not the methodology is appropriate for this task domain. In fact the methods actually used here differ from the linguistic ones in several ways. This section attempts to motivate the theory's methodology from first principles.

It is now a fairly routine matter to build computer programs that can act like a human subject while the subject is performing some formal task, such as solving a puzzle or a mathematics problem. However, even if a program's behavior is very similar to the subject's, the program is still only a component of the ideal theory. The program itself is a complicated expression in some formal programming language. Much of it consists of psychologically irrelevant details. Indeed having one program that fits the data well, it is a relatively simple matter to generate an equivalent set of programs that fit the data equally well, even though no part of them is identical to the original program. Of course all these programs, although objectively quite distinct, implement the same *computation*. It is the computation, not the program, that is the model of the subject's cognition. It would be theoretically convenient at least to have a notation for the subject's computation per se rather than a program (or an equivalence class of programs).

The technology of formal specifications and proofs of correctness can be viewed as one attempt at notating computations. A popular technique for proving the correctness of programs is based on formulating a set of axioms that specify the computation per se and proving formally that the program implements the computation. Although there are other paradigms for notating computations, the axiomatic approach has particular advantages for psychological modeling. Each axiom can be taken as a distinct hypothesis. One can then ask about the relationship between hypotheses (for example, are they independent?), and, more important, one can ask about the relative importance of the hypotheses for explaining the subject's behavior. Indeed all the standard methodology of nomological theories can probably be adapted for computational theories that specify their computations axiomatically (Hempel 1966).

In particular one can ask what would happen to the fit of the model if a hypothesis were removed, modified slightly, or replaced with a competing hypothesis. By perturbing the individual hypotheses, one can uncover which hypotheses make major contributions to the program's predictive ability, and which hypotheses have small (or no) influence on the program's fit with the data. This type of scrutiny of individual computational hypotheses has been called a *competitive argument* (VanLehn, Brown, and Greeno 1984), because it argues by taking various competitors to a hypothesis and contrasting their effects when they are substituted for the original hypothesis. There are many reasons to believe that competitive argumentation would improve cognitive theorizing, but they are not reviewed here. (See Pylyshyn 1984 for a general discussion of computational theories and their methodological problems.)

The methodological objective for this theory is, naturally, to approximate as closely as possible the ideal theory I have sketched. This means building the following components:

1. A set of hypotheses, expressed as axioms in a formal specification language
2. A program
3. A proof that the program implements the computation expressed by the axioms
4. A demonstration that the program's behavior matches human behavior over a reasonably large sample of task instances and subjects
5. For each hypothesis a competitive argument that shows what happens when the hypothesis is removed or replaced by competing hypotheses.

The rest of this section deals with the form that these components have taken in the present theory.

The theory has a program, Sierra, and a demonstration that its behavior matches the behavior of a very large number of subjects over a small range of tasks. Sierra takes in a lesson sequence and constructs all the procedures that the theory predicts students will acquire while learning from that lesson sequence. There are many different procedures because students vary in how they learn. In particular some of the predicted procedures will have bugs. The measure used to evaluate the match between predictions and data is the overlap between the set of predicted bugs and the set of observed bugs. That is, if P is the set of predicted bugs and O is the set of observed bugs, then

- $P \cap O$ is the predicted bugs that have been observed. It should be large
- $O - P$ is the observed bugs that are not explained by the theory. It should be small.
- $P - O$ is the predicted bugs that have not yet been observed, but might be observed if more subjects were tested.

It does not matter how large the set $P - O$ is, but all of its members must be plausible. This proviso is a logically necessary component of the evaluation because a bad theory could look quite good by generating an enormous set of predictions, thus making $P \cap O$ large at the expense of introducing hundreds of implausible bugs into $P - O$. Not only is this proviso a logical necessity, it is a practical necessity as well. During the course of development Sierra often generated implausible bugs. For instance, it once generated a bug that goes into an infinite loop on borrow-from-zero problems. Because students are never driven into a catatonic state by borrow-from-zero problems, this bug is quite implausible. Such bugs are called *star bugs*, by analogy to the linguists' tradition of marking with a star those sentences that would never occur naturally. When Sierra generates a star bug, it is missing some kind of constraint. Star bugs indicate that the theory needs revision. So avoiding the generation of star bugs is just as important as generating observed bugs.

The theory has a set of hypotheses, but they are not expressed formally, although they could be. The formality was dispensed with because unfortunately there is no way to prove that Sierra implements the hyotheses. Sierra is a very large program with many tricks built into it that make it fast and easy to use (VanLehn 1987a). Its complexity places it well beyond the state of the art in proving programs correct. Nonetheless the intent in building Sierra was to make it a mere implementation of the hypotheses, and this intent is reflected in its design. For instance, when modeling learning, Sierra generates a large set of candidate knowledge structures and then removes knowledge structures from the set that do not conform to specific hypotheses, which are implemented as predicates in the programming language. This generate-and-filter design, although inefficient, makes it easier to see that some of the hypotheses, namely, those implemented as filters, are provably correct descriptions of the learning module's output. Because Sierra uses such generate-and-filter designs whenever the inefficiency is tolerable, I have a reasonable degree of confidence that it is a correct implementation of the theory's hypotheses.

Last, and most important, the theory has competitive arguments. Forging these arguments required more effort than building Sierra or collecting the data. Much was learned about the impediments inherent in realizing this component of the ideal theory. Perhaps the most important lesson is that hypotheses depend on each other in such a way that truly solid competitive arguments are possible only for the most specific hypotheses. A typical hypothesis has other hypotheses that depend on it, so it cannot be changed without changing the hypotheses that depend on it. Only a few hypotheses can be replaced without needing to replace any other hypotheses. To put it in more practical terms, the hypotheses that have really solid competitive arguments to back them up are those that are implemented as filters in Sierra. This implementation makes it easy to substitute new hypotheses and measure their effects.

Because of this interdependency of hypotheses, the overall argument must be organized fairly carefully to avoid introducing circularities. The argument is organized into three stages. Briefly put, the first stage (chapter 2) explicates how students use their knowledge, the second stage (chapter 3) explicates the representation of knowledge, and the third stage (chapters 4, 5, and 6) explicates how they acquire that knowledge. The final chapter summarizes the overall argument, emphasizing the interdependencies among the arguments. The next section previews the argument.

1.3 An Overview of the Argument

This section sketches the three stages of argumentation—the execution of cognitive procedures, their representation, and their acquisition. It mentions most of the major hypotheses of the theory enroute.

Beginning with this section, I describe the execution of procedures as if the subjects were actually engaged in the processes described— that is, reaching impasses, making repairs, pushing goals onto stacks, and so forth. This is a convenient way to talk, but it makes it seem that the theory is describing processes that could actually be observed with, for instance, protocol analysis or eye tracking. As I mentioned, describing the actual psychological mechanisms of execution is not an objective of this research. The goal is only to explain the solution paths generated by those mechanisms. As it happens, the interpretation function used by the theory is itself a process/ mechanism, but it might not be the same process/mechanism as the one used by people. Only their inputs and outputs are supposed to correspond. So, although I use "process talk," I do not really mean it.

1.3.1 How Do Students Use Procedural Knowledge?
The first stage of the argumentation makes assumptions about how subjects convert their knowledge into problem-solving activity. In particular it assumes that the basic activity consists of following (or more technically, interpreting) a procedure. However, when the procedure calls for an action that cannot be performed in the current situation, an *impasse* occurs. The impasse is treated as a meta-problem: How can this impasse be resolved or circumvented to allow

continued execution of the procedure? The solution strategies for this metaproblem are usually very simple actions, such as skipping the action that cannot be performed. The metaactions used to overcome the impasse are called *repairs,* and the strategies used to generate repairs are called *repair strategies.* If a repair succeeds (that is, solves the problem of being stuck), then the subject resumes ordinary problem solving, which consists of merely executing the procedure. Because of impasses and repairs the behavior exhibited by subjects does not always correspond directly to the procedure they are actually following. It is helpful to have some nomenclature to differentiate the procedure that they seem to be following from the one they are actually following. The procedure actually being followed is called a *core procedure.* The key concepts introduced in this first stage of argumentation are procedure following, core procedure, impasses, and repairs. (When technical terms are introduced, they are italicized. The index lists all technical terms.)

The hypotheses of the first stage are discussed informally and motivated by the bug data. The second stage of argumentation takes this interpretation function as a given and uses it to argue for a specific representatioin of procedures.

1.3.2 How is Procedural Knowledge Represented?

Cognitive science has produced a myriad of proposed representations for procedural knowledge, ranging from stimulus-response bonds to production systems to networks of schemata. Rather than deal with each proposed representation individually, I define two general dimensions of variation and assume that they are more or less independent:

- The first dimension concerns the type of control structure or control regime employed. For instance, some representations (for example, SR bonds) do not permit recursive procedures, whereas others do.
- The second dimension concerns the representation of referring expressions. To guide actions that take place in the real world, procedures must have expressions that refer to objects and properties of the real world. If a procedure has an action that means "pick up the next block in the current row," then "the current row" and "the next block in the current row" are referring expressions. Tests for a property, such as "Is the current row empty?" often are used to control the flow of control.

At the conclusion of the second stage of argumentation, a specific knowledge-representation language has been assembled. Its control structure is hierarchical and partially recursive. Internal information is passed via instantiation, that is, goals can pass arguments to subjoals, but subgoals can neither return values to the goals that called them nor send values to sibling or cousin subgoals. Referring expressions are represented by abstract, intentional "patterns," which are like expressions in predicate calculus. Patterns contain mostly visual features, such as adjacency (A is next to B), relative orientation (A is left of B), and inclusion (A is a part of B). Procedures are notated in a rule-based language similar to a production system.

A by-product of the second stage of argumentation is a set of specific procedures, expressed in the representation language, that seem to exist among the subject population because when these procedures are executed by the interpretation function, with its impasse-repair component, they generate the same bugs that subjects generate. This set of procedures is assumed to be the result of the subjects' learning processes.

1.3.3 How Do Students Learn Procedures?

The third stage of argumentation aims to specify the learning process. By "specify" I mean the technical sense of the word mentioned in connection with specification of programs. That is, the objective is *not* to describe the learning process itself but rather to describe the *constraints* obeyed by the process.

The third stage assumes that the output of the learning process consists of the procedures elucidated by the second stage of argumentation. However, it must make a major assumption about the nature of the input to the learning process, that is, what part of the instruction given to students drives the learning process. It is assumed that examples, exercises, and other concrete episodes of problem solving are the most salient part of instruction. The verbal and textual explanations that often accompany such concrete episodes of problem solving have a secondary, indirect effect on learning. This assumption seems necessary to account for the ubiquity of misconceptions among procedure learners and more important to account for the particular types of misconceptions that occur. The third stage of argumentation then assumes that the learning process takes in specific episodes of problem solving and constructs general procedures. The technical term for a process that produces a generalization given many concrete instantiations is *induction*. So the assumption is that learning proceeds by induction.

The main effort in the third stage is to find out which kind of induction characterizes human skill acquisition in this domain. In the machine learning literature a constraint on an inductive process is called a *bias* because it makes the learning algorithm tend to learn certain things rather than others or because it blocks the acquisition of certain concepts altogether. It is universally accepted that all inductive learning processes must be biased, on philosophical grounds as well as computational ones. The central question is not whether students are biased, but what those biases are.

The biases governing the acquisition of patterns turn out to be different from those governing the acquisition of control structures. The main pattern bias is that subjects acquire patterns that are maximally specific conjunctions of primitive visual relations. That is, the learning process retains all and only the common visual features of the situations that exemplify the application of a pattern. This simple result is muddied by the finding that mathematical features of situations (for example, the top digit in the column is less than the bottom digit) sometimes occur in patterns, and when they do, their induction is governed by different biases than the maximal specificity bias.

With respect to the biases governing the induction of control structures, there are unfortunately two competing biases that both successfully specify which kinds of control structures subjects learn. The bug data are not the right kind of data for determining which bias is better. One bias is based on the idea of structural simplicity. It asserts that students learn the procedures with the fewest productions possible. The second bias is based on the idea of *felicity conditions* (Austin 1962), which is borrowed from studies of natural-language conversations and applied to the instructional setting, where a teaching system (that is, the combination of teacher, textbook, peers, and so forth) communicates knowledge to a student. The idea is that a curriculum is felicitous only if it obeys certain conventions. The conventions relate the format of the curriculum to the format of the knowledge that the curriculum is intended to teach. When students learn from a curriculum, they do not know what that knowledge is, so they must infer it from the curriculum's format and content. It is always the case that many kinds of knowledge are consistent with the curriculum, and inductive inference alone is insufficient for disambiguating them. However, the students are like listeners in a conversation. They choose an interpretation for the curriculum such that the curriculum is felicitous with respect to that interpretation. That is, they assume the teaching system teaches felicitously, and they use that assumption to determine which of the many possible interpretations of the instruction to make.

The particular felicity condition that may govern the learning of procedural skills is that each production is a procedure will be taught in its own lesson, where a lesson consists of an uninterrupted sequence of demonstrations, examples, and exercises. The length of a lesson varies. A lesson could fill a whole 50-minute mathematics period in elementary school, or even a whole week's worth of mathematics classes. In high school a single lesson might occupy only 15 minutes of class time and the homework that corresponds to it. Regardless of its length a lesson teaches just one topic, where "topic" in the arena of skill acquisition corresponds roughly to a production. It would be infelicitous, for instance, to introduce carrying and borrowing together in the same lesson by alternating between examples of each. From the students' point of view, this means that they can assume that all the examples, exercises, and the like in a lesson exemplify the *same* production. This is a very strong assumption in that it significantly reduces the number of procedures that are consistent with a given lesson sequence. For instance, the number of productions in the procedure will be less than or equal to the number of lessons in the curriculum. It will be shown that the felicity condition account is consistent with the bug data. However, the account based on structural simplicity is also consistent with the data, and there is no way to tell which is better without further research.

1.4 An Introduction to the Model: Explaining Always-Borrow-Left

The preceding section presented the theory's assumptions in a general form, mentioning each individually. To show how they work together to handle specific cases, this section presents the theory's account of how a particular subtraction bug, Always-Borrow-Left, is acquired. Although this particular bug is typical of a large class of bugs, the members of which are enumerated in chapter 4, the exposition is much easier to follow when it deals with just a single bug rather than the whole class. Always-Borrow-Left will be used throughout this book as a prototype for the whole class.

Students with Always-Borrow-Left always borrow from the leftmost column in the problem no matter which column originates the borrowing. Problem A shows the correct placement of borrow's decrement. Problem B shows the bug's placement.

$$
\begin{array}{cccccc}
& 5 & & 2 & & 5 \\
\text{A.} & 3\ \not{6}^{1}5 & \text{B.} & \not{3}\ 6^{1}5 & \text{C.} & \not{6}^{1}5 \\
& -1\ 0\ 9 & & -1\ 0\ 9 & & -1\ 9 \\
\hline
& 2\ 5\ 6 & & 1\ 6\ 6 & & 4\ 6 \\
\end{array}
$$

Always-Borrow-Left is moderately common. In a sample of 375 students with bugs, 6 students had this bug (VanLehn 1982). It has been observed for years (Buswell 1926, p. 173, bad habit number s27). Although this theory is the first to offer an explanation for it, explaining a single bug in isolation is easy. The trick is to explain all the bugs that occur. The purpose of this example is to present the main ideas of the theory in a concrete context. The explanatory power of the theory lies in its ability to account for a set of bugs, not just a single bug.

The explanation begins with the assumption that students use induction in learning the pattern that describes where to place the borrow's decrement. Induction is learning from concrete instances, such as the teacher's or text's examples or the students' own practice exercises. The explanation for this bug depends on the fact that subtraction curricula use a skewed selection of examples and exercises when they introduce borrowing. All the textbooks used by students in our sample introduce borrowing in the context of only two-column problems, such as C. Multicolumn problems, such as A, are not used. Assuming that the student uses only the examples and not the verbal explanations that accompany them, the student has insufficient information to determine which of all possible patterns to use for describing where to place the borrow's decrement. The correct placement is in the left-adjacent column, as in A. However, two-column examples are also consistent with decrementing the leftmost column, as in B.

The next assumption of the theory is that when a student is faced with such an underdetermined induction, the student saves all the relevant descriptive relations as one large conjunction. When inducing from two-column problems (for example, C), the student describes the borrow-from column as "a column that is both left-adjacent to the current column and the leftmost column in the problem."

Suppose that our student is given a diagnostic test at this point in the lesson sequence and that the test contains borrowing problems of all kinds. Suppose the student is faced with solving problem D:

D.   3 6 5   E.   3 6^{1}5
    − 1 0 9   − 1 0 9
   ‾‾‾‾‾‾‾   ‾‾‾‾‾‾‾

The student starts to borrow, gets as far as E, and is suddenly stuck. The student's pattern fails to refer to any object in the situation because there is no column that is *both* the left-adjacent and the leftmost column. In the terminology of the theory the student has reached an *impasse*.

An important assumption of this theory is that whenever students reach an impasse on a test, they make a *repair*. The process of finding a repair and making it is just like classical problem solving (Newell and Simon 1972) in that there is an initial state, a desired final state, and state-change operators. Here the initial state is being stuck, and the desired final state is being unstuck. Unlike traditional problem solving, however, most of the state-change operators of the repair process don't change the state of the exercise problem. Instead they change the *state of the interpreter* that is executing the procedure. The operators do things like pop the stack of goals or relax the criterion for matching a description to the exercise problem. They do not do things like writing digits on the test paper. Because the repair process modifies the state of the procedure's interpretation, it is a kind of *metalevel* problem solving. Returning to our stuck student, three common repairs to the impasse are illustrated by these problems:

$$
\begin{array}{llll}
& \begin{matrix} 2 \\ \text{F.} \quad \not{3}\,6^1 5 \\ \underline{-1\,0\,9} \end{matrix}
& \begin{matrix} 5 \\ \text{G.} \quad 3\,\not{6}^1 5 \\ \underline{-1\,0\,9} \end{matrix}
& \begin{matrix} \\ \text{H.} \quad 3\,6^1 5 \\ \underline{-1\,0\,9} \\ 6 \end{matrix}
\end{array}
$$

In F the student has relaxed the pattern by ignoring the restriction that the column be left-adjacent to the current column. The remaining restriction, that the column be the leftmost column in the problem, has the student decrement the hundreds column, as shown in F. This is one repair. It generates the bug Always-Borrow-Left. Another repair is shown in G. Here the student has relaxed the pattern by ignoring the leftmost requirement. The decrement is placed in the left-adjacent column, yielding G. This repair generates a correct solution to the problem. In H the student has chosen to skip the borrow-from entirely and go on to the next step in the procedure. This repair generates a bug that is named Borrow-No-Decrement-Except-Last because it executes a borrow-from only when it is unambiguous where to place the decrement, and that occurs only when the borrow originates in the last possible column for borrowing. To sum up, three different repairs to the same impasse generate two different bugs and a correct version of subtraction.

Students' bugs, unlike bugs in computer programs, are unstable. Students shift back and forth among bugs, a phenomenon called bug migration. The theory's explanation for bug migration is that the student has a stable underlying procedure but that the procedure is incomplete in such a way that the student reaches impasses on some problems. Students can apply any repair they can think of. Sometimes they choose one repair and sometimes another. The different repairs manifest themselves as different bugs. So bug migration

A.	B.	C.	D.	E.
7 12	4 10			12
8̸2̸	5̸0̸	109	1564	10̸2̸
− 43	− 23	− 70	− 887	− 39
39	27	39	187	73

F.	G.	H.	I.	J.
1 17				
2̸7̸	900	716	311	885
− 8	− 688	− 598	− 214	− 205
19	222	118	97	680

K.	L.	M.	N.	O.
4			2	
5 15 11		6 10 11	3 10 15	
6̸5̸9̸1̸	8355	8̸0̸0̸1̸	4̸0̸1̸5̸	637
− 2697	− 3	− 43	− 607	− 35
2904	8352	6068	2418	602

P.	Q.	R.	S.
4 10	6 12	12	6 12
5̸0̸0̸	7̸0̸2̸	1̸0̸0̸1̸2̸	7̸4̸2̸
− 4	− 103	− 214	− 136
406	609	208	616

1.3
Verbatim presentation of a test by subject 8 of class 17 showing three repairs to the same impasse. On problems D, E and G one repair generates the bug Borrow-No-Decrement-Except-Last. (The subject does not always use scratch marks to indicate borrowing.) On problems H and I another repair generates the correct borrow-from placement. On problems K, M, N, P, Q, R, and S, a third repair generates the bug Always-Borrow-Left. There are slips on problems D, K, Q, and S. On problem R a second impasse occurs. While processing the hundreds column, the subject tries to decrement the zero in the ten thousands column. A repair to this impasse ultimately leads to the answer of 2 in the hundreds column.

comes from varying the choice of repairs to a stable, underlying impasse. In particular the theory predicts that the three repairs just discussed ought to show up as a bug migration. In fact there is evidence of just such a bug migration. A verbatim presentation of a diagnostic test showing the predicted bug migration is shown in 1.3.

The discussion of the bug Always-Borrow-Left illustrates many of the important claims of the theory. First, procedures that lead to bugs are the result of generalization of examples rather than, say, memorization of verbal or written recipes. Evidence for this claim comes from the fact that this and many other bugs depend on accidental, visual characteristics of the examples, namely, the placement of the decrement. A nonexample source of instruction, such as a verbal recipe, would not mention these features. The appearance of these visual characteristics in the acquired procedure is evidence that they were learned by induction. (See VanLehn 1986 for further discussion.)

A second claim is that many bugs are caused by testing beyond training, that is, testing students who are in the middle of the lesson sequence on exercise types that they have not yet been taught how to solve. Always-Borrow-Left illustrates this claim. It seems to be caused by testing with three-column problems when the students have seen only two-column problems.

Another set of claims involves procedure following, impasses, and repairs. A particularly important assumption is that repairs occur at the metalevel and change only the state of the interpreter. This assumption predicts the existence of bug migration. In fact this prediction was made before any evidence of bug migration had been found (Brown and VanLehn 1980). The surprising success of this forecast and the fact that it is an almost unavoidable consequence of the assumption provide welcome support for the theory.

1.5 The Organization of the Rest of the Book

Structurally this book consists of this introductary chapter, a body, and two concluding chapters. Chapter 2 through 6 present the main argument, which was sketched in section 1.3. It is organized into three stages, which answer these questions: How is procedural knowledge utilized to solve problems (chapter 2)? How is procedural knowledge represented mentally (chapter 3)? How is procedural knowledge learned (chapters 4, 5, and 6)?

The first of the two concluding chapters is a detailed evaluation of the empirical accuracy of the theory. It presents the computer model, Sierra, in some detail. It presents a particular study of subtraction bugs, the Southbay study. It discusses the predicted bugs that the model generates when it is given the same curriculum as the students in the Southbay study. Finally, it compares the predicted bugs to the observed bugs, and contrasts this degree of accuracy with similar measures for two previous versions of this theory (Young and O'Shea 1981, Brown and VanLehn 1980).

As mentioned, there are two objectives for the theory. One is to explain where bugs come from, and the other is to test competitive argumentation as a methodology. The first concluding chapter evaluates the theory with respect to the first objective. For symmetry's sake the second concluding chapter should evaluate the theory with respect to the second objective. Evaluating a methodology, however requires trying it on more than one theory. Indeed the only sensible measure of a methodology is whether it produces lasting, useful theories over a course of many decades. So it is premature to evaluate competitive argumentation.

It is possible, however to show what competitive argumentation has produced by being applied to this theory, so the final chapter consists of a summary of all the argumentation that emphasizes the interconnections between the assumptions. It classifies assumptions into three types and the dependencies among them into five types. These ad hoc classifications serve to explicate the overall structure of the theory.

Last, there are two appendixes. The first, in chapter 9, is a glossary of all known subtraction bugs. It includes observed bugs, star bugs, and bugs that have been predicted but not yet observed. The second appendix, in chapter 10, lists all the bug sets that were observed in the Southbay study. An index of technical terms and assumptions is included.

Chapter 2
The Interpretation of Procedural Knowledge

This chapter presents a taxonomy of the ways that procedural knowledge can be used to solve problems and locates within the taxonomy the type of knowledge acquired by arithmetic students. The taxonomy is a traditional one in cognitive science. A summary of it is presented in 2.1.

The top-level distinction in the taxonomy concerns the amount of search the subject does. Newell and Simon (1972, p. 822ff) have pointed out that this distinction is a matter of degree:

> When a subject is using a highly specific algorithm (e.g., the simplex algorithm for linear programming) to solve a problem in a highly mechanical way and with a low error rate (hence with little occasion to use procedures that stand outside the formal algorithm), it adds little to our knowledge about him to say that "he is engaged in problem-solving activity." We might as well say that "he is carrying out the XYZ algorithm.". . . If we wish to have a term to refer to these arbitrarily varied sequences of behavior that are carried out under control of specific algorithms, we can call them *programmed activity*. They take place in problem spaces, but are to be distinguished (at least as a matter of degree) from the *unprogrammed activity*—i.e., less stereotyped and mechanized activity, involving search and backup—that we have treated in this book as problem-solving behavior.

> Problem solving within the context of a plan has somewhat the same flavor as executing a specialized algorithm, for plans are structurally identical to programs . . . [and] plans involve exactly the same kind of commitment that we find in following algorithms like the simplex algorithm. [However,] there is no rigid boundary between behavior in which the subject is searching in the problem space (unprogrammed activity) and his behavior when he is following a predetermined plan (programmed activity).

Unprogrammed behavior (search)
Programmed behavior (procedure following)
   Knows procedure and understands it
   Understands procedure, but must follow written recipe
   Knows procedure but does not understand it
      Impasse-free procedure following
      Impasses occur during procedure following
         Subject selects repair at the time of the impasse
         Choice of repair uniquely determined by subject's knowledge
         Both: some impasses have fixed repairs, some require choice

2.1
A taxonomy of procedural knowledge types

In short Newell and Simon proposed a scale with procedure following on the programmed-behavior end, search on the unprogrammed-behavior end, and plan-governed problem solving ranging about somewhere in the middle. In section 2.1 I argue that arithmetic problem solving falls on one end of the scale, under the taxonomic category of procedure following.

Newell and Simon (1972, p. 882) presented a four-step theory of how algorithmic knowledge is acquired, pointing out that there are two types of knowledge about an algorithm:

(1) At the outset the algorithm is followed by reference, step by step, to a recipe stored in External Memory. (2) The recipe is memorized (stored internally), but still has to be executed by step-by-step interpretation. (3) The memorized recipe is "mechanized"—that is to say, compiled in the internal language of programs, so that it can now be executed directly and without interpretation. (4) More or less independently of the previous sequence, and understanding may be acquired of the logical justification for the algorithm—of why it works. Observe that a high level of mechanization can be achieved in executing the algorithm, without any evidences of understanding; and a high level of understanding can be achieved at a stage where the algorithm still has to be followed from an externally stored recipe. (The latter is likely to be true only of relatively elaborate algorithms—e.g., the simplex algorithm for linear programming.) . . . The level of understanding is likely to affect performance primarily in recovery from error or interruption. Over longer periods of time it also affects the ease with which the subject acquires or retains the algorithm in memory. . . . Finally, it may be exhibited in the

subject's flexibility in adopting shortcuts and adapting the algorithm to special cases. A high degree of mechanization, on the other hand, may actually inhibit the use of special procedures for special cases.

Although this quote is rich in hypotheses that I examine later (in particular I show that memorization of recipes may not be how students learn arithmetic), the relevant point for this chapter is that a subject's knowledge can include the algorithm alone, an understanding of the algorithm, or both. This is the second tier of the taxonomy (see 2.1). In section 2.2 I argue that arithmetic students know the algorithms, but do not understand them.

The next tier of the taxonomy distinguishes two types of architectures for execution of procedures. One type is like early production systems in that procedures can never reach an impasse. Early production systems were designed so that some production always matched and was executed no matter what. This represented the fact that people never seemed to halt. Some more recent systems, such as Soar (Laird, Newell, and Rosenbloom 1987), are designed to reach impasses and react appropriately to them. In section 2.3 I argue that arithmetic students do in fact reach impasses, and I proposed a set of strategies, called repair strategies, that represent appropriate reactions to the types of impasses that occur.

In principle subjects' choice of repair strategy could be fixed in advanced by their knowledge or their cognitive architecture. On the other hand it could also be that subjects actively choose a repair strategy when an impasse occurs. In section 2.4 I argue that both cases occur. Stable bugs result when the choice of repair strategy is fixed in advance by the subjects' knowledge. Unstable patterns of bugs (bug migrations) result when subjects choose a repair each time the impasse occurs. This distinction, between the presence or absence of repair selection, constitutes the last tier of the taxonomy (see 2.1).

Each of arguments in this chapter culminates in a hypothesis about the structure and execution of the subjects' procedures. Beginning with this chapter hypotheses are named and given explicit, albeit sketchy, statements. This will make it easier to refer to them later. The index lists each hypothesis under both its name and the heading "Assumptions."

2.1 Searching versus Following a Procedure

In folk psychology as well as early cognitive psychology, it is common to distinguish between two types of goal-directed behavior. Newell and Simon (1972) labeled these two types "programmed activity" and "unprogrammed activity." Programmed activity consists of repetitious, routine sequences of actions. Usually there is no uncertainty about what action to take next at any point in the sequence. Unprogrammed activity consists of variable, nonroutine sequences of actons. Although the actions are directed toward achieving a goal, the relationship between the goal and the choice of actions is obscure, and there may be great uncertainty about what action to take next. The prototypical example of unprogrammed activity is solving a puzzle, such as the Tower of Hanoi, that one has never seen before.

According to Newell and Simon (1972), the prototypical example of a programmed activity is solving an arithmetic problem, such as 1492×1762. That assumption still seems valid today. Because the rest of this section involves splitting some pretty fine hairs in dealing with this topic, readers may wish to skip ahead to the next section.

The hair splitting is due to Newell's (1980) *problem space* hypothesis, which asserts that all goal-directed activity consists of search in a problem space. On this hypothesis programmed activity is just a very tightly directed form of search. Here I review the problem space hypothesis and show that it does not apply well to arithmetic. Instead the original Newell and Simon (1972) conception of search as being fundamentally different from procedure following seems more appropriate, with arithmetic being a prime case of procedure following.

A *problem space* includes at least three components: (1) an initial state, (2) a finite set of operators such that applying an operator to a state produces (or moves to) another state, and (3) an efficient test for whether or not a state is a desired final state. Often the test for a final state is simply a description of the final state that can be matched against a given state. The goal of the search is to find a sequence of operators that will transform the initial state into an acceptable final state. During the search the choice of operators and states is governed by *search control knowledge*. Some people have more task-specific search control knowledge than others. A person with a great deal of search control knowledge may know enough about the task that their search always succeeds with no backtracking or any other signs of what a layperson would call search. Thus they would appear to be following a procedure, and their search control knowledge can be equated with the procedure that they appear to be following.

The problem space hypothesis comes along with a general theory of skill acquisition. According to Newell (1980, p. 704), "The problem space hypothesis asserts that skilled, routine behavior is organized within the problem space by the accumulation of search control knowledge. . . . Though how the accumulation occurs is not given, the final result consists simply of the addition of search control knowledge." In other words first students have the final state description and lack the search control knowledge; later they have both.

Several investigators have developed learning models that instantiate the problem space hypothesis. Anzai and Simon (1979) showed that a subject's acquisition of skill in Tower of Hanoi could be explained by accretion of search control knowledge (among other things). Ohlsson (1980) showed that subjects' acquisition of skill in the three-term series problems could be modeled by acquisition of search control knowledge. Several AI programs have shown that the same mechanisms could be used to acquire skill in subtraction (Langley and Ohlsson 1984), integral calculus (Mitchell, Utgoff, and Banerji 1983), college-level algebra (Silver 1986), and other task domains (Laird, Rosenbloom, and Newell 1986, Langley 1987).

In all of these learning models the novice and expert perform essentially the same search, but the novice has underconstrained (weak) search control knowledge, whereas the expert's search control knowledge is deterministic: it uniquely determines all (or almost all) choices. Thus learning is modeled as increasing determinism in the subject's search control knowledge.

The main problem with applying the problem space hypothesis to subtraction is that the hypothesis requires the subject to have a test that can tell the search process when the final state is achieved. In the case of subtraction the only plausible final state tests are (1) to ask a teacher, parent, peer, textbook, or pocket calculator whether the subtraction problem is solved correctly, or (2) to see if the answer has superficial properties, such as being a string of digits of approximately the right length, or (3) to add the answer to the subtrahend and see if it equals the minuend. Suppose we assume subjects learn subtraction as the problem space hypothesis says, by accreting search control knowledge as they search. Which of the three tests could be used to guide this search? Test 3 is implausible because the use of addition as a check is readily visible to observers (it must be written addition because mental addition of such large numbers is implausible at this stage of the child's development), yet students are notorious for not checking their answers. Test 2 is implausible because it places such weak constraints on acceptable final states that it would predict that students would to learn a much larger class of systematic errors than are actually observed. This leaves test 1, which is, broadly speaking, plausible. Thus let us assume for the sake of argument that students acquire search control knowledge by searching through a problem space where final statehood is determined by consulting an expert, where by "expert" I mean books and calculators as well as people. So far the problem space hypothesis is holding up just fine.

When students are tested, however, they are not permitted to ask for an expert's judgment on the correctness of proposed answers. If they search during test taking, they must be searching a problem space different from the one they searched while learning. Perhaps their test-taking problem space has test 2 as its test for final statehood, but it certainly does not have test 1. However, test 2 places only the weakest constraints on the choice of operators. We could not explain the systematicity in students' errors if we assumed that they used just weak, task-general methods and test 2. Indeed the only plausible assumption is that students try to apply the search control knowledge that they acquired while learning, even though the appropriate final state test is not currently available. That is, they are doing a sort of "open-loop" search—they select operators based on their search control knowledge, but they have no way (or only a weak way) to check whether their selections have (or will) lead them to a correct final state. That is, they are more or less blindly following their search control knowledge. This kind of behavior is, I believe, exactly what Newell and Simon (1972) meant by programmed behavior. The subject is following a prefabricated plan (search control knowledge) rather than searching for operations that achieve a known final state.

In short, even if we assume a problem-space style of learning, we end up having to assume that the final state test used during learning is not used during testing, so students must rely almost exclusively on the procedure they acquired previously. Indeed the assumption that the procedure is acquired via accretion of search control knowledge is immaterial to the conclusion. The point is basically that subtraction does not have a final state test that can be used during test taking and is strong enough to guide search in ways that replicate the observed behaviors.

This line of argument leads to

The procedure-following assumption
During test-taking situations, students solve arithmetic problems by following a procedure (or trying to) rather than by searching for a sequence of operators to transform the problem's initial state into a final, desired state.

To put it another way, the knowledge that students carry into the test-taking situation (or any other situation where an expert is not readily available) consists of a procedure (or plan or search control knowledge) and perhaps some weak specifications of the syntax of the final state (for example, how long the answer should be). When their procedure fails to uniquely specify what to do next (that is, they reach an impasse), then it would be irrational of them to abandon their procedure and rely exclusively on their final state description because, in the case of subtraction, that final state description is very weak. Thus even if search control knowledge fails, then students probably do not search in the traditional sense of finding operations to achieve a known final state. Rather they perform a search of a different kind, which seeks an expedient way to overcome the impasse and return control to the procedure/search control knowledge. Thus the motive behind the students' activity is not so much to achieve a final state, because they do not have a good specification of what that is. Rather their motive is to follow a procedure as closely as possible.

This argument relies on the fact that subtraction's procedure is easier to specify that its final state test, so people take the procedure, rather than the final state test, as the defining the problem. In other task domains, such as the puzzles that are often used in cognitive science, the final states are easily described, so subjects take them as defining the problem. I suspect that these are two extremes, and that many skills lie between these extremes. That is, the subject takes into a test-taking situation (or other nonpedagogical situation) a moderately strong description of the final state and moderately strong advice about how to get there. For instance, welders know what a good weld looks like, and they know how to make one. However, they also know that even a weld that looks good can in fact be quite weak because the proper procedure was not followed. That is, the operative specification of the problem is both the appearance of the weld and the procedure for making a weld. Neither procedure nor appearance alone is sufficient to specify the welding problem; both are required.

This suggests that the problem space hypothesis should be generalized somewhat. Currently the hypothesis holds that the problem space is given, and the student derives search control knowledge via general mechanisms, such as production compilation (Anderson 1987) or chunking (Laird, Rosenbloom, and Newell 1986). There is no logical reason why this has to be the only way that students have problems defined for them. It could also be that students are given the search control knowledge (procedure) instead of the final state information or in addition to the final state information. The argument suggests that subtraction students are given a procedure instead of a correct, succinct final state description. Welding and other skills may be more toward the middle, where students are given both procedures and final state descriptions.

2.2 Pure versus Teleological Understanding of Procedures

A person who knows a procedure and follows it may also know the design or justification for that procedure. For instance, one might know the procedure for the simplex algorithm of linear programming as well as the reasons why it has the steps that it has, why it has certain conditions on its applicability, and why it always succeeds when those conditions are met and the steps are followed accurately. If subjects understand the design behind a procedure, then they may be able to reconstruct parts of the procedure that they have forgotten, or adapt the procedure to novel situations, or use it as a basis for intelligent analogies (Carbonell 1986), or in general exhibit competence in many tasks other than simply executing the procedure. This section considers whether subtraction subjects might know the design of their procedures as well as the procedures themselves. Subjects who know the design of a procedure are said to have a *teleological* understanding of it. It will be concluded that subtraction subjects generally do not have a teleological understanding.

Again this is a fairly uncontroversial assumption. As Haugeland (1978, p. 223) so aptly put it, "As any teacher of arithmetic or logic knows, many students can learn the routines for getting the right answers, without the slightest insight into what's going on." To this observation one can add with assurance that students who have mastered routines for getting the *wrong* answers are even less likely to have a slight insight into what's going on. In view of the lack of controversy readers may wish to skip ahead to the next section.

It is simplest to explain teleological understanding with a concrete illustration. Consider a procedure for making white sauce. A novice cook often knows only the pure procedure for the white sauce recipe—which ingredients to add in which order. The expert cook realizes that the order is crucial in some cases but arbitrary in others. The expert also knows the purposes of various parts of the recipe. For instance, the expert understands a certain sequence of steps as making a flour-based thickener. Knowing the goal, the expert can substitute a cornstarch-based thickener for the flour-based one. More generally, knowing the teleology (design) of a procedure allows its user to adapt the procedure to special circumstances (for example, running out of flour). It also allows the user to debug the procedure. For instance, if the white sauce comes out lumpy, the expert cook can infer that something went wrong with the thickener. Knowing which steps of the recipe make the thickener, the cook can discover the bug: the flour-fat mixture (the roux) was not cooked long enough. The purpose of cooking the roux is to emulsify the flour. Because the sauce was lumpy, this purpose was not achieved. By knowing the purposes of the parts of the procedure, people are able to debug, extend, optimize, and adapt their procedures. These added capabilities, beyond merely following (executing) a procedure, can be used to test for a teleological understanding (compare Greeno, Reily, and Gelman 1984).

Having made the distinction between pure and teleological knowledge, it is appropriate to ask which kind of knowledge is acquired by arithmetic students.

There is uniform agreement that most students of mathematics do not acquire teleological understanding (for a recent collection of articles on the subject, see Hiebert 1986). It would be nice, however, to have more concrete evidence in the case of arithmetic. Such evidence is readily available for the students who are the focus of this study, those students with bugs. They must lack knowledge of the underlying design of the procedure because such knowledge would allow them not only to see that their buggy procedure was wrong but also to understand how to rectify it. For instance students are sometimes asked to solve borrow-from-zero problems (for example, $508 - 29$) when they have been taught only how to borrow from non-zero digits. As shown later, this causes students to reach an impasse and repair. If they understood the procedure teleologically, however, they would never reach an impasse, because the same design principles underlie both types of borrowing. The assumption that students lack teleological knowledge helps explain why they have bugs. To put it colloquially, students with bugs have learned a "symbol-pushing" procedure.

These assumptions leave open the question of what type of knowledge is possessed by students *without* bugs. Intuition suggests that some bug-free students may have a quite sophisticated understanding of the algorithm, whereas others do not. On the other hand the learning processes I describe certainly suffice to allow learning of correct as well as buggy procedures, so parsimony suggests that all students, even the bug-free ones, have pure procedural knowledge. Unfortunately the bug data are powerless to determine what type of knowledge bug-free students have. Rather than have separate assumptions for the buggy students and the bug-free students, we simply make the following assumption:

The ateleological assumption
Students do not have knowledge of the design (teleology) of mathematical calculation procedures. Their knowledge consists only of the procedure itself.

Mathematical procedures are perhaps a little different than other human procedures in that their teleology is quite complex. This complexity results in part from the fact that the procedures manipulate a representation (for example, base-10 numerals) rather than the objects of interest themselves (for example, numbers). A procedure for making white sauce does not have this problem. Cooks do not manipulate representations of flour and fat; they manipulate the real stuff. An added complexity with arithmetic procedures is the way their teleologies merge loops to accomplish several goals at once (VanLehn and Brown 1980). The teleology of merged loops is so complex that only in the last decade has AI made much progress in analyzing it (Waters 1978, Rich 1981). In task domains other than mathematics, more students might show evidence of teleological knowledge. In the present domain it is safe to assume that students' knowledge is purely procedural, with no teleology.

2.3 Impasses and Repairs

In computer programming there are two kinds of runtime errors: those that the machine can detect and those that it cannot detect. For instance, a computer can detect an attempt to divide by zero. However, if the programmer meant to divide by X, but instead wrote into the program a division by Y, then the computer cannot detect the error. Later this error may cause detectable problems, but the error itself will pass by unnoticed by the machine.

When people execute a procedure that they have learned, the same distinction applies. Some errors can be detected by the person, and some cannot (at least immediately). We call the detectable errors impasses. To illustrate the concept and establish some convenient terminology for later use, four classes of impasses are presented in subsequent paragraphs.

2.3.1 Classes of Impasses

Suppose, for example, that I am selling my house in Pittsburgh. According to the procedure, my water meter should be read shortly before closing the sale. Suppose I do not know when my water meter was last read, so I do not know whether or not to read the meter. This is typical of one class of impasses: the procedure calls for a decision

("Has the meter been read recently?"), and I cannot make the decision. So I must suspend execution of the procedure, resolve the impasse (for example, call Allegheny County and ask when my meter was last read), then resume the procedure. Impasses in this class are called *decision impasses*.

Another class of impasses consists of *reference impasses*. We have all experienced the frustration of assembling a piece of equipment whose instructions say something like "Push the large yellow tab through the hole on the main support tube," and we find either no holes on the main support tube or several of them. These are reference impasses because the description "the hole on the main support tube" does not uniquely identify an object in the problem state.

A third class of impasses consists of *primitive impasses*. Descriptions of procedures always have primitive acts. Examples of primitives are getting someone to read the water meter or tightening a screw. Primitives are mentioned but not described by the procedure. It is assumed that one already knows how to carry out primitive actions. If a primitive action cannot be performed, then the impasse is classified as a primitive failure. An example is having a screw's head break off while one is tightening it.

A fourth kind of impasse is the *critic impasse*. The term *critic* derives from Sussman's (1976) Hacker program. A critic is a prohibition based on compiled hindsight or common sense. A critic is triggered when the procedure is about to do something that is known to be wrong. For instance, one possible critic for subtraction is that all the digits in the subtrahend and the minuend must be used at some time during the course of problem solving. If the procedure tries to finish before using all the digits, the critic triggers, and an impasse occurs. A possible critic for buying a house prohibits accepting a personal check as the form of payment. If someone tries to give you a personal check for such a large sum of money, the critic fires, and the house sale reaches an impasse. Critics are knowledge that is difficult to circumscribe in the theory because they seem to depend so much on common sense, a notoriously open-ended body of knowledge. Fortunately critic impasses are relatively rare in arithmetic, and the theory has been able to model much of the data without including critics in the model. However, in other task domains that are less isolated from common sense than arithmetic, critics are probably much more important.

Procedures can get stuck in many ways, but these four classes of impasses—decision, reference, primitive, and critic—cover many of the common cases.

2.3.2 *Classes of Repairs*

When computers reach an impasse, they do not just turn themselves off (although some early computers tended to do that, unfortunately). Instead they start executing an error-handling routine instead of the main program. Similarly when people are executing a procedure and reach an impasse, they do not simply turn themselves off (what a thought!), but instead handle the impasse in some fashion. In particular the assumption that seems most plausible is

> **The impasse-repair assumption**
> When people reach an impasse while executing a procedure, they treat the impasse as a problem, solve it, and continue executing the procedure.

The solution to an impasse is called a *repair*. The problem-solving method used to find or construct the repair is called a *repair strategy*. Repairs and repair strategies are intended to inherit all the properties of solutions and problem-solving methods. Thus just as one can ask whether the same solution derived from different methods, one can ask whether the same repair results from application of different repair strategies. Just as the application of a problem-solving method yields different solutions when applied to different problems, the same repair strategy yields different repairs when applied to different impasses. Just as students may or may not recall their solutions to previous presentations of a problem, students may or may not recall repairs to earlier instances of an impasse.

The impasse-repair assumption is definitely a hypothesis and not a tautology. Some theories of problem solving, such as the ones by Anderson (1983) or Newell and Simon (1972), do not sanction impasses and repairs, whereas other theories, notably Soar (Laird, Newell, and Rosenbloom 1987), do. The success of the impasse-free models indicates that the existence of impasses and repairs is not forced on us by logic or computational necessity. Their existence is an empirical issue.

It is not, however, an easy issue to settle because it hinges on whether the subject is focused on solving the main problem, say $234 - 105$, or on solving an impasse. We could simply ask the subjects or collect verbal protocol—this might settle the issue. However, informal interviews have indicated that third graders are not sufficiently articulate for this method to work in the arithmetic task domain. So indirect methods must be used. For this purpose a new assumption is introduced.

2.3.3 Repair Strategies Are Common Knowledge

Suppose that we assume that all repair strategies are task general rather than acquired as part of a procedure. In terms of the computer analogy introduced previously, this is like asserting that programs do not have program-specific error-handling code in them; all impasses are handled by default, program-general routines. Clearly this is an empirical assumption and is not forced on by computational necessity.

Let us also assume that although repair *strategies* are not associated with specific procedures, individual repair *episodes* can be. A student might store the repair that was derived by some repair strategy on one occasion, then recall and reuse that repair whenever the procedure reaches that impasse on subsequent occasions. Thus although stored repairs are procedure specific, repair strategies are not.

Suppose we make the further assumption that repair strategies are common knowledge, in that most subjects will know most of the repair strategies. For future reference let us label this

The common-knowledge assumption
Repair strategies are task-general methods, most of which are familiar to most subjects.

This assumption implies that it should be possible to find a set of "common" repair strategies such that all observed repairs can be derived by the application of a common repair strategy, and most common repair strategies are widely used, that is, repairs generated by them are found in response to many types of impasses and in the work of many students.

This means that we should be able to find a specific pattern in the bug data. Suppose that some of the observed bugs can be analyzed as being derived from repairs to impasses. If repair strategies are common general methods as assumed, then we ought to see the same impasse being repaired by several different repair strategies, with different bugs being derived from different strategies. That is, it should be possible to formulate a set of impasses I and a set of repairs R such that the Cartesian product $I \times R$ generates a set of predicted bugs, most of which occur in the data. The set R is a first approximation to the set of common repair strategies. The existence of such a Cartesian product pattern in the bug data would be evidence for both the original impasse-repair assumption and the assumption that repair strategies are common knowledge. Failure to find such a pattern would mean that one or both of the assumptions are false.

If we fail to find such a pattern, it could also be that subjects are displaying common preferences in their choice of repair strategy. For instance, if *all* subjects prefer to use repair strategy A for one type of impasse, repair strategy B for a second type, and repair strategy C for a third type, then few of the cells of the $R \times I$ matrix would be filled in with occurring bugs. The issue of how subjects select repair strategies is important and is discussed at length in a following section. However, common selection preferences would only *hide* the existence of repair strategies; if we find that most of the cells of the matrix are filled in, then we can assume that repair strategies exist and that different subjects have different selection preferences.

Before going on to see whether such a pattern exists in the bug data, it is worth pointing out that this is a classic case of an auxiliary hypothesis (the common-knowledge assumption) being adopted to test a main hypothesis (the impasse-repair assumption) (Hempel 1966). In a following section a different auxiliary hypothesis is stated so that a different test can be performed.

2.3.4 A Cartesian Product of Impasses and Repairs

This section has several purposes beyond merely demonstrating that a Cartesian product of impasses and repairs exists. First, it defines three repair strategies, which are used throughout this book. Second, it defines several impasses, which are also used frequently in subsequent illustrations. Third, it demonstrates that the Cartesian product pattern is not a simple matrix but a nested collection of impasse-repair combinations. This nesting occurs when a particular repair to an impasse allows the procedure to continue only a short time before suffering a second impasse. Different repairs to the second impasse manifest themselves as different bugs. Indeed some repairs to the second impasse might cause a third impasse to occur, and so on. Thus the pattern of bugs that impasse-repair independence predicts is actually quite complicated.

The particular Cartesian product that is the topic of this section is shown in 2.2. It is a product of three impasses and three repair strategies. Bugs from the same impasse are in the same column. Repair strategies label the rows of the bugs they generate. Some cells have more than one bug in them because they cause secondary impasses, and different repairs to the secondary impasses cause differerent bugs. The remainder of this subsection deals with the derivation of each bug in the product. Enroute the repair strategies and impasses are defined and illustrated. The appendixes contain statistics on how often these bugs occurred and in what contexts.

The bug Stops-Borrow-At-Zero is generated by assuming that the student has not been taught how to borrow from zero. When the

| Repair | Impasses | | |
Strategies	Primitive	Reference	Decision
No-op	Stops-Borrow-At-Zero	Borrow-No-Decrement-Except-Last	Blank-When-Borrowed-From
Barge-on	Borrow-Add-Decrement-Instead-of-BFZ	Always-Borrow-Left	SFL-When-Borrowed-From
	Zero-Borrow-From-Zero	OK	OK
Back-up	SFL-Instead-of-BFZ	SFL-Except-Last	Quit-When-Borrowed-From
	Zero-Instead-of-BFZ		

2.2
Cartesian product of three repair strategies and three Impasses. OK = a bug-free procedure; SFL = Smaller-From-Larger; BFZ = Borrow-From-Zero.

student tries to use simple borrowing on Borrow-From-Zero problems such as

$$\begin{array}{r} 2\,0\,7 \\ -\,1\,6\,9 \\ \hline \end{array}$$

an attempt is made to decrement the zero. The student discovers that either her knowledge of arithmetic facts does not contain an entry for $0-1$ or such a question doesn't make sense. Accessing knowledge of arithmetic facts is a primitive, so this failure to execute a retrieval of $0-1$ causes a *primitive impasse*. The student has detected a metaproblem that needs to be solved before any more of the procedure can be executed. Stops-Borrow-At-Zero results from a repair strategy called *No-op*, in which a student simply skips the stuck decrement action (that is, it turns the action into a "null operation" or "no-op" in computer programmers' jargon). This leads the student to finish the units column with the problem in state A. State B shows the completed problem:

A.
$$\begin{array}{r} 2\,0^1 7 \\ -\,1\,6\,9 \\ \hline 8 \end{array}$$

B.
$$\begin{array}{r} 1 \\ \not{2}^1 0^1 7 \\ -\,1\,6\,9 \\ \hline 4\,8 \end{array}$$

Let us proceed down the first column of 2.2, discussing the effects of different repairs to this same impasse. The next cell in the same column indicates that two bugs, Zero-Borrow-From-Zero and Add-Borrow-Decrement-Instead-of-Borrow-From-Zero, are caused by the *Barge-on* repair strategy. The basic idea of the Barge-on repair is to interpret the specification of the procedure in a more relaxed way, thus approximating the action it specifies rather than performing it exactly. In this case the specified action is to find $0 - 1$. One approximation is to reason that whatever the answer to $0 - 1$ is, it must be pretty small, and zero is the smallest possible number (negative numbers have not yet been introduced at the time subtraction is taught), so $0 - 1 \approx 0$. This generates the bug Zero-Borrow-From-Zero, which always borrows from a zero by crossing out the zero and writing a zero over it, as in

$$
\begin{array}{cc}
0 & 4^1 0^1 0 \\
7\ \not{0}^1 3 & \not{5}\ \not{0}\ \not{0}^1 3 \\
-9 & -1\ 2\ 3\ 4 \\
\hline
7\ 0\ 4 & 3\ 8\ 7\ 9
\end{array}
$$

Zero-Borrow-From-Zero gives exactly the same answers as Stops-Borrow-At-Zero, but the pattern of scratch marks is different. The bug Add-Borrow-Decrement-Instead-of-Borrow-From-Zero is generated by either of two different relaxations. The student can approximate $0 - 1$ by $0 + 1$, by $1 - 0$, or by $|0 - 1|$. Any of these approximations yields a one, which is written over the zero:

$$
\begin{array}{cc}
1 & 4^1 1^1 1 \\
7\ \not{0}^1 3 & \not{5}\ \not{0}\ \not{0}^1 3 \\
-9 & -1\ 2\ 3\ 4 \\
\hline
7\ 1\ 4 & 3\ 9\ 8\ 9
\end{array}
$$

Notice that Barge-on generates different bugs depending on how it is applied. Of course we could just as well have several different versions of Barge-on, each of which applies uniquely and generates just one bug. Nothing important hangs on the choice of a generic Barge-on rather than a set of specific ones.

Perhaps this is as good a time as any to point out that forming a taxonomy of repair strategies is just like forming a taxonomy of problem-solving methods—a subtle and at times arbitrary endeavor, engaged in mostly for expository convenience and as a prelude to precise theories. This particular taxonomy—which divides repair strategies into No-op, Barge-on and Back-up—is designed around process models for the repair strategies that I present later. (It turns out that Barge-on is implemented by partial matching of patterns, and that Back-up and No-op are implemented by popping a stack of goals.) The taxonomy used in earlier reports (Brown and VanLehn 1980, VanLehn 1983a, b) was different than this one because the early representation of procedures forced repair strategies to be implemented as ad hoc processes. This ad hoc set of repairs generated star bugs. Avoiding these absurd predictions was one of the motivations for revising the representation language.

The next cell in the matrix contains two bugs, Smaller-From-Larger-Instead-of-Borrow-From-Zero and Zero-Instead-of-Borrow-From-Zero. Actually it contains many other bugs as well, but they are not discussed here. The bugs in this cell of the Cartesian product are generated by the *Back-up* repair strategy. Back-up is a simple repair strategy, although it is difficult to describe. The essence of the Back-up repair strategy is retreating in order to take an alternative path. In most cases using Back-up causes a secondary impasse. This is just what happens with Smaller-From-Larger-Instead-of-Borrow-From-Zero. Here's how that bug is generated. Suppose the student is solving

$$703 \\ \underline{-\quad 9}$$

The student reaches an impasse trying to decrement the zero in the tens column. The Back-up repair strategy gets past the decrement-zero impasse by backing up to the last decision. In this case the last decision was whether to borrow for the units column. So the student backs up to that decision and takes another alternative. Suppose he takes the alternative of doing the units column without borrowing. Almost immediately he hits a second impasse because he finds that he cannot take a larger number from a smaller one. Suppose this second impasse is repaired by Barge-on. If the student approximates $3 - 9$ as $9 - 3$, then the bug Smaller-From-Larger-Instead-of-Borrow-From-Zero is generated. This bug solves columns that require borrowing from a zero by taking the absolute difference instead:

$$\begin{array}{r} 703 \\ -\quad 9 \\ \hline 706 \end{array} \qquad \begin{array}{r} 4 \\ \cancel{5}^{1}0\,0\,3 \\ -1\,2\,3\,4 \\ \hline 3\,8\,3\,1 \end{array}$$

If the Barge-on repair strategy is implemented by approximating $3 - 9 \approx 0$, then the bug Zero-Instead-of-Borrow-From-Zero is generated. Perhaps the student rationalizes this relaxation by reasoning that if he has three apples, and the teacher tries to take nine away, he certainly will not have any apples left. Zero-Instead-of-Borrow-From-Zero solves borrow-from-zero columns by merely entering a zero as their answer:

$$
\begin{array}{r}
7\ 0\ 3 \\
-\quad\ 9 \\
\hline
7\ 0\ 0
\end{array}
\qquad
\begin{array}{r}
\overset{4}{\cancel{5}}{}^{10}\ 0\ 3 \\
-1\ 2\ 3\ 4 \\
\hline
3\ 8\ 0\ 0
\end{array}
$$

These two bugs illustrate that some cells in the Cartesian product have more than one bug in them because the original repair strategy, Back-up in this case, causes secondary impasses.

The second column of 2.2 presents bugs generated from a new impasse. This impasse occurs when a student has a procedure that has an overly specific description of where to place the decrement of borrowing. In all subtraction curricula that I have seen, borrowing is first taught with two-column problems. In such problems the decrement always occurs in the tens column, which is both the leftmost column of the problem and the column that is left-adjacent to the column that causes the borrow. Suppose that this idiosyncratic choice of training examples causes some students to believe that the correct place to situate a decrement is in a column that is both left-adjacent to the current column and the leftmost column in the problem. On a problem like

$$
\begin{array}{r}
3\ 4\ 5 \\
-1\ 1\ 9 \\
\hline
\end{array}
$$

the student starts to borrow from the units column and discovers that her description, leftmost and left-adjacent, does not refer to any column in the problem, because there is no column that is both leftmost and left-adjacent. This causes a *reference impasse*.

The first cell of the matrix shows that the No-op repair strategy causes the bug Borrow-No-Decrement-Except-Last by simply omitting the decrement action whenever the reference impasse occurs. Perhaps the student reasons that if she cannot figure out where to place the decrement, she is better off not doing it at all. This means that the bug will perform decrements only when the borrow is caused by the penultimate column in the problem:

$$
\begin{array}{r}
3\ \overset{}{4}{}^{1}5 \\
-1\ 1\ 9 \\
\hline
2\ 3\ 6
\end{array}
\qquad
\begin{array}{r}
\overset{4}{\cancel{5}}{}^{1}1{}^{1}3 \\
-1\ 6\ 7 \\
\hline
3\ 5\ 6
\end{array}
$$

The next cell of the matrix contains two bugs because the Barge-on repair strategy can be applied in two ways. If the description "leftmost and left-adjacent" is approximated by "leftmost," then the bug Always-Borrow-Left is generated. It places all decrements in the leftmost column regardless of the position of the column causing the borrow:

$$
\begin{array}{cc}
 & 3 \\
2 & \not4 \\
\not3\;4^15 & \not5^11^13 \\
-1\,1\,9 & -1\,6\,7 \\
\hline
1\,3\,6 & 2\,5\,6
\end{array}
$$

On the other hand if the Barge-on repair strategy is implemented by relaxing the "leftmost and left-adjacent" description to "left-adjacent," then the correct placement of the decrement is generated. This leads to a bug-free procedure (except that the procedure may not have a routine for borrowing across zero, in which case the bugs in the first column will be generated). This illustrates that repair strategies need not always cause bugs. Sometimes correct procedures are generated.

The last cell in the column indicates that the Back-up repair generates Smaller-From-Larger-Except-Last. (It also generates several other bugs that are not shown in the figure.) When the reference impasse occurs, the Back-up repair strategy has the student shift attention back to the decision about how to process the column that caused the borrow. In the case of 435 − 119, this means returning to the decision about processing the units column. If the student chooses the alternative method of trying to process the column without borrowing, he reaches a second impasse because he cannot calculate 5 − 9. Suppose he takes the Barge-on repair strategy and implements it by approximating 5 − 9 by 9 − 5. This generates a bug that takes the absolute difference in all columns except those columns that require a borrow from the last column:

$$
\begin{array}{cc}
 & 4 \\
3\,4\,5 & \not5^11\,3 \\
-1\,1\,9 & -1\,6\,7 \\
\hline
2\,3\,4 & 3\,5\,4
\end{array}
$$

The third column of 2.2 presents bugs derived from a *decision impasse*. The impasse occurs when a procedure has an overly specific description of when it is appropriate to borrow. The procedure seems to derive from teaching students how to borrow, but neglecting to show them training examples where borrows occur in adjacent columns. Many curricula place adjacent-borrow problems in a distinct lesson, so there is often a period of time just before this lesson when students have been trained on many types of borrowing but not on problems that require adjacent borrows. Students tested during this period might have the procedure discussed here. In problems that have adjacent borrows, such as

$$
\begin{array}{r}
7\ 2\ 3 \\
-1\ 8\ 5 \\
\hline
\end{array}
$$

the second borrow is caused by a column that has had a decrement placed in it by the preceding borrow. In this case the tens column is $1 - 8$ because the two has been decremented. Apparently some students' description of when to borrow specifies that the column be "plain," that is, free of scratch marks, and that the top digit be less than the bottom digit. On the other hand if the top digit is greater than the bottom digit, then the students believe that it is appropriate to do the column without borrowing, even if the column has scratch marks in it. Thus when they come to the tens column of this problem, they are unsure whether to borrow. Their description of borrowing-columns does not match because it specifies a plain column, but the tens column is not plain. The description of nonborrowing-columns does not match either because it specifies a column whose top digit is greater than the bottom digit, but 1 is not greater than 8. So neither description matches. This causes a decision impasse because the student is unsure which column-processing method to apply.

The top cell in the third column of 2.2 indicates that the No-op repair strategy produces the bug Blank-When-Borrowed-From. This bug skips columns that are borrowed from and require a borrow:

$$
\begin{array}{r}
1 \\
7\ \not{2}^{1}3 \\
-1\ 8\ 5 \\
\hline
6\quad\ 8 \\
\end{array}
$$

The second cell shows that Barge-on produces two bugs, depending on how it is applied. Application of Barge-on to a decision impasse means choosing one of the methods that one is having trouble deciding between. If the student takes the borrowing method of column processing, a bug-free procedure is generated. If the student takes the nonborrowing method of column processing, the bug

Smaller-From-Larger-When-Borrowed-From is generated eventually (via the usual impasse and a second application of Barge-on):

```
      1
    7 ²13
  - 1 8 5
  -------
    6 7 8
```

The third cell of the column shows that Back-up produces the bug Quit-When-Borrowed-From. This bug quits working the problem when a borrowed-from column is encountered that requires a borrow:

```
      1
    7 ²13
  - 1 8 5
  -------
        8
```

The explanation is that Back-up retreats to the most recent decision, which is presumably whether to process this column or go on to the next problem in the problem set. It takes the alternative that was not taken before, which is to move on to the next problem.

This completes the description of the bugs in the Cartesian product of 2.2. This Cartesian product is extended in chapter 7 by adding more columns and rows until it covers all the bugs generable by the theory.

This section began by adopting an auxiliary hypothesis—that repair strategies are common knowledge. This led to the prediction of a Cartesian product pattern in the data, on the argument that if repair strategies are common knowledge, then for each repair strategy and each impasse someone will eventually be found who chooses to use that repair strategy on that impasse. Obviously this is making some assumptions about how subjects select repair strategies, so in the next section I examine that issue.

2.3.5 Selection of Repair Strategies: Individual versus Group Data

The impasse-repair assumption is that the choice of a repair strategy is like the choice of a problem-solving method. Presumably this is a matter of some deliberation on the part of the subject. What can the bug data tell us about how subjects select a repair strategy?

In several years spent examining bug data, I have not yet observed a pattern in the choice of repair strategies. This has led me to suspect that although individual subjects probably do not guess randomly, I

	Larger from Smaller	Decrement Zero
Barge-on	119	58
No-op	1	16
Back-up	0	6
Total	120	80

2.3
Frequency of repair strategies for two different impasses

just do not have enough data on any one subject to detect a pattern in their responses.

On the other hand there is fairly strong evidence that subjects have a large variety of selection strategies, because when the selection data are aggregated over many subjects, the overall "group-selection strategy" can be approximated by random choice. That is, the finding is that choice of repair is statistically independent of the type of impasse because the data analysis deliberately commits the well-known sin of averaging over disparate strategies, as 2.3 demonstrates. It shows the number of times the two most common impasses occurred and the number of times each repair strategy was applied to them.[4] These figures show that there is a substantial preference for Barge-on over the other two repair strategies, regardless of the type of impasse. According to the chi-square test, the choice of repair is independent of the type of impasse ($p < .005$).

Statistics such as these should be taken with a large grain of salt because the quality of the frequency data is poor. The worst problem is that many bugs have more than one derivation. For instance, 2.3 shows 119 occurrences of the bug Smaller-From-Larger, which can be generated by applying the Barge-on repair strategy to the larger-from-smaller impasse. However, there is another possible derivation for the bug, which is based on the idea that the student always ignores the relative locations of a column's digits and thus ends up taking absolute difference in every column without ever suffering an impasse. The bug data provide no clue as to how many of the 119 occurrences of the bug come from impasses and how many come from misunderstanding the nature of column difference. If none comes from impasses, then that cell of 2.3 is zero, and the chi-square test fails. If 25 percent of the bugs are generated by repairs to impasses, then the resulting frequencies give some reason to believe in independence ($.01 < p < .05$).

There are other problems with frequency data. For instance, when a subject has several bugs, one bug can mask another by destroying the contexts that would normally allow it to be seen, thus leading to an underestimate of the masked bug's true frequency of occurrence. In short, for several reasons, using statistical arguments is in general a poor method for analyzing the bug data.

Nonetheless I currently believe that the subjects use a set of selection heuristics diverse enough that when the data are averaged, the influence of individual heuristics becomes so blurred that selection can be approximated as random choice. Thus, as a working rule of thumb, if a new impasse is discovered, then one should expect to eventually find all the repair strategies with it, with Barge-on occurring more frequently than No-op, and Back-up occurring least frequently. For future reference, this rule of thumb will be recorded as

The impasse-repair independence assumption
Subject strategies for selecting repair strategies at impasses are so variable that aggregate selection data can be aproximated by random choices that are independent of the type of the impasse and the surrounding situation.

In particular, given any impasse and any repair strategy, as we find more and more subjects with that impasse, the probability approaches certainty that at least one of the subjects will apply that repair strategy to the impasse.

Combining an unpopular repair with an uncommon impasse often predicts a bug that has not yet been observed. In fact repair-impasse independence predicted several bugs before they were observed. When the theory was first tested in September 1979, it predicted sixteen bugs that had not yet been observed. When its predictions were tested against newly collected data in December 1979, six of the predicted bugs were discovered (Brown and VanLehn 1980). Since then another of the predicted bugs has been discovered, even though few new data have been acquired in the interim. Such prediction is, to me at least, one of the most convincing arguments for the impasse-repair assumption.

Impasse-repair independence gives us an empirical criterion for judging the existence of proposed impassses and repairs. Sometimes it is tempting to explain a particular bug by postulating a new impasse or a new repair. However, the independence of impasses and repairs means that the new impasse or repair can now be combined with all the old impasses and repairs. If all these new combinations generate bugs that either exist or could plausibly be observed in larger samples, then one is justified in assuming that the newly invented impasse or repair does in fact exist. On the other hand if some or all of the combinations generate star bugs (implausible bugs—see section 1.2), then there is reason to doubt that the newly invented impasse or repair exists, so one should seek a different explanation for the bug that precipitated their invention. This tool will be used extensively in analyses of particular bugs.

2.3.6 Bug Migration

The previous sections tested the impasse-repair assumption by adopting an auxiliary hypothesis that led to the successful prediction of a pattern in the bug data. This section applies the same method, with a different auxiliary hypothesis and different data. The data involve *bug migrations*, a term coined by Brown and VanLehn (1980) for the phenomenon of a student switching among two or more bugs during a short period of time with no intervening instruction. The bugs the student switches among are called a bug migration class.

One general characteristic of problem solving is that a subject may try different means to the same end on different occasions. That is, if you give the same subject the same problem on different occasions, she may apply different methods to solve it. Sometimes she will use the same method, of course because she either always prefers that method for this type of problem or remembers the previous episode of problem solving and wants to apply the method she used then. As a general rule of thumb, however, some subjects will be found who select different methods for the same problem. Although this is an empirical hypothesis, it is so obviously a component of the common view of problem solving that it does not deserve a name of its own. This hypothesis will be used as an auxiliary hypothesis for testing the impasse-repair assumption.

The impasse-repair assumption and the hypothesis together imply that we should see a particular kind of bug migration wherein a student has the same core procedure during the period of observation— and therefore the same impasses—but she chooses different repair strategies at different occurrences of the impasses. On such occasions all the bugs in the bug migration class result from *applying different repairs to the same impasse*. This is the hallmark of bug migrations caused by choosing different repairs to the same impasse.

If the data show such bug migrations, then both the impasse-repair assumption and the auxiliary hypothesis are supported. If the data never show the predicted bug migrations, then either the impasse-repair assumption is false or there is something that causes all subjects to always use the same repair strategy for every occurrence of their impasse.

```
                             7
  6 4 7     8 8 5      8̸ 3      8 3 0 5
-   4 5   - 2 0 5    - 4 4    -       3
  6 0 2     6 8 0      3 9      8 3 0 2


   4  10                3  12      0  10
  3̸ 0̸      5 6̸ 2̸     7 4̸ 2̸     1̸ 0̸ 6
             5  12
- 2 3     -     3   - 1 3 6    -   7 0
  2 7       5 5 9      6 0 6      3 6


  6  10 16   0 14 15  14   5 14 15 11    2 10 11
  7̸ 1̸ 8̸    1̸ 3̸ 6̸ 4̸   6̸ 3̸ 9̸ 1̸   3̸ 1̸ 1̸
- 5 9 8   -   8 8 7   - 2 6 9 7   - 2 1 4
  1 1 8       6 6 7     3 8 9 4      9 7


       7  10 13    0 10 12    8 10 10     3 10 0 15
  1 8̸ 1̸ 3̸    1̸ 0̸ 2̸    9̸ 0̸ 0̸ 7    4̸ 0̸ 1̸ 3̸
-   2 1 5   -   3 9   - 6 8 8 0   -   6 0 7
  1 5 9 8       7 3     2 2 2 7    3 4 0 8


  6  0 12   1  0 10    0 0 10 0 12    0 10 11
  7̸ 0̸ 2̸    2̸ 0̸ 0̸ 6   1̸ 0̸ 0̸ 1̸ 2̸   8 0̸ 0̸ 1̸
- 1 0 8   -     4 2   -     2 1 4   -     4 3
  5 0 4     1 0 6 4         8 0 8    8 0 6 8
```

2.4
Solution to a test by student 22 of classroom 34 showing intratest bug migration

Some cases of the predicted bug migrations have been found. An example is shown in 2.4, which reproduces a test taken by a student in the Southbay sample. (The Southbay study is discussed in detail in chapter 7.) This student missed only six problems, namely, the ones that required borrowing from zero. The first two problems that she missed (the second and third problems in the fourth row) she answered as if she had the bug Stops-Borrow-At-Zero. That is, she got stuck when she attempted to decrement a zero and used the No-op repair strategy to skip the decrement operation. The next two problems that she missed (the first two problems on the last row) she answered as if she had the bug Borrow-Across-Zero. This bug can be generated by a series of repairs to the impasse, but I will not pause here to explain them. On the third problem of the last row, she used two repairs within the same problem. For the borrow originating in

36	Stable correct algorithm
3	Stable bugs
12	Stable impasses and unstable repairs (plus perhaps some stable bugs)
10	Unstable impasses and repairs (plus perhaps some stable bugs)
6	One or both tests cannot be analyzed
67	Total

2.5
Categories of two-test stability

the tens column, she used Back-up to retreat from the decrement-zero impasse. She wound up writing a zero as the answer in the tens column (as if she had the bug Zero-Instead-of-Borrow-From-Zero). In the hundreds column she took the same repair strategies that she used on the preceding two problems. On the last problem she used No-op and Barge-on.

This subtraction test, like many others that could be shown, provides evidence for bug migration. Unfortunately Debuggy is not equipped to find cases of bug migration, so it is difficult to estimate the frequency of occurrence or to assemble a data base of bug migrations. However, hand analysis provides the results shown in 2.5 (see VanLehn 1982, for details). These results are from a group of 67 students who were tested twice a short time apart, with no intervening subtraction instruction. Half of the students were bug-free on both tests. Of the remainder about a third (12 of 32) exhibited the kinds of bug migrations predicted by the theory. A few students (3 of 32) showed exactly the same bugs on both tests. Some students (10 of 32) showed bug migrations that cannot be explained by the theory. Six students could not be analyzed, probably because they made slips so frequently that their underlying knowledge of the task could not be reliably determined given the brevity of the tests.

The general finding then is that bug migration is rather common, and about half of the observed bug migrations are consistent with the theory's predictions. This finding supports the impasse-repair hypothesis.

2.4 The Stable Bugs Problem

As 2.5 shows, bugs are often stable. Sometimes stable bugs occur in the context of a bug migration. For instance, a student may have bug A on both tests, but switch from bug B to bug C. Some bugs are extremely stable and persist for months or years. In one study (see appendix 6 in VanLehn 1982) 154 students were tested several months apart. Of these students 34 (22 percent) had bugs on both tests. Of these 34, 17 (50 percent) had the same bugs on both tests.

As mentioned previously; some bugs are generated by repairing impasses, and some are generated directly, without going through an impasse-repair process. If we assume that procedures are stable, but the choice of repair strategies is not, then the stable bugs should be mostly those bugs that are generated without going through the impasse-repair process. However, this is not the case. Of the 17 students that held the same bugs for several months, 8 had bugs that can only be generated (as far as I know) by repairs to impasses. Thus the stable bugs problem is to explain how it is that some students always end up exhibiting the same repair on every occurrence of an impasse. Three possible explanations are:

1. The student has strong preferences for the choice of repair strategy. A stable bug results when the student always chooses to use the same repair strategy for the given impasse. Preferences for a specific repair strategy may have existed before the initial occurrence of the impasse, or the preference may have developed as a result of trying different repair strategies and deciding that one is preferable to the others for this impasse.
2. Before the bug became stable, the student may have tried one or more repair strategies. But now, rather than applying a repair strategy, the student merely recalls an earlier repair and reuses it.
3. At some previous occurrence of the impasse, the student's repair strategy was implemented by editing the procedure then executing the revised procedure. Now the procedure runs without reaching an impasse because it traverses the code generated by the repair strategy rather than the older code that caused the impasse.

The bug data simply do not provide any way to split these hypotheses. Indeed some of them may not be empirically distinguishable at all. Rather than make some arbitrary choice among these potential explanations, the stable bug problem is left hanging. Eventually an assumption may fill this gap in the theory, but it is too early to tell what the right assumption is. As a place holder the term *patch* was coined (Brown and VanLehn 1980, VanLehn 1988). A patch is some kind of lasting change to the student's knowledge—such as a preference for a specific repair strategy, the memory of a repair, or an edit to the procedure—that causes the student to behave as if the same repair strategy is always selected at a given impasse. The appropriate assumption to record is

The patches assumption
Subjects' knowledge of a procedure may include patches.

2.5 Summary

To summarize the main argument, two predictions are implied by the impasse-repair assumption, and both of these seem to hold in our data. The first is that bugs can be arranged in a Cartesian product of impasses and repairs such that most cells of the product are filled in. The second is that some bug migrations result from differing repairs to the same underlying impasse.

We have finished the first of the three stages of argumentation that I mentioned in the introduction. At this point several assumptions have accumulated, the most important of which are the impasse-repair assumption and the procedure-following assumption. Together these describe in general terms the relation between what people know and what they do when they are solving procedural tasks in domains like arithmetic. The major surprise is that execution of a procedure is not as simple as one might think. Impasses and repairs complicate the picture considerably.

We have also accumulated some minor, domain-specific assumptions about what kinds of impasses occur in subtracton procedures (for example, there is an impasse when a student attempts to decrement a zero) and what kinds of repair strategies are typically used. These assumptions prove quite useful when the bug data are examined in more detail.

Most important we have developed an empirical tool. The impasse-repair hypothesis provides a method for interpreting observables—that is, the bug data—in terms of unobservables—that is, the core procedures. Granted, the lack of formality in both the description of the execution process and the knowledge structures makes these inferences somewhat weak. But one has to start somewhere. Indeed it is necessary for this particular theory to begin its argumentation with informal representations because the formal representations later play a crucial role in the learning theory. For instance, some of the hypotheses in the learning theory state that students prefer procedures that are structurally simple, where simplicity is based on the procedure's formal representation. Thus the formal representations for procedures are not just an arbitrary notation but an important component of the theory. The next stage in the argumentation proposes specific formal representations and defends those proposals by using the empirical tools developed in this first stage.

2.6 A Comparison with Soar

The basic idea of impasses was developed independently of the research presented here by John Laird, Allen Newell, and Paul Rosenbloom in their general architecture for intelligence, Soar (Laird, Newell, and Rosenbloom 1987). When it became apparent that Soar and Sierra were doing the same thing, Laird and colleagues graciously changed their terminology to correspond to mine and relabeled difficulties (Laird 1983) as impasses. Although both Sierra and Soar have impasses, they differ in many other respects. This section is a comparison of the two models' view of impasses.

The major difference between Sierra and Soar is that Soar specifies a more detailed model of cognition than Sierra. For instance, Soar has a model of long-term memory. Because Soar allows impasses to occur at any point in its processing, impasses can occur during retrieval from long-term memory because the cue is not sufficient for unambiguous access. When such impasses occur, Soar can apply strategies such as elaboration of the retrieval cue. When the impasse is finally resolved, the retrieved information is associated with the original impasse-causing cue. Thus Soar enriches its access paths to long-term memory via impasse-driven processing. This sort of learning occurs frequently, perhaps once every few seconds. This is just one example of how Soar uses impasse-driven processing. In contrast Sierra has no models of long-term memory or any other detailed, fine-granied cognitive processes. The only kinds of procedures that can suffer an impasse in Sierra are procedures like subtraction. If Soar were used to model subtraction execution, it is likely that only a small subset of its impasses would correspond to Sierra's impasses. Soar has more impasses per unit time than Sierra has and a larger variety of impasses because its process model is much more detailed than Sierra's. Thus the major difference between Soar's impasses and Sierra's impasses is due to the scale of their models.

Some less important differences exist between Soar and Sierra's treatment of impasses. Soar maintains a last-in–first-out stack of impasses, so that if a new impasse occurs while an old impasse is being handled, work on the old impasse is suspended while work on the new one takes place. When the new impasse in finally taken care of, the stack pops and the work resumes on the old impasse. Sierra cannot stack impasses in its present implementation because no arithmetic bugs have been found that require stacking impasses to explain them. However, it is not difficult to find cases from outside the arithmetic task domain where stacking of impasses seems to be required. What follows is a long anecdote that both illustrates the occasional necessity of stacking and reviews some of the earlier comments about how the basic ideas of impasses and repairs can be applied outside the task domain of arithmetic.

I once assembled a barbecue grill using an instruction manual that listed 44 steps. I experienced the usual variety of impasses (reference, decision, primitives, and critic) and was able to handle most of them by reinterpreting the instructions (the Barge-on repair, loosely speaking). On one occasion I had to do a major Back-up repair because I had mistakenly assumed that all the bolts that looked about the same length were in fact the same length. Actually some were 1 inch long, and others were $\frac{7}{8}$ inch long. I had mistakenly used up the longer bolts, so I had to disassemble the grill to get them back. Nonetheless even this sophisticated repair required no stacking of impasses. However, some other repairs did. On one occasion the instructions called for inserting a bolt in a hole in a certain steel tube, and I could find no such hole. I first tried to reinterpret the instructions, hypothesizing that I had gotten the wrong tube. However, all the other tubes with holes were inappropriate. The Barge-on repair failed. I contemplated skipping the step (the No-op repair), but that would have left a crucial strut unsupported. Without trying Back-up, I gave up on repair strategies based on changing my interpretation of the procedure and decided to perform the repair strategy of last resort: change the situation itself. With my electric drill I started to drill a hole and got the drill bit stuck, thus reaching an impasse inside the handling of another impasse. Needless to say, this impasse could only be repaired by changing the situation, so I wrenched the drill bit free of the hole with a pair of pliers. Applying a little more cutting oil, I was able to successfully drill the hole, finish up the first impasse, and continue that aggravating 44-step procedure. This last episode of impasses and repairs illustrates that occasionally it is necessary to suspend the processing of one impasse to deal with a new one. Thus the Soar architecture seems justified in stacking impasses.

Another difference between Soar and Sierra is that Sierra has a goal stack, and Soar does not. Although the goal stack is not discussed until the next chapter, it is worth mentioning here. Sierra theory assumes people use a goal stack because they seem to remember the dynamic, hierarchical relationship among past goals and use this information during the Back-up repair. Thus students who are working on the decrement of a borrow that originated in the tens column know exactly that they are working on a subgoal of the borrow goal.

The simplest organization that permits a parsimonious explanation of the bug data is that the memory of past suspended goals is organized as a last-in–first-out stack. There is nothing particularly unusual about this assumption; goal stacks are often used in models of problem solving (Newell and Simon 1972, Simon 1975, Anderson 1983). However, Soar does not have a goal stack, so a Soar model of subtraction would probably use the impasse stack. (Although there are other kinds of memory in Soar, the impasse stack seems to be the most suitable for this application.) This means that every time subjects perform a borrow, they must suffer an impasse. Without the impasse there is no record of the fact that a borrow is in progress. I am not expert enough on Soar to say what the consequences of this are, but it just does not seem right. Intuitively an impasse is a genuine problem, whereas a borrow is just a routine segment of activity. This leads me to suspect that Soar's ability to handle many types of novel problems (Newell 1987) is balanced by an inability to handle routine problems in the same way that people do. That is, it appears that Soar's forte is classical, search-based problem solving, whereas Sierra's forte is procedure following.

Chapter 3
The Representation of Procedural Knowledge

This chapter presents a particular representation language for expressing knowledge about procedures. The argument is quite unlike the usual sorts of arguments for representation languages. A standard argument proposes a representation language and a learning mechanism and shows that the two together can account for some acquisitional data. However, the methodological objective of this research is to avoid postulating large sets of assumptions all at once, because that makes it hard to assign explanatory credit to the individual assumptions. The preferred route is to postulate only a few assumptions, use these to raise issues, enumerate some plausible solutions for each issue, and use the data to decide which solution to incorporate into the theory. In this case there are four ways to do this:

1. Assume a representation language then find a learning process that maximizes coverage of the acquisition data.
2. Assume a learning process and find a representation language that maximizes coverage of the acquisition data.
3. Use an independent source of data to uncover the representation language then find a learning process that maximizes coverage of the acquisition data.
4. Use an independent source of data to uncover the learning process then find a representation language that maximizes coverage of the acquisition data.

The third method is pursued in this research. The independent source of data comes from the details of the impasse-repair process. The key idea is that there are two processes that read the expressions in the representation language. One is the ordinary interpretation process, which reads a procedure and acts on it. The other is the repair process, which reads the state of the interpretation and changes it in such a way that the procedure can continue. By examining the kinds of repairs that occur, we can infer what information must be present in the interpretation at the time the repair occurred.

We then assume that this information is available because the interpretation process uses it in the course of its ordinary processing of the procedure. This then tells us what kind of interpretation process the subject is using. That in turn tells us what class of representation languages the subject's language lies within. This type of argument does not completely fix the representation language, but it does indicate a class of representation languages that subjects could have. This is not perfect independent evidence for the language, but it is much better than none.

In this chapter the strongest arguments are those that determine what kind of interpretation process that subject is using. These arguments appear mostly in sections 3.3 through 3.6, where control-structure issues are discussed. The other arguments are like the usual sort of argument that one finds in discussions of representation languages, where a language design is chosen because it is simple yet sufficient for writing programs that predict the data. Most of these arguments appear in the last two sections of the chapter, sections 3.7 and 3.8. The first two sections present arguments about how information inside a procedure interfaces with information outside the procedure. The arguments here are based partly on repairs and partly on computational sufficiency and parsimony. Thus they are halfway between the strong arguments of sections 3.3 through 3.6 and the weaker arguments of sections 3.7 and 3.8.

3.1 The Decomposition Assumption

One can safely assume that knowledge of a mathematical calculus, such as arithmetic, involves knowing at least three types of things: (1) mathematical facts, such as $15 - 7 = 8$, (2) the syntax of the notation, and (3) the procedures for manipulation of that notation. This theory is concerned with only the third type of knowledge, the manipulation procedures. When a procedure executes, however, it uses specific mathematical facts and specific pieces of the notation. For instance, it might need to find out what $15 - 7$ is and what part of the page constitutes the numerator of $x/(2 + x)$. How such questions are answered could be quite complicated. For instance, Siegler and his colleagues (Siegler and Shrager 1984, Siegler 1987, 1988) have discovered that students use a variety of strategies for answering questions like $5 + 7$ and have developed an interesting theory of the acquisition of competence in the retrieval of such basic mathematical facts. Although little is known about how people parse mathematical notation, studies of bugs in linear algebra indicate that notational knowledge can be a nontrivial component of the overall competence (Matz 1982, Sleeman 1982, Sleeman 1984a,b).

The procedure needs a way to pose the appropriate questions to the factual and notational processes and to receive their answers. It does not need to know how they arrive at such answers, nor anything about the knowledge representation involved in generating the answers. All it needs is a way to state the questions and receive the answers. This implies that there must be a language in which such questions and answers can be stated. Specific notational questions (for example, What is the numerator of $x/3y$?) are expressions in the notational interface language, and specific factual questions (for example Is $5 \leq 7$?) are expressions in the factual interface language. Thus we make

The decomposition assumption
The representation language for procedure has sublanguages for representing questions posed to the processes that handle mathematical notation and mathematical facts. A procedure is an expression in the procedure representation language, pieces of which may be expressions in the interface languages for notation and facts.

This assumption breaks down the task of finding out what the representation of procedural knowledge is into the three subtasks of finding out what each of the three sublanguages is. In the next section I examine the representation of the two interface sublanguages. The remainder of the chapter deals with the representation of control structure, which is that part of the procedure not involved in interfacing.

3.2 The Representation of Interfaces

An interface expression is like the kind of concept used in concept-formation experiments. Instead of concepts such as "The stimulus has a black dot over a white triangle," interfaces express ideas such as "The column has a nonzero digit over a blank." There is a large literature on how people represent concepts and use them, including work in psychology, philosophy, and artificial intelligence. But there is as yet no consensus on how concepts should be represented.

The lack of such consensus suggests trying to duck the issue of representing interface concepts. This was the approach taken in previous versions of this theory (Brown and VanLehn 1980). Interfaces in procedures were represented as black boxes (actually as Lisp functions). This approach failed because it led to an ad hoc set of repair strategies. To see how this occurred and to set the stage for a better representation, consider the bugs of 2.2 that are listed as being generated by the Barge-on repair.

The bug Always-Borrow-Left seems to be caused by an impasse that occurs when the procedure is trying to find the proper column for the decrementing action of borrowing. It tries to find a column that is both leftmost and left-adjacent to the current column, but there is no such column (unless the borrow occurs in the second to the last column). The bug Always-Borrow-Left is generated by a repair that causes the decrement to be relocated to the leftmost column. Suppose the interface that describes what kind of column to find is atomic, in that neither the normal interpretation nor the repair strategies can decompose it into parts. Because the description is just a black box, the repair strategy that generates the bug Always-Borrow-Left must contain the bias toward moving left. So the repair strategy is something like "relocate to the left." There is another bug in 2.2, Smaller-From-Larger-When-Borrowed-From, that seems to require a repair that relocates attention vertically by swapping the roles of the top and bottom digits when taking a column difference. Thus a second repair strategy is needed, "relocate vertically." But each repair strategy can be applied to the other's impasses, according to the impasse-repair assumption. Applying the swap-vertical repair strategy to the impasse that generates Always-Borrow-Left generates a bug that has not been observed, but is somewhat plausible. However, applying the move-left repair strategy to the impasse that generates Smaller-From-Larger-When-Borrowed-From generates a star bug. (This star bug skips to the leftmost column when it encounters a column that has been borrowed form. It is not clear what happens after that. Execution might continue, eventually leading to an attempt to answer the leftmost column a second time.) Plainly the theory's empirical fidelity would be improved if the unobserved bug and the star bug were not generated. Thus it appears that the set of repair strategies has been characterized incorrectly.

A better approach requires using nonatomic, composite representations of interface expressions. This allows the repair strategies to act on components of the expressions. In particular if the description of where to decrement is represented as a conjunction of the concepts leftmost and left-adjacent, then the repair strategy can cause one of the conjuncts to be ignored. Suppose it is the left-adjacency property that is ignored. Now the expression refers quite nicely. Of course the column it refers to is the leftmost column in the problem, which means a buggy solution occurs. If the student had been luckier and had relaxed the leftmost property, a correct solution would have been generated. In short by ignoring parts of the interface expressions, the Barge-on repair strategy can generate appropriate repairs and avoid generating repairs that lead to star bugs.

Deciding to ignore a portion of an expression as that expression is being matched is often called partial matching, to distinguish it from exact matching, where all elements of an expression are matched. It might seem plausible, on the basis of the story given, that partial matching is what *always* occurs. However, this suggestion makes it difficult to explain all the bugs in the second and third columns of 2.2. It would predict that only bugs in the Barge-on row would appear. The bugs in the No-op and Back-up rows could not be explained because when partial matching is the default interpretation of interfaces, there would be no impasses for the bugs in columns 2 and 3. Consequently there would be no opportunity to apply No-op and Back-up. So it appears that interface expressions are matched exactly, and that a variety of repair strategies can be applied to the resulting impasses.

In short the need to explain where impasses come from, plus the need to have interface concepts that the Barge-on repair can perform surgery on, motivates

The pattern assumption
Interfaces are represented as *patterns*, which are expressions in predicate calculus. They are matched according to standard rules for the interpretation of logical formulas.

Predicate calculus is used here as a placeholder. There are many plausible representations that are equivalent to predicate calculus or to a well-defined part of predicate calculus. For instance, the discrimination trees used to represent concepts, by, for example, Hunt, Marin, and Stone (1966), are equivalent to propositional calculus, which is a part of predicate calculus. The assumption is meant to include discrimination trees and other variants of predicate calculus, while excluding sets of instances, prototypes and other fuzzy concept representations.

The assumption is written to include interfaces with mathematical facts as well as interfaces with the external situation. This generality has some support. Notice that two different bugs are generated by applying the Barge-on repair to the impasse of column one in 2.2. One bug is Zero-Borrow-From-Zero. This bug seems to be caused by a repair that causes the students to act as if $0 - 1 = 0$. The other bug, Borrow-Add-Decrement-Instead-of-Zero, is caused by a repair that makes them act as if $0 - 1 = 1$. Suppose we represent the interface expression that accesses the student's knowledge of number facts as

"The number desired is one away from and smaller than the given number." Dropping the first property, "one away from," gives $0 - 1 = 0$, whereas dropping the second property, "smaller than," gives $0 - 1 = 1$. Thus it seems that the Barge-on repair works on interfaces to mathematical facts as well as interfaces to the situation, provided that both are represented as patterns.

3.3 Serial Systems

Having settled on a representation for interfaces, let us turn now to the question of how to represent the rest of the procedure, which is sometimes called the control structure of the procedure. Because this structure is not as directly connected to the external situation as the interfaces are, it is more difficult to infer from data what its properties are. The investigation begins in this section and continues through the remainder of the chapter.

Throughout the history of computer science and cognitive science, many representation languages for procedures have been devised. Some, like the programming languages Fortran and Cobol, were never intended to represent human procedural knowledge. Some languages, such as Sage (Langley 1982), Caps (Just and Carpenter 1987), Pups (Anderson and Thompson 1986), and Soar (Laird 1986), are held to be psychologically plausible.

The intent of this research is not simply to propose yet another language, show that empirically accurate simulations can be written in it, and assert on that basis that the language corresponds to the human procedural knowledge representation language. In general the ability to write accurate simulations is often not a strong enough test to support the claim of psychological reality *for the language*. It does show that the theorist has discovered and encoded a psychologically plausible *computation*, but it often takes a great deal of extra work to ascertain whether the particular *encoding* of it is psychologically plausible as well.

The intent here is to formulate and test *specifications* for a procedural representation language. Specifications act as axioms that describe a mathematical structure in that many concrete representation languages may be sanctioned by those specifications. Thus the discussion is in terms of *classes* of representation languages, all the members of which share specific properties.

Computer science has developed a fairly rich classification scheme for programming languages. The top level of the classification scheme differentiates between logic programming languages, production systems, object-oriented programming languages, ordinary sequential programming languages, and a variety of languages for parallel processing. The differences among these languages is so vast that it would be well beyond the scope of this book to even delineate those differences, let alone argue the merits of each language as a representation for knowledge of subtraction. So, after a few brief remarks, a class of languages is adopted simply by fiat.

Only two of these general types of languages are actively being explored as psychologically plausible: production systems and connection systems. (For articles on production systems and connection systems, see Klahr, Langley, and Neches 1987, Rumelhart, McClelland, et al. 1986, and VanLehn 1990.) If one had to choose between production systems and connection systems as a representation language for knowledge about subtraction, then production systems seem much more plausible. Indeed it is not easy to see how a connection system could possibly generate the kind of extended, sequential problem-solving behavior that characterizes students solving subtraction problems.

On the other hand the class of production systems is not exactly right either. It is too narrow for it excludes conventional sequential languages, which seem plausible for representing "rote" procedures like subtraction. On the other hand it is too broad because it includes both parallel and serial systems. A parallel production system can fire many rules at the same time, whereas a serial system is like a conventional programming language in that only one rule can be executed at a time. Subtraction seems to be a quintessential serial procedure. Thus we arrive at

The seriality assumption
Procedures are represented by serial systems, a class of languages that is intended to include serial production systems and conventional sequential programming languages.

3.3.1 Focus Flow Is Necessary
Most serial languages have variables, and the programs written in them use variables profusely. However, it is worth a moment of defend the use of variables in representing subtraction because variables become important in other arguments.

Suppose that subtraction procedures have no variables. This would put the whole burden of indicating the locations of actions onto the procedure's interface patterns with the situation. To traverse columns, instead of passing the current column in a variable the patterns would have to describe the focus of attention as the "rightmost unanswered column" or some other description that mentions only visi-

345	345	207
− 102	− 129	− 169
243	22 x	1 x

3.1
Three problems answered by the bug Blank-Instead-of-Borrow. Incorrect answers are marked with an X.

ble aspects of the situation, and not some internally held index or pointer into the situation. So far this variableless approach seems to be working. Let us examine it a little further.

This technique succeeds in representing correct subtraction procedures because there is a visual marker for where focus of attention needs to be, namely, the boundary between answered and unanswered columns. However, there are subtraction bugs that leave answers blank. These cannot be represented by using the boundary between answered and unanswered columns. For instance, one observed bug skips columns that require borrowing (3.1). This bug can be explained by assuming that the student has not learned how to borrow. When the student attempts to take a larger number from a smaller one, an impasse occurs. The repair to this impasse is the No-op repair. It causes the column-difference action to be skipped. If the procedure is using the boundary between answered and unanswered columns to determine the focus of attention, then after the No-op repair the procedure returns to focus on the column that it just finished. It does not shift its attention to the next column left. Instead the procedure goes into an infinite loop examining the same column over and over again. This is clearly a star bug. Not only does the no-variables hypothesis prevent the generation of an observed bug, it causes a star bug to be generated.

Beyond subtraction there are procedures that clearly need some kind of current-focus-of-attention variable. For example, children can add long columns of digits. This seems to require a variable to hold a pointer into the column of digits and a variable to hold the running total. This illustrates that variables can have at least two kinds of bindings: those that refer to the situation and those that refer to numbers. Presumably these bindings are the answers to questions posed by expressions in the interface languages. These arguments justify

The variables assumption
Procedures have variables. In particular variables can be bound to numbers or to pointers into the situation.

3.4 The Control Regime Issue

There are many kinds of serial systems in the literature. They can be classified along many dimensions. With respect to execution alone the most important dimension seems to be whether the system is hierarchical. This distinction is most easily described by using production systems as a running example to stand for the whole class of serial systems.

A hierarchical production system distinguishes goals from other kinds of items in working memory. It has special built-in facilities for managing goals. In most contemporary production systems for cognitive simulation, this facility is a goal stack.[5] The goal stack is a last-in-first-out list of goals. The most recently added goal is called the currently active goal. Only productions whose left sides mention a goal that matches the currently active goal are permitted to run. Two special actions are provided. The *push* action adds a new goal to the stack, which automatically causes it to become the currently active goal. The *pop* action causes the currently active goal to be removed from the stack, which automatically causes the goal behind it in the stack to become the new currently active goal. The goal stack mechanism makes it simple to represent hierarchical procedures, where routines call subroutines, which in turn call subsubroutines, and so forth.

More significant, the stack mechanism permits recursive procedures to be simply encoded. A recursive procedure is one that calls itself. For instance, to travel from point A to point B, I might find airports near A and B and set the subgoal of traveling from point A to the airport near A. This is a recursion. The subgoal has the same type as the goal. ("Goal" is sometimes used to mean goal instance—that is, an item in working memory—and sometimes to mean a goal type—for example, a class of instances sharing some property. I use "goal" to mean goal instances.) The nice thing about a stack is that when a subgoal is finished—for example, I am at the airport near A—execution automatically resumes at the higher goal. That is, I do not have to work out again what to do now that I am at the airport. I simply continue the subprocedure I selected for getting from point A to point B. That subprocedure's second step is to fly from one airport to the other. Its third step is to push the subgoal of traveling from the airport near B to B. This third step constitutes another recursive call of the travel-to goal.

Although hierarchical production systems are useful in many tasks, that is no argument for their psychological validity. Indeed some production systems are not hierarchical (for example, PSG (Newell 1973),

HPSA78 (Newell 1978), Caps (Just and Carpenter 1987)). In the next section I present an argument based on bug data for assuming that procedures are hierarchical.

One last comment is in order before going into the argument. The discussion so far has been in terms of production systems, but the issue of recursive versus nonrecursive control is much more general. It is really an issue of what control regime the procedural representation language supports. In computer science the control regime of a programming language is the system of facilities built into the language for controlling the flow of execution of the program. Older programming languages (for example, early Fortran) had nonrecursive control regimes. One could write a recursive procedure, but only if the program created a stack and maintained it itself. Most modern programming languages are recursive because recursive procedures are quite often the simplest way to express a computaton. There are other, more sophisticated control regimes. For instance, some languages (for example, Sail (VanLehn 1974)) support *coroutining*, a way to simulate parallelism on a serial machine by using more than one stack. A process (that is, a set of procedures that uses the same stack) executes for a while then can suspend itself and send control over to another process. If control gets sent back to it, it continues from where it left off. Similar capabilities are now available by using *continuations*, a more elegant control regime than the one used by Sail and its contemporaries. The point here is that the control regime issue is actually much more complicated than just whether or not a language is recursive. The following arguments just scratch the surface; much more research is needed.

3.4.1 *The Back-up Repair Pops the Goal Stack*
The argument presented in this section shows that the Back-up repair strategy's behavior can only be captured if there is a goal stack and a repair that pops it. This of course is an argument for the existence of the goal stack, but it also develops Back-up as a tool for "seeing" the goal stack pop that can be used in later arguments.

First, it is necessary to present the repair in more detail than it has been presented previously. Because the discussion of the previous chapter demonstrated its existence, the details of its operation can be demonstrated with just one example. An idealized protocol of a subject who has the bug Smaller-From-Larger-Instead-of-Borrow-From-Zero is shown in 3.2. The (idealized) subject does not know about borrowing from zero. When this subject tackles the problem 305 − 167, he begins by comparing the two digits in the units column. Because five is less than seven, he makes a decision to borrow (epi-

a.	305 − 167	In the units column I can't take 7 from 5, so I'll have to borrow.
b.	305 − 167	To borrow, I first have to decrement the next column's top digit. But I can't take 1 from 0!
c.	305 − 167 ――― 2	So I'll go back to doing the units column. I still can't take 7 from 5, so I'll take 5 from 7 instead.
d.	²¹ ƺ05 − 167 ――― 2	In the tens column I can't take 6 from 0, so I'll have to borrow. I decrement 3 to 2 and add 10 to 0. That's no problem.
e.	²¹ ƺ05 − 167 ――― 142	Six from 10 is 4. That finishes the tens. The hundreds is easy, there's no need to borrow, and 1 from 2 is 1.

3.2
Idealized protocol of a student performing the bug Smaller-From-Larger-Instead-of-Borrow-From-Zero

sode *a* in 3.2), a decision that he later comes back to. He begins to tackle the first of borrowing's two subgoals, namely, borrowing-from (episode *b*). At this point he gets stuck because the digit to be borrowed from is a zero, and he believes that it is impossible to subtract a one from a zero. He has reached an impasse. Back-up gets him past the decrement-zero impasse by backing up, in the problem-solving sense, to the last decision that has some alternatives open. The backing-up occurs in episode *c*, where the idealized subject says, "So I'll go back to doing the units column." In the units column he hits a second impasse and says, "I still cannot take 7 from 5," which he repairs ("so I'll take 5 from 7 instead"). He finishes up the rest of the problem without difficulty. His behavior exemplifies Smaller-From-Larger-Instead-of-Borrow-From-Zero.

This idealized protocol illustrates one story for a certain bug. However, it can be demonstrated that it is the right story by showing that the decrement-zero impasse exists and that the second impasse, at episode *c*, also exists. The existence of the decrement-zero impasse was demonstrated during the discussion of 2.2. The existence of the

A.

$$\begin{array}{r} \scriptstyle 1 \;\; \scriptstyle 7\,1 \\ 8\cancel{8}5 \\ -\,205 \\ \hline 680 \end{array}$$

B.

$$\begin{array}{r} \scriptstyle 7\,1 \\ \cancel{6}47 \\ -\;\;45 \\ \hline 702 \end{array}$$

C.

$$\begin{array}{r} 8305 \\ -\quad 3 \\ \hline 8302 \end{array}$$

D.

$$\begin{array}{r} \scriptstyle 1\,1 \\ \scriptstyle 6\,3\,1 \\ 7\cancel{4}2 \\ -\,136 \\ \hline 606 \end{array}$$

E.

$$\begin{array}{r} \scriptstyle 1\,1 \\ \scriptstyle 3\,0\,0\,1 \\ 4\cancel{0}15 \\ -\;607 \\ \hline 3408 \end{array}$$

F.

$$\begin{array}{r} \scriptstyle 1 \;\; \scriptstyle 7\,1 \\ 8\cancel{8}5 \\ -\,205 \\ \hline 680 \end{array}$$

G.

$$\begin{array}{r} \scriptstyle 1 \;\; \scriptstyle 3\,1 \\ \cancel{6}47 \\ -\;\;45 \\ \hline 602 \end{array}$$

H.

$$\begin{array}{r} \scriptstyle 1 \;\; \scriptstyle 2\,1 \\ 8\cancel{3}05 \\ -\quad 3 \\ \hline 8302 \end{array}$$

I.

$$\begin{array}{r} \scriptstyle 1\,1 \\ \scriptstyle 6\,3\,1 \\ 7\cancel{4}2 \\ -\,136 \\ \hline 606 \end{array}$$

J.

$$\begin{array}{r} \scriptstyle 1 \\ \scriptstyle 1\,0\,1 \\ 4\cancel{0}15 \\ -\;607 \\ \hline 4708 \end{array}$$

3.3
Repairs to an answer-overflow impasse

second impasse is documented in appendix 9 of VanLehn 1983c with data from students who took a variety of repairs at that impasse.

When a student backs up in Smaller-From-Larger-Instead-of-Borrow-From-Zero, the decision that she returns to is chronologically most recent (see 3.2). This kind of backing-up is called *chronological Back-up* (or chronological backtracking) in AI. However, that decision is also the hierarchically closest. That is, the decision about whether to borrow immediately dominates the impasse; no other decisions lie on the subgoal calling path between them. So it could also be that the student is popping the control stack back to the last decision and resuming from there. This kind of backing up does not have a standard name, so it is dubbed *hierarchical Back-up*. This particular bug does not allow us to tell whether the Back-up repair is chronological or hierarchical. However, if we could show that it was hierarchical, we would have an argument for the existence of the goal stack. (Indeed the notion of a hierarchical Back-up cannot even be stated without assuming the existence of a goal stack, which may have made the preceding definition of it a little hard to swallow.)

Problems shown in 3.3 were solved by student 1 of class 2, who was given the same test twice, two days apart. The top row is from the first testing session; the bottom row is from the second session. These problems are all the problems that require subtracting a column with two equal digits (that is, an $N - N$ column). This student has induced incorrectly that the test for borrowing is $T \le B$ rather than $T < B$, where T and B stand for the top and bottom digits of the current column. Consequently the student borrows for $N - N$ columns. This generates an impasse when it comes time to write the answer: two digits do not fit in a space that usually holds just one. On most problems the student carries. On other problems (*B* and maybe *E* and *J*) the student merely answers with a zero. This is a classic bug migration: the student is switching between two repairs to the same impasse. In particular the repair that results in a noncarry, zero answer is probably Back-up: the student realizes that a two-digit answer is too big for one column and backs up to the decision to borrow, where she takes the alternative choice and solves the column the ordinary way, $N - N = 0$. The decision point that she backs up to is hierarchically closest. However, it is not *chronologically* closest. The most recent decision took place when she decided to do a normal borrow-from instead of a borrow-from-zero. That is, the sequence of decisions for problem *B* was

1. In the units decide to do the column without borrowing.
2. In the tens decide to do a borrow.
3. In the hundreds decide to do the borrow-from in the usual way (however, she mistakenly does an increment instead of a decrement, a common slip)

The student backed up to decision 2, not the chronologically most recent one. On the other hand decision 2 is just where she would return to if she popped the stack.

A skeptic might not believe that Back-up is responsible for the noncarry, zero answers in the test. Even so the independence of repairs at impasses permits Back-up to be applied at that impasse. And if Back-up is chronological Back-up, then it would return to the borrow-from decision (for example, number 3 in the list). Although it is not worth tracing through the details, consistently doing such chronological Back-ups results in an infinite loop. That is surely a star bug. So applying chronological Back-up to this impasse generates a star bug. On the other hand a hierarchical Back-up from this impasse generates an observed bug.

A plausible way to salvage the chronological Back-up hypothesis in the face of this evidence is to suppose that students have free choice in how far back they back-up. But this supposition just weakens the model without fixing the problem because it still permits students to back up to the most recent decision. In particular it still allows backing up to decision 3, so the star bug can still be generated. To fix the chronological Back-up, one has to specify how far to back up in any given impasse situation and do it in such a way that the most recent decision point is excluded in situations like the ones described. Of course this is exactly what hierarchical Back-up does.

To put it bluntly, every instance of Back-up in the data is faithfully predicted by hierarchical Back-up. In the places where chronological

Back-up differs from hierarchical Back-up in its predictions, the data show students going with hierarchical Back-up, which means skipping past the chronologically most recent decision in a certain way. It is doubtful that this is an accident. So an accurate, plausible implementation of the Back-up repair requires a goal stack.[6]

It is conceivable that the goal stack that Back-up uses is there solely for repairs and not for regular execution. This seems so unlikely, however, that it will simply be assumed that the control storage accessed by Back-up is the same as the one used by regular execution. Thus we arrive finally at

The recursion assumption
The control regime for procedures is recursive. At minimum, a goal stack is required for the interpretation of procedures.

The reason that the assumption says "at minimum" is that there are other kinds of data structures for holding goals that permit procedures to be recursive. For instance, Grapes (Anderson, Farrell, and Saurers 1984) uses a tree of goals. Back-up corresponds to ascending the tree from the currently active goal to some supergoal instead of popping the stack. The argument shows only that some manner of getting back to the hierarchically most recent goals is available. This mechanism, whatever it is, is just exactly what is needed for making a procedural language recursive. Recursion means the unconstrained ability to return to caller and continue it. So the right level of generality for stating the result of the argument is that procedures can be recursive.

3.5 The Back-up Repair Pops the Bindings of Variables

Variables are for passing noncontrol information between parts of the procedure. One can identify noncontrol information by whether it refers to something outside the program, like a piece of the situation or a number. Computer programmers tend to call such information "data," and the mechanisms for moving it about are called data flow mechanisms or regimes. Like the notion of control regimes, the idea of a data flow regime is a very general concept. However, I discuss it in a parochial way, as constraints on the way variables are used.

Over the years computer science has tried many types of data flow regimes for variables, ranging from simple substitution as used in the lambda calculus, to odd combinations of variables referring to other variables indirectly. At present the field seems to have settled on four major types as being the most useful:

- *Global variables* are variables that can be accessed by any part of the program at any time.
- *Local variables* can be accessed only within a given procedure or module of code. Subprocedures called by the procedure cannot access the procedure's local variables.
- *Dynamically scoped fluid variables* are owned by one procedure, but they can be accessed by any procedure called by that procedure, as well as by the procedure itself.
- *Lexically scoped fluid variable* make sense only when it is possible to write a procedure "inside" another procedure, regardless of the calling relationships between them. This allows the programmer to indicate when procedures are relevant to each other in a way that is independent of the calling structure. Given such a facility, a lexically scoped fluid variable can be accessed by a procedure and all the procedure written inside it.

Arguments to procedures are local or fluid variables that are initialized by values passed to the procedure from its caller.

Of the four types of variables, global variables and local variables are by far the most widely used. Fluid variables are useful only in special circumstances. For instance, to return several values from a procedure, one can use fluid variables that are owned by the caller and set by the callee.

Hierarchical production systems do not use fluid variables. They provide only global and local variables. Local variables correspond to the arguments to goals, and global variables correspond to the arguments of other items in working memory. For an illustration consider the production

If [Goal is travel from A to B], and
[Airport F is near place A]
then Push [Goal is travel from A to F].

The variables A and B are arguments to the goal. They can only receive values when matched against a goal token in working memory. Because this is a hierarchical production system (by the recursion assumption), only productions whose goals are [travel from A to B] can access this same information. Thus the arguments are local to a procedure, where "procedure" means all the productions that have the same goal. When the procedure pops (that is, one of the productions calls a Pop action), then the information present in the local variables is lost. This is exactly the behavior of a local variable in a standard programming language.

On the other hand the variable F occurs in a condition element that matches nongoal items from working memory. The information accessed by it could be written by any production, not just the productions that belong to this procedure. Moreover when the procedure is popped, any information written by it in this form remains in working memory for other procedures to access. Popping does not destroy the values of variables as it does for local variables. These properties make the arguments of nongoal items correspond to global variables.

Because fluid variables are seldom useful in regular programming languages and are not even available in production systems, it is simply assumed that the procedural knowledge representation language lacks fluid variables. This leaves us to consider only whether procedures need global variables, local variables, or both. This section addresses that question with an argument from bug data.

It was argued that procedures must have variables to hold pointers into the situation and to hold numbers. This section concerns only the variables that hold pointers to situations, because unfortunately the subtraction procedures that were taught to the subjects do not require them to hold numbers in memory for any extended length of time, as column addition does, so the acquired subtraction procedures probably have no variables for holding numbers. Even if they do, no evidence for them shows up in the bug data, and consequently there is no way to tell what their properties are. Perhaps by studying addition bugs one could learn how the variables for numbers work. I strongly suspect that they obey constraints different from those for the variables for pointers into situations.

For easy reference variables that hold pointers into situations are called "focus" variables, because they hold the procedure's focus of external attention, so to speak.

3.5.1 Back-up pops the Values of Focus Variables

In this section it is shown that Back-up can be simply implemented only if focus variables are local. Evidence comes from the bug Smaller-From-Larger-Instead-of-Borrow-From-Zero, which was introduced in a previous section. The bug is generated by a core procedure that has no routine for borrowing from zero. Two procedures shown in 3.4 are implementations of such a core procedure. Both use a goal stack, but one uses local variables, and the other uses global variables.

When these procedures are given a subtraction problem that requires borrowing from zero, they both reach an impasse in the BorrowFrom routine. Suppose the Back-up repair is applied. This causes

For each column in the problem, 1. SubICol (the column).	For each column in the problem, 1. C ← the column, 2. SubICol.
SubICol (C): 1. If the top digit of column C is smaller than the bottom digit, then Borrow (C), 2. else subtract the two digits and write their difference in the answer of C.	SubICol: 1. If the top digit of column C is smaller than the bottom digit, then Borrow, 2. else subtract the two digits and write their difference in the answer of C.
Borrow (C): 1. Add 10 to the top digit of column C. 2. BorrowFrom (the next column left of C). 3. Subtract the bottom digit of C from the top digit and write the difference in the answer of C.	Borrow: 1. Add 10 to the top digit of column C. 2. C ← the next column left of C. 3. BorrowFrom. 4. C ← the next column right of C. 5. Subtract the bottom digit of C from the top digit and write the difference in the answer of C.
BorrowFrom (C): 1. Decrement the top digit of column C by one.	BorrowFrom: 1. Decrement the top digit of column C by one.

3.4
Two implementations of subtraction. Local focus variables are used on the left. Global focus variables are used on the right.

A.	305	B.	305	C.	305
	− 167		− 167		− 167
			6		26

3.5
Back-up without a focus stack

the goal stack to pop back to Sub1Col, where the hierarchically closest decision was made. The local focus variable implementation is constructed so that popping the goal stack also pops the focus stack. Thus the stack popping restores the focus of attention to the column that originated the borrow. This restoration occurs in Smaller-From-Larger-Instead-of-Borrow-From-Zero, as 3.1 shows. The global focus variable implementation does not cause Back-up to automatically restore the focus. In the problem of 3.1 the variable would be left set to the tens column, yielding the sequence of actions shown in 3.5.

The decrement-zero impasse occurs in state A of 3.5. The Back-up repair pops the stack back to Sub1Col and causes the alternative to borrowing, ordinary column subtraction, to be taken. Because focus variable C is still pointing to *the tens column*, this causes an ordinary column subtraction to be attempted on the tens column. This is very strange behavior. Anyway because $0 < 6$, a second impasse occurs. State B results from applying one of the several repairs that could be applied. The rest of the problem is finished uneventfully. The absurdity of "forgetting" to restore the focus of attention when backing up is highlighted by this star bug.

The local focus variable implementation generates an *observed* bug, and the global focus variable implementation generates a *star* bug. This casts doubt on the hypothesis that focus flow is global, but it is not yet a full-fledged refutation. There are other implementations of global focus variable borrowing that do not generate the star bug. One such implementation is shown in 3.6.

A second register, BFC, has been used to store the focus for the borrow-from column. Now a Back-up from BorrowFrom causes an observed bug (that is, Smaller-From-Larger-Instead-of-Borrow-From-Zero) and not the star bug. In short, depending on which routines are allocated their own global variables, one either does or does not get good predictions. This is going to make it complicated to decide which kinds of data flow regimes govern focus variables.

There is one kind of procedure, however, that global focus variables cannot express. This procedure allocates a different global focus variable *per instantiation* of a routine. If a routine is called recursively,

For each column in the problem,
1. C ← the column.
2. SublCol.

SublCol:
1. If the top digit of column C is smaller than the bottom digit, then Borrow,
2. else subtract the two digits and write their difference in the answer of C.

Borrow:
1. Add 10 to the top digit of column C.
2. BFC ← the next column left of C.
3. BorrowFrom
4. Subtract the bottom digit of C from top digit and write the difference in the answer of C.

BorrowFrom:
1. Decrement the top digit of column BFC by one.

3.6
A two register implementation of subtraction

as is BorrowFrom in the left procedure of 3.4, there is a different focus stored with each instance of BorrowFrom in the recursion. For instance, if the left procedure of 3.4 procedure is solving 8003 − 7, then there will be, when the stack is at its deepest, three instantiations of BorrowFrom on the stack: one for borrowing from the eight and two for borrowing from the zeros. Moreover the more zeros there are, the more instances of BorrowFrom there are. Because there can be arbitrarily many instances, no global variable scheme can represent a procedure like this one that stores a different focus with each instance. To refute the global variable hypothesis, all that has to be done is to demonstrate that such a procedure exists. This can be done using the Back-up repair in the same way as before. However, the details are burdensome and have been published elsewhere (VanLehn 1983a, appendix 9), so that part of the argument is omitted.

3.5.2 The Instantiation Hypothesis
So far all that has been shown is that for one procedure, local variables work and global variables do not. This only rules out the hypothesis that procedures use only global variables. So the theory is

stuck with guessing whether people use only local variables or both local and global variables in their procedures. In the interests of theoretical parsimony and increased refutability, it is assumed that they use only local variables.

This assumption, however, leaves a number of loose ends. In the examples the local variables always appear as arguments of procedures. They appear as arguments in order to receive their values from their callers. In computer programs not all local variables are arguments. Some are given their initial value from inside the procedure that owns them. They are used simply as temporary storage, rather than as a way to pass information from caller to callee. From the examples we can infer that the language must have arguments, but we have no information about whether it need also support temporary local variables. Again parsimony and refutability justify assuming that *only* arguments are supported.

Another property of the examples is that no procedure resets the values of its arguments. The initial value of the argument is used unchanged throughout the lifespan of the procedure. Let us assume that this property also characterizes all procedures: variables are initialized and never reset.

These assumptions together imply that the only variables in the language are the arguments of goals (in production system terminology) or procedures (in programming language terminology), and moreover once a goal's arguments are initialized, the values are never changed. One way to refer to such a convention is to say that the goal is *instantiated*, which means that its arguments are bound, thus creating a goal/procedure instance, and never rebound. Thus the essence of this long argument is captured by

The instantiation assumption
The only way that focus flows is via instantiation of goals.

This means that for a procedure to shift its focus of attention, it must create a new goal instance that has the new focus of attention as its arguments' values. To put the point in production system terms, the working memory has only items that are goal instances, and moreover once a goal instance is placed in working memory, its arguments cannot be changed.

3.6 Types of Goals

The instantiation assumption in combination with the Back-up repair strategy provides a tool for discovering more properties of the representation of procedural knowledge. In this section I discuss one important property: that there seem to be multiple types of control constructs akin to the conditionals, iterations, and sequential control constructs of programming languages.

Because the preceding sections covered general control regimes and data flow regimes, they could be rather sloppy about the terms for the components of the formal expressions that represent procedures. This section deals with the actual expressions themselves as well as properties of their execution, so it is time to clarify the terminology. A procedure is composed of units that are referred to sometimes as goals and sometimes as procedures, reflecting the mixed ancestry of this representation, which combines production system notation and traditional programming language notation. When a goal/procedure calls another goal/procedure, the one called is termed a subgoal or subprocedure of the caller. Thus Subtract is a goal that calls "Sub1Col, and Sub1Col is a procedure that calls several subprocedures, one of which is Borrow, and so on. So far the term goal/procedure is just an undefined word. However, assumptions will soon be made concerning its representation, its execution, and its relationship to the Back-up repair. The chapters on learning add even more assumptions that use the same terms. Thus the term is defined by the assumptions, rather than given a concise initial characterization.

The Back-up repair strategy pops the goal stack. Thus it can be used to see what goals are on the stack. A rich source of Back-up episodes is the decrement-zero impasse, which occurs when a procedure that does not know how to borrow from zero is used to solve a borrow-from-zero problem. In 3.7 the bugs that occur at this impasse are shown with repair strategies that generate them, provided certain assumptions are made about the goal stack. (The bug Stops-Borrow-At-Zero comes from applying a No-op repair to the impasse. However, the No-op repair is the same as popping the stack exactly once. Nonetheless the name No-op is retained for continuity with previous publications on the theory.) In particular these bugs can be generated if the stack at the time of the impasse is assumed to be, from top to bottom,

Decrement (tens-column)
Borrow (units-column)
Sub1Col (units-column)
Subtract (all-columns)

At the time of the impasse the current goal is the top of the stack, decrement. This illustration assumes the impasse occurs when trying to decrement a zero in the tens column. The Barge-on repair strategy

Repair	Bugs
Barge-on	Borrow-Add-Decrement-Instead-of-Zero
	Zero-Borrow-From-Zero
Back-up: pop 1	Stops-Borrow-At-Zero
Back-up: pop 2	Smaller-From-Larger-Instead-of-Borrow-From-Zero
	Top-Instead-of-Borrow-From-Zero
	Zero-Instead-of-Borrow-From-Zero (unobserved)
Back-up: pop 3	*Blank-Instead-of-Borrow-From-Zero (unobserved)
Back-up: pop 4	Borrow-Won't-Recurse (unobserved)

3.7
Bugs generated by repairs to the decrement-zero impasse

causes that goal to be tried again with some elements of its description relaxed. For instance, Borrow-Add-Decrement-Instead-of-Borrow-From-Zero is generated by relaxing the sign of the decrement operation, allowing an increment to be substituted.

Popping the stack once causes Borrow to become current. If Borrow is assumed to be similar to a sequential construction in a programming language (for example, the Progn in Lisp or the Begin-End block in Algol) in that it has an ordered list of subgoals, then resuming it causes the next subgoal in its list to be executed. Assuming its list is [Decrement, Add-ten, take-column-difference], the bug Stops-Borrow-At-Zero is generated. This bug merely skips the stuck decrement and does only the Add-ten half of borrowing before taking the column difference.

Popping the stack twice causes Sub1Col to become current. If Sub1Col is assumed to be like a Cond in Lisp, in that it selects which subgoal is appropriate for the solution of the particular column it is given, then resuming its execution causes it to try another subgoal, because the Borrow subgoal failed. If it chooses the subgoal for answering columns with blank bottoms, which merely writes the top digit in the answer, then the bug Top-Instead-of-Borrow-From-Zero is generated. If it chooses the subgoal for answering columns with equal digits (that is, $N - N = 0$), then the bug Zero-Instead-of-Borrow-From-Zero is generated. If it chooses the subgoal for answering regular columns, then an impasse occurs because a larger number cannot be taken from a smaller one; if the impasse is repaired by Barge-on, the bug Smaller-From-Larger-Instead-of-Borrow-From-Zero is generated. Assuming that Sub1Col is like a three-way Cond is important for generating these bugs.

If Back-up pops the stack three times, then the goal Subtract becomes current. Assuming this goal is some kind of iteration over the columns means that execution resumes by calling Sub1Col on the tens column. This generates a star bug called *Blank-Instead-of-Borrow-From-Zero. The bug leaves a column with a blank answer if that column requires borrowing from a zero. It has never occurred and seems quite unlikely to ever appear because no student would bother to continue a problem that is blatantly wrong, and a blank answer column is quite blatantly wrong. This bug is assumed to be filtered by a critic (see Brown and VanLehn 1980). The present treatment of the theory has little to say about critics because it is not clear how they are acquired. The point here is only that Back-up would generate a bug, except that another piece of knowledge prevents it from occurring.

If Back-up pops the stack four times, then the stack is empty. This means the student has given up on the problem. This generates the bug Borrow-Won't-Recurse, which answers a problem only up to the first column that requires borrowing from zero.

In the course of describing how the decrement-zero bugs were generated, several assumptions were slipped in. It was assumed that Borrow was like a Progn in Lisp, whereas Sub1Col was like a Cond. That is, Borrow is conjunctive in that it succeeds only when *all* its subgoals have been executed, whereas Sub1Col is disjunctive in that it succeeds as soon as *one* of its subgoals succeeds. Let us name these two execution conventions the AND execution type and the OR execution type, respectively. Then Borrow's representation must bear some indication that it is an AND goal, whereas Sub1Col's representation must indicate that it is an OR goal.

The existence of AND and OR goal types is no surprise. Even the simplest procedural representation languages have both types. For instance, finite state automata express OR goals as a state with several paths exiting it; an AND goal is a path with several states along it. To take a second example, a production system can express an AND goal as a rule with several actions on the right side. An OR goal can be expressed as several rules whose conditions mention the same goal name. For example, Sub1Col would be notated as three rules, with each rule's condition including the element [CurrentGoal Sub1Col]. Thus the existence of distinct execution types for AND and OR is not surprising because most other representation languages use them too.

However, this discussion slipped in a third execution type. It was assumed that Subtract is an iteration that called Sub1Col on each column in the problem. This is a new execution type, named FOREACH because it calls the same subgoal on each object in a designated set of objects. Most production systems do not have such an execution type.[7] When they need to express an iteration, they use a tail recursion, such as

> If the goal is [Subtract Remaining-columns],
>   and there are two or more columns in Remaining-columns,
>   and C is the first column of Remaining-columns,
>   and R is the rest of the columns of Remaining-columns,
> Then push the subgoal [Sub1Col C],
>   and push the Subgoal [Subtract R].

> If the goal is [Subtract Remaining-columns],
>   and there is only one column in Remaining-columns,
>   and C is that column,
> then push the subgoal [Sub1Col C].

In our terminology an AND/OR goal pair is used to get the same effect as the iteration. However, this means that the stack will be different. Suppose that the decrement-zero impasse occurs in the hundreds column. Then the stack will be

> Decrement (hundreds-column)
> Borrow (tens-column)
> Sub1Col (tens-column)
> Subtract ({tens-column, hundreds-column, thousands-column})
> <Or goal corresponding to choice between the two productions>
> Subtract ({units-column, tens-column, hundreds-column, thousands-column})
> <Or goal corresponding to choice between the two productions>

The lowest three frames of the stack correspond to the initial portion of the tail recursion, where the units column is processed, and control moves on to the tens column. If Back-up returns to them, then various impasses and bugs are predicted to occur, all of which are unobserved, and some are quite bizarre. The problem with tail recursions is that even though a column is "done" in that no student would consider returning to it to fix an impasse in a subsequent column, the tail recursive implementation causes the stack to contain goals for each of the "done" columns, and thus Back-up could return to them, contrary to what people seem to do.[8] To avoid predicting star bugs, it is best to assume that a tail recursion is not how the procedure is encoded by the students. Rather the procedure seems to be encoded as an iteration across columns. These arguments motivate

The goal types assumption
There are (at least) three execution types for goals. An AND goal executes all its subgoals. An OR goal executes just one of its subgoals. A FOREACH goal executes its subgoals on each object in a designated set of objects.

These types play important roles in the learning component. In particular the existence of a FOREACH type makes it possible to bias the learning element so that it tends to learn iterations. This accounts for the observation that students who have seen only two-column problems can solve problems with three or more columns without suffering an impasse. If they have no FOREACH goal, they would represent the Subtract goal as an AND goal with two subgoals, a Sub1Col for the units and a Sub1Col for the tens. This core procedure reaches impasses on three-column problems, whereas students do not appear to do so. So the assumption that there is a FOREACH goal type has independent support from the evidence about biases during learning.

3.7 A Specific Representation for Procedural Knowledge

The preceding sections developed several general assumptions about the representation of procedures. The specifications developed there define a large class of specific representation languages. For the sake of concreteness, however, this section presents one particular representation language that obeys the specifications. It is the language used by Sierra, the program that calculates the theory's predictions. The main purpose in presenting Sierra's representation language is to show how much of the language is *not* specified by the assumptions developed so far.

The procedure in 3.8 is for a version of subtraction that can borrow, but not across zero. It exhibits several notational conventions. There are six goals. Each has a header that shows the goal type, the arguments, and the execution type. Following the header are the rules. A rule's pattern is displayed in square brackets preceding the arrow, and the action is displayed after the arrow. All pattern variables are bound by wide-scoped existential quantifiers unless otherwise indicated. Arguments of the procedure that appear in patterns are treated like constants by the pattern matcher. An empty pattern always matches.

Subtract (P) FOREACH
1. (Lambda (C)
   [And (Column C) (Part-of CP)])
2. (Lambda (C1 C2) (Not (Ordered P C1 C2)))
3. (SublCol C)

SublCol (C) OR
1. [And (Digit T) (Part-of T C) (First T C)
         (Digit B) (Part-of B C) (Middle B C)
         (Ordered C T B) (Adjacent C T B)
         (Value-of TV T) (Value-of BV B) (LessThan TV BV)]
   →   (Borrow C)
2. [And (Digit T) (Part-of T C) (First T C)
         (Digit B) (Part-of B C) (Middle B C)
         (Ordered C T B) (Adjacent C T B)
         (Value-of TV T) (Value-of BV B)
         (Less-Than-or-Equal BV TV)]
   →   (Diff C)

Diff (C) AND
1. [And (Digit T) (Part-of T C) (First T C)
         (Digit B) (Part-of B C) (Middle B C)
         (Cell A) (Part-of A C) (Last A C)
         (Ordered C T B) (Adjacent C T B) (Ordered C B A)
         (Adjacent C B A)
         (Value-of TV T) (Value-of BV B)
         (AbsoluteDifference TV BV AV)]
   →   (Write AV A)

Borrow (C) AND
1. [And (Problem P) (Part-of C P)
         (Column N) (Part-of N P) (Adjacent P N C) (Ordered P N C)]
   →   (Decr N)
2. [] → (Add10 C)
3. [] → (Diff C)

Decr (C) AND
1. [And (Cell T) (Part-of T C) (First T C)
         (Value-of TV T)
         (One-away TV AV) (LessThan AV TV)]
   →   (Overwrite AV T)

Add10 (C) AND
1. [And (Cell T) (Part-of T C) (First T C)
        (Value-of TV T)
        (Count-up-by-ten TV AV)]
    →   (Overwrite AV T)

3.8
A simple procedure written in Sierra's representation

The interpretation of a goal depends on the goal's type. An OR goal executes only one of its rules. The patterns of all the rules are matched, and if only one pattern matches, that rule is executed. (If more than one rule's pattern matches, or if no rule's pattern matches, an impasse occurs.) When the chosen rule is done executing, the goal is done. For AND goals the rules are executed in the order given. The goal is done when all the rules have been executed. Thus an AND goal is like a Progn in Lisp.

Patterns on AND goal rules are not used to control the flow of execution as they are in OR goals. Rather they are used to refer to parts of the situation or to mathematical facts. They are called *fetch* patterns. On the other hand patterns in OR goals are not permitted to fetch objects from situations or the fact knowledge base. They can only be used as predicates for deciding which rule to execute. They are called *test* patterns. There are good empirical reasons for separating patterns into these two types. It is shown in section 6.5 that the two types of patterns are acquired by two distinct learning mechanisms. This finding motivates a further hypothesis about the representation called the *two-pattern assumption*.

The syntax of FOREACH goals differs slightly from the syntax of AND and OR goals. A FOREACH goal has three parts: a predicate of one argument, a predicate of two arguments, and an action. The first predicate defines a set of objects, namely, those objects that the predicate is true of in the situation that is current at the time the goal is instantiated. The second predicate imposes an order on those objects. The action is applied to the objects in the specified order. Thus the Subtraction goal of 3.8 first finds all the columns in the problems, orders them from right to left, then calls Sub1Col on each column, starting from the right.

3.7.1 *Primitives*

Patterns contain primitive predicates, such as (Digit T) or (Ordered P C1 C2). The vocabulary of primitive predicates has an important explanatory role in the theory. For example, the bug Always-Borrow-

Left depends crucially on the existence of a primitive predicate that differentiates the left most columns from all others. If such a predicate were missing, then Sierra could not generate the bug. The presence and even the absence of specific primitive predicates is part of the explanation for why some bugs exist and others do not. Clearly there should be an assumption concerning the vocabulary.

Such an assumption, however, basically amounts to a theory of perception (for situational primitives) and declarative knowledge (for arithmetic facts). These subjects are too vast to attack in any thorough way. So I have made a guess about what kinds of primitives are important for mathematical notation. The resulting assumptions are discussed in this section.

The situation assumption
Situations are represented as a typed part-whole tree, where sibling parts are related by a fixed set of primitives: First, Last, Ordered, and Adjacent. The knowledge representation for interpreting the external world as situations is a two-dimensional grammar that can recognize sequence arranged in one of the four compass points: horizontal, vertical, and the two diagonals.

This assumption reflects the fact that mathematical notations make use of a very limited repertoire of visual elements. For instance, a column is a vertical sequence of digits, a subtraction problem is a horizontal sequence of columns, exponents (for example, x^{2^3}) are a diagonal sequence, and a polynomial is a horizontal sequence of terms alternating with plus and minus signs. These examples also illustrate that situations are represented as a typed part-whole tree. A subtraction problem is a tree whose top node is typed "subtraction problem." Its parts are typed "column." The parts of a column are "cells," where a cell can be either a digit, or a blank that could have a digit written in it, or a digit that has been overwritten with another digit. A simple grammar for this conception of subtraction problems is shown in 3.9. The situation constructed by this grammar in interpreting the subtraction problem $57 - 9$, shown in 3.10, is expressed as a set of relations.

The preceding discussion has concerned primitives for situations. A similar assumption is needed for the primitives that access the subject's knowledge about arithmetic facts. In a preceding section it was shown how the bugs Zero-Borrow-from-Zero and Borrow-Add-Decrement-Instead-of-Borrow-From-Zero could be explained by making appropriate assumptions about what primitives are contained in the pattern for accessing the facts about decrementing. It was shown

SubProblem → Column⁺	Horizontal
Column → Cell Cell Cell	Vertical
Cell → Digit	
Cell → Blank	
Cell → Overwritten-digit	

3.9
A two-dimensional grammar for subtraction problems

that the patterns should contain the primitives "One-away-from" and less-than."[9] Based on similar episodes of Barge-on repairs, the following set of factual primitives seem plausible:

The factual primitives assumption
The following primitives are used to access knowledge about number facts: One-away-from, Less-than, Equal, Less-than-or-equal, Absolute-difference, Count-up-by-ten, Zero?, One?, and One-or-Zero?.

Primitives with a question mark suffix are unary predicates, and the others are binary, except Absolute-difference, which is ternary.

Lastly an assumption is needed to characterize actions. Again a domain-specific assumption is made:

The action assumption
There are three types of actions: writing a character in a blank, erasing a character, or overwriting a character with another character.

3.8 Where Do Impasses Occur?

One last piece of business is to specify where impasses can occur. The assumptions made here have been implicit in much of the discussion. Because we now have a formal representation of procedures, they can be made explicit. There are three types of impasses:

The impasse assumption
1. In an OR goal, if more than one rule has a true pattern, or if no rule has a true pattern, a decision impasse occurs.
2. If a fetch pattern binds variables that are used in the action of its rule, and the pattern matches in such a way that there is either more than one possible binding or no possible binding for those variables, then a reference impasse occurs.

(Problem 1)	Object 1 is a subtraction problem
(Column 2) (Column 3)	Objects 2 and 3 are columns
(Part 1 2) (Part 1 3)	The columns are part of the problem
(First 1 3)	Column 3 is the leftmost part of the problem
(Last 1 2)	Column 2 is the rightmost part of the problem
(Adjacent 1 2 3)	The columns are adjacent
(Ordered 1 3 2)	Column 3 is right of column 2
(Cell 4) (Cell 5) (Cell 6)	Objects 4, 5, and 6 are cells
(Digit 4) (Digit 5)	Cells 4 and 5 are also digits
(Blank 6)	Cell 6 is a blank
(Part 2 4) (Part 2 5) (Part 2 6)	They are part of column 2
(First 2 4) (Last 2 6)	Cell 2 is on top, and 6 on the bottom
(Adjacent 2 4 5)	Cells 4 and 5 are adjacent
(Ordered 2 4 5) (Ordered 2 4 6)	Cell 4 is above 5 and 6
(Adjacent 2 5 6)	Cells 5 and 6 are adjacent
(Ordered 2 5 6)	Cell 5 is above 6
(Cell 7) (Cell 8) (Cell 9)	Objects 7, 8, and 9 are cells
(Digit 7)	Cell 7 is also a digit
(Blank 8) (Blank 9)	Cells 8 and 9 are blanks
(Part 3 7) (Part 3 8) (Part 3 9)	They are part of column 3
(First 3 7) (Last 3 9)	Cell 3 is on top, and 9 on the bottom
(Adjacent 3 7 8)	Cells 7 and 8 are adjacent
(Ordered 3 7 8) (Ordered 3 7 9)	Cell 7 is above 8 and 9
(Adjacent 3 8 9)	Cells 8 and 9 are adjacent
(Ordered 3 8 9)	Cell 8 is above 9

3.10
The situation for 57 −9

3. Each primitive action has associated with it some preconditions that specify the conditions under which the processes that implement it will successfully carry out the action described by the primitive. If a precondition is not true when the primitive is called, a precondition violation impasses occurs.

The three primitive actions mentioned in the primitives assumption have the following preconditions:

- Writing into a blank fails if the number to be written has more than one digit or if the blank already has something written into it.
- Erasing a digit never fails.
- Overwriting a digit never fails.

In the preceding chapter I mentioned that impasses could be caused by critics that detect when the notation is ill-formed. Currently these are only partially implemented in Sierra, because they have not proved particularly useful in explaining bugs. One of them is the answer overflow critic, which is implemented as the precondition on writing into a blank that insists on only one digit per blank. Most of the other critics specify constraints on the form of the solution, that is, that the answer not have blanks in the middle of it. These cannot easily be implemented as preconditions, so they have not been incorporated into Sierra.

Chapter 4
Induction

This chapter marks the halfway point in the development of the theory. The preceding chapters investigated how procedures are represented and used by the subjects. The next three chapters investigate how procedures are learned. One could say that this chapter marks the transition between repair theory and step theory, insofar as those two theories can be separated.

The first section of this chapter covers the objectives of the learning theory. The middle sections begin the development of the theory by presenting a few basic assumptions. The last section sets the stage for a detailed treatment of learning by reviewing all the bug data and grouping them into classes according to the learning mechanisms that seem to be involved in their acquisition.

4.1 Objectives of the Learning Theory

As mentioned in chapter 1, the research strategy for uncovering the acquisition function is to (1) make an informed guess about the kinds of instructional information that play the most crucial roles, (2) find all possible procedures that could be learned from such information, and (3) find constraints on that set of possible outputs such that the constrained set matches the set of observed core procedures. The products of this research strategy are the constraints. They serve as general specifications that seem to be obeyed by the fine-grained learning process, whatever it is.

An advantage of this research strategy is that it seems to average out the details of teaching and leave only the essential constraints in view. There are so many subjects in our samples that we can safely assume that most teaching styles and learning styles are represented in the sample. If we succeed in finding constraints that hold across all these methods of teaching and learning, then we can plausibly assume that they are general principles that govern many kinds of instructional situations. In contrast investigators in typical protocol studies of subjects learning (for example; Anderson, Farrell, and Saurers 1984, Pirolli and Anderson 1985) must temper their conclusions by the fact that only a few teaching methods were used. The larger sample of methods taken in this study justify making more general assumptions.

Although the objective is to view learning as a constrained function that maps curricula into procedures, the lesson sequence cannot be entirely ignored. In previous chapters it has often been necessary to assume that some of the subjects in the sample had been tested before they had completed the lesson sequence. Thus their core procedures were missing exactly the subprocedures that are taught later in the curriculum. At the end of this chapter, a list of such missing subprocedure bugs is presented and discussed. At this point the relevant implication of these bugs is that they demonstrate that students learn *incrementally*. That is, students have well-formed, operable procedures even before they have finished the lesson sequence. Of course those procedures are incomplete, in that they lack subprocedures taught later in the lesson sequence.

The bug data were collected in such a way that the set of observed core procedures contains some procedures that are intermediate results in the learning process. Although the data could be considered polluted by such intermediate results, they actually serve a very important function by indicating the learning processes, albeit at a very large grain-size of observation. Thus the following assumption is not only warranted, it is welcome:

The incremental learning assumption
The set of core procedures includes the set of incomplete procedures P_i, where P_i is an incomplete procedure if and only if $P_i \epsilon$ Learn (P_{i-1}, L_i) and P_{i-1} is an incomplete procedure.

L_i stands for the ith lesson in the lesson sequence. The initial procedure P_0 is left unspecified because it depends on the task domain. For subtraction, P_0 might contain only primitive actions. For multiplication it might contain a procedure for addition.

The incremental learning assumption mentions an undefined function, Learn. This is the function whose input/output mapping the learning theory seeks to understand. The subsequent sections begin the characterization of it.

4.2 Consistency with the Examples or with the Explanations?

The objective of the learning theory, as modified by the incremental learning assumption, is to first find a function Learn that generates all "possible" P_i consistent with the given L_i and P_{i-1}, then find constraints on Learn that make it produce only the procedures that human learners acquire. This section and the next are concerned with the first objective, finding a Learn function that generates all possible P_i. This section considers what it means for P_i to be consistent with L_i. The next section considers the relationship between P_i and P_{i-1}.

The basic intuition behind the incremental learning assumption is that students actually learn something from their lessons. Thus the new procedure is "consistent" with the information contained in the lesson that generated it. The key question is: What kind of information is consistency based on? Clearly it must be some kind of information that is in fact a part of the classroom situation, the homework situation, or some other instructional situation. However, this hardly answers the question at all, because many kinds of information are present.

Leinhardt's work is one indicator of types of information that are present (Leinhardt 1987). Leinhardt videotaped and analyzed seven hours of subtraction instruction by a master second-grade teacher. The instruction took place on eight consecutive class days, and each day's instruction lasted about fifty minutes. This eight-day unit, which would be called a lesson, in the vocabulary of this book, introduced borrowing using two-column problems exclusively. Leinhardt's teacher used the term "renaming" for the actions of decrementing and adding ten. Thus the solution of $34 - 17$ consists of a renaming following by two column differences. The teacher called a problem a "fooler" if it required renaming. On the first day the teacher "demonstrated both the need for and possibility of subtracting the special types of problems she called foolers. Second, she moved laterally (in an intellectual sense) and developed the renaming procedure and the proof of legitimacy of its algorithm. (This proof rested on the fact that the value of the quantity in the minuend was unaltered by the notational transformation.)" (Leinhardt 1987, p. 276). The teacher used concrete numerals (for example: sticks and bundles of ten sticks) crucially throughout the first day. On the second day "She moved back to the initial fooler problem and showed how the new renaming procedure could be utilized" (Leinhardt 1987, p. 276). Again concrete numerals were used extensively. The remaining six days were spent reviewing the material introduced during first two days, drilling the students on the procedure, and using the procedure in a variety of contexts, such as word problems. The teacher also included examples where the borrowing was not needed.

The instruction appears to have been quite successful, although not perfect. On a posttest all but one student correctly solved all the two-column subtraction problems. Several students correctly solved three-column problems that required simple, nonzero borrowing in one or two columns. No student correctly solved a problem that required borrow from zero (G. Leinhardt, personal communication, August 1988). Thus the unit on simple two-column borrowing seemed to have succeeded in teaching that subprocedure, as well as teaching it in a general enough form that some students could apply the subprocedure in unfamiliar contexts (that is, the tens column of three-column problem). However, no student seemed to have developed a deep enough understanding of renaming to recognize that borrowing from zero problems can be solved by a second call to renaming from inside the renaming procedure. This is consistent with the ateleological assumption. Furthermore it is consistent with the assumption that even bug-free students lack a teleological understanding of the procedure.

As Leinhardt's study shows, explanations and examples seem to dominate the instruction. The remainder of this section defines two hypotheses, corresponding to learning from examples and learning from explanations, and weighs their merits.

By an *example* I mean any solving of a problem with the procedure, regardless of whether the solution was performed by the student, the teacher, another student, a parent, or a textbook. An example consists of the sequence of observable actions taken while solving a problem. By an *explanation* I mean any sort of natural language or analogical information, even if it accompanies an example and refers to it. Let the *examples hypothesis* be that the procedures that students learn are some subset of all procedures consistent with the examples. Let the *explanation hypothesis* be that the students' procedures are a subset of all procedures consistent with the explanations. Clearly both hypotheses could be true at the same time. This would mean that students' procedures are consistent with both the examples and the explanations.

Although some of the explanations are mere natural-language renditions of the procedures, it is reasonable to suppose that *some* of the explanations are general principles of the procedure, such as the principle that borrowing moves a ten from one place value to another while preserving the overall value of the number. Textbooks always mention such general principles, and one can assume that teachers do too. Leinhardt's master teacher certainly did. Yet, as Resnick (1982) and other have noted, if the students actually understood and obeyed such principles, they could not have the bugs that some of them do have. Also they might be able to solve transfer problems, such as seeing that borrowing from zero problems can be solved by a recursive call to renaming. Such principles are part of the teleology (design knowledge) of a procedure. The ateleological assumption is that students either do not know the teleology of procedures or they do not use it even if they do know it.

The ateleological assumption implies that procedures are not consistent with the teleological portions of explanations, but perhaps students encode only the recipe portion of explanations, where a procedure is described step by step, just like a cookbook's recipe. Although such recipes are rare in textbooks, the teachers might utter them in class, perhaps in partial form, as advice to students who get stuck while solving a problem at the blackboard. A revised version of the explanation hypothesis is that students learn by translating procedures from natural language to mental language. There is a substantial literature on the characteristics of such learning, which is reviewed briefly.

From the beginning of computer science, people have tried to invent translators that convert natural-language descriptions of procedures into programs. These attempts have succeeded only when the types of programs being written are confined to a very narrow domain. For instance, the LUNAR system (Woods, Kaplan, and Nash-Webber 1972) translated natural-language queries, such as "What is the ratio of calcium to silicon in samples with magnesium?" into small data base query programs. LUNAR can only write programs that access a certain data base about samples of moon rocks. Although general-purpose translators are commercially available now, they must be strongly constrained for the customer's application before they will function reliably. This general finding is usually interpreted to mean that natural language is not as precise a communication medium as a formal programming language, so translating from one to the other requires information from some source to be added to obtain the requisite precision. Strong prior expectations about the content of utterances is one such source of extra information. Examples could be another such source, although not much is known about the performance of natural language understanding systems that expect to receive examples as well, because few have been built (Badre (1972) described one for learning arithmetic procedures). Although it is not plausible that students have strong prior knowledge about arithmetic procedures, it is plausible that they use examples to help them understand the recipes they are given. So from a computational standpoint the revised explanations hypothesis cannot stand on its own (that is, that students learn from recipes in isolation), but it could stand if combined with the examples hypothesis.

On the other hand computer science's attempts to induce programs from examples have had more success. The success of early attempts were limited, because they tried to induce procedures from input/output pairs (Amarel 1971). When the learning program is given a sequence of actions to generalize from, it was found that programs of moderate complexity could be acquired using a variety of techniques (Bauer 1975, Biermann 1972, 1978, Neves 1981, Shaw, Swartout, and Green 1975, Siklossy and Sykes 1975).

Turning now to the psychological evidence, several recent studies show that examples are more important than recipes when both are available. In tutoring student programmers, several studies found that subjects tend to attend more to the examples than the explanations (Anderson, Farrell, and Saurers 1984, Pirolli and Anderson 1985). When subjects are given examples and instructions that describe different procedures for solving a series completion task and are led to believe that they describe the same procedure, the subjects' performance indicates that they followed the examples and disregarded the recipes, even if it was stressed that the instructions were very important (LeFevre and Dixon 1986).

In the preceding studies students had a choice of whether to study written examples or written explanations. Different results are obtained when students are asked to study examples and generate the explanations *themselves*. Chi, Bassok, Lewis, Reimann, and Glaser (1989) found that students who self-generated explanations while studying physics examples learned more than students who merely read the examples. Several studies (Gagne and Smith 1962, Davis, Carey, Foxman, and Tarr 1968, Wilder and Harvey 1971) of subjects learning the Tower of Hanoi puzzle showed that requiring subjects to explain their moves as they made them increased transfer from training trials to test trials.

From all these results the general conclusion can be drawn that explanations have an influence on learning only when they are explanations of specific examples rather than abstract statements or general discussions, and when the explanations are self-generated, rather than being provided to the students in written form. Unfortunately these results do not bear directly on the mathematics classroom situation, where it can be assumed that most explanations are spoken to students, and students can ask questions if they find the explanations confusing. It could be that explanations are disregarded or ambiguous when they are delivered in written form, but effective when delivered in a conversational setting (or self-generated).

In the experiments where explanations proved pedagogically effective, however, the retention of this learning was not tested. Even if verbal explanations might help a student acquire an initial understanding, because subsequent practice in the typical mathematics classroom drills students on performing the procedure rather than explaining it, it seems likely that students will forget the content of the explanations, and their knowledge structures will eventually be dominated by the content of the examples. Thus although initial learning of the procedure might be best modeled as a combination of learning from examples and learning from explanations, the eventual state of knowledge can be approximated by learning from examples alone, because the intervening drill dealt mostly with examples rather than explanations.

Instead of relying on conjectures and dubious generalizations from laboratory experiments, it would be preferable to seek evidence from the products of the classroom enviroment, the procedures. This requires making some plausible assumptions about the entailments of the examples and explanations hypotheses with regard to the procedures. Suppose we assume that procedures derived from examples have mostly visual and spatial descriptions in their patterns, because those patterns are derived from visual entities, the examples. Suppose we also assume that procedures derived from recipes have linguistic descriptions in their patterns, such as "the tens place" or "the subtrahend." Given these temporary, auxiliary assumptions, the bug data can be used to check the contents of the observed procedures' patterns, thereby settling the issue of whether learning is more influenced by examples or explanations.

Consider students who have been shown how to borrow on examples/explanations that use only two-column problems, such as A:

$$
\begin{array}{llll}
& \quad 2 & \quad\quad 4 & \quad\quad\quad 4 \\
\text{A.} & \not{3}14 \quad \text{B.} & \not{5}\,3^14 \quad \text{C.} & 3^14\,\not{5}\,6 \\
& -\,1\,7 & -\,1\,2\,7 & -\,1\,7\,1\,1 \\
\hline
& \;\,1\,7 & \;\,3\,1\,7 & \;\,2\,7\,4\,5
\end{array}
$$

Such partial training seems to cause bugs, such as Always-Borrow-Left (B), that seem to be caused by patterns that contain the primitive descriptions "leftmost and left-adjacent." These are presumably induced from examples such as A, where the decrement's position is indeed the leftmost column in the problem. These are spatial features because they reference salient visual features (for example, the left end of the block of columns). However, the decrement's position in problems like A is always in the tens column. It is possible that the pattern could contain "tens column" instead of leftmost. The descriptor "tens column" is most likely the way that a teacher would refer to the decrement's position when explaining the examples, so its presence in patterns would be predicted by the explanations hypothesis.

If "tens column" were in the pattern, then a bug would be generated (via Barge-on) that always borrows from the tens column, no matter where the borrow originates (see C). No such bug has been observed, and in my opinion it is a star bug. Thus we have some support for the examples hypothesis in the existence of Always-Borrow-Left and other bugs, and no support (or disconfirmation, if one accepts the star bug judgment) for the explanations hypothesis.

The foregoing demonstrates the form of the argument from bug data, but it references only a small number of bugs. In VanLehn 1986 it is shown that 85 percent of all the observed bugs can be described with a small set of visual/spatial features. No bug requires linguistic features for its description. Thus the bug evidence is unequivocally in favor of the examples hypothesis, which henceforth is assumed.

The examples assumption
If $P_i \epsilon$ Learn (P_{i-1}, L_i), then P_i is consistent with the positive examples of L_i, but not necessarily with the explanations of L_i.

This statement of the assumption uses some terms that need proper definitions. A procedure is *consistent* with an example if it produces the same sequence of actions that the example produces when it solves the same problem as the example. If the procedure is non-deterministic (that is, it can solve some problems in more than one way), then one of the action sequences that it is capable of generating for solving the problem must match the example's action sequence.

An example is a *positive* example if the explanatory material indicates that it is a correct solution to the example's problem. A *negative* example is marked as an incorrect solution. Arithmetic textbooks virtually never use negative examples of procedures. In the classroom, however, incorrect solutions generated by a student working problems on the chalk-board for the rest of the class could be considered negative examples. A student's homework exercise constitutes a negative example when it is marked wrong. Although negative examples do occur in arithmetic lessons, they are much less common than positive examples. Moreover the textbooks (and probably the teachers as well) put much less emphasis on negative examples. Although the examples assumption could be made stronger by requiring that the acquired procedures be inconsistent with the negative examples, a better approximation to the instructional situation is that negative examples are simply ignored.

Induction is the technical term for the class of functions that produce generalizations of examples. The examples assumption could be restated as saying that P_i is induced from the examples of L_i. Indeed this was how the assumption was stated in earlier reports on this theory

(VanLehn 1983a, 1986). Induction includes, as a special case, learning from analogies. An analogy involves two examples: one is well understood, and the other is less well understood. A mapping is formed, and the knowledge about the well-understood example is translated and applied to the other example. Usually it is assumed that using an analogy in this way somehow modifies the knowledge structures, making them more general. There have been several recent protocol studies where analogical problem solving was clearly evident and seems responsible for the learning that occurred during the course of the protocol. Anderson, Farrell, and Saurers (1984) found that novice Lisp programmers would solve an exercise problem by drawing an example to a solved exercise in the textbook. Chi and colleagues (1989) found the same thing for physics students. In these cases, as in the general view of learning from analogy, subjects acquire a generalization or abstraction of the examples. Thus learning by analogy is a subclass of the class of all inductive learning functions. Unfortunately there are no accepted terms for the residual classes, namely, inductive learning programs that are not explanation-based or skill acquisition strategies that are not analogical. Sometimes these residual classes are called *induction*. Thus the meaning of the term has varied depending on the context of its usage. In the sequel the term induction is used with its original meaning, which includes all forms of learning from examples, including those termed analogical.[10]

4.2.1 The Scandal of Induction
One of the problems with induction, as philosophers have pointed out, is that it sanctions irrelevant inferences as well as relevant ones. This problem is sometimes called "the scandal of induction." Given an example of a black crow, one would logically induce that all crows are black, or one could logically induce that all crows are black and the moon is made of green cheese. Clearly the latter logically correct inference is not what people do. Although philosophers of science have investigated various constraints on induction that are aimed at getting only the scientifically acceptable inferences to come out (see, for example, Hempel 1945), these investigations are tangential to the needs of this theory, which aims to capture what people actually infer rather than what they should infer. Nonetheless some constraint is needed on induction a priori to rule out wild, irrelevant inferences that people would never make.

The constraint that seems best is based on the idea that students only add new structure to their procedure if they have to. Having just seen a borrow example with some relatively small numbers, they could add the extra rule "If the column is in the millions place or higher, then finish the problem by adding." However, they would have no reason to add this rule because such a rule would not be used in producing the solution of the borrowing example. The assumption is that no student would ever add such irrelevant rules to their procedure. This assumption is a variant of *reducedness*, a constraint on formal grammar acquisition that has some interesting properties (VanLehn and Ball 1987).

The reducedness assumption
If $P_i \in$ Learn (P_{i-1}, L_i), then P_i is reduced with respect to the positive examples of L_i in that all the rules added to P_i are used in some solution of some example of L_i.

It can be shown that there are only finitely many simple context-free grammars that are consistent and reduced with respect to finite set of positive examples (VanLehn and Ball 1987). It is shown in the next chapter that the procedural representation language makes a procedure equivalent to a context-free grammar, except for the patterns. If a few additional constraints are placed on the procedural representation, it can be shown that there are only finitely many procedures consistent with any given curriculum. Although comforting in a mathematical sense, these finiteness results tell us little about how people learn. The number of procedures consistent with N examples is an exponential function of N. It grows so fast that it is nonsense to suggest that people generate all possible procedures then select the one they like best. What is important about the finiteness results is that it is possible, at least in principle, for a theorist to generate all possible procedures consistent with a given lesson sequence, then see which correspond to the observed behavior. Indeed Sierra is designed to be exactly that sort of generator, although for efficiency's sake some extra constraints are built into it a priori.

4.3 Assimilation versus Radical Modification

The output of a lesson, P_i, is assumed to be a function of two inputs, the lesson L_i and the procedure P_{i-1}. In the preceding section I discussed the relationship between P_i and L_i. This section deals with the relationship between P_i and P_{i-1}.

Typically, incremental learning is dichotomized as major changes due to radical restructuring versus minor changes due to assimilation of new material (Rumelhart and Norman 1978). During assimilation the existing knowledge is added to or changed in minor ways. During restructuring the content of the existing knowledge is maintained, but the way it is organized or formatted changes radically, which in turn causes its content to be viewed in an entirely new way.

Fortunately there is every reason to believe that learning arithmetic lessons is a paradigmatic case of assimilation. The only question is how to formalize this assumption.

The standard way to formalize the idea of assimilation within inductive theories is to assert that the new concept is a *generalization* of its predecessor. Generalization is standardly defined in terms of the denotations of concepts, where the denotation of a concept is the set of all possible instances (positive examples) of it. Concept A is a generalization of B if its denotation includes the denotation of B. This version of assimilation, based on the idea of growing denotations. captures the basic intuition that as you learn, you never lose abilities that were previously learned. However, this version of assimilation does not work for this theory. Although denotation and generalization can be defined for procedures, they do not yield the right relation between P_i and P_{i-1}. P_{i-1} might generate a buggy solution to a certain problem, but P_i might generate a correct solution to the very same problem. Thus distinct instances (examples) of the procedures occur with the same problem, so P_{i-1}'s denotation is not a subset of the denotation of P_i. A nonstandard definition of assimilation is needed.

The approach taken here is syntactic. The idea of a small addition or change to a procedure is defined in terms of small additions or changes to the representation of the procedure. The previous arguments, however, only specified a class of representations, including certain types of production systems, transition nets, and goal graphs. To state the assimilation assumption, it is convenient to fix on just one of these representations, the production system. In this representation goals are folded into the condition sides of rules, for example,

If Goal = (Sub1Col C), and
(Part-of T C), and (Part-of B C), and . . .
(Value-of TV T), and (Value-of BV B), and (Less-than TV BV),
then
(PushGoal (Borrow C))

When procedures are written in this fashion, the basic notion of assimilation can be captured by assuming that rules are never deleted. New rules can be added, or existing rules can have their patterns modified. This captures the basic idea of assimilation that learning preserves the abilities that were present, although it might make minor modifications in how they are deployed.

The assimilation assumption
If $P_i \epsilon$ Learn (P_{i-1}, L_i), and procedures are expressed in production system notation, then the productions of P_{i-1} are subset of the productions of P_i.

Note that the assumption allows the two sets of productions to be equal. This typically occurs when the lesson does not introduce a part of the skill, but merely shows the student that an existing part can be extended to handle more complicated problems. Such a lesson might not add any rules, but instead would cause the conditions on existing rules to be changed.

4.4 Deletion

A convenient way to introduce the last assumption in this chapter is with some anecdotes. I once followed a procedure manual for replacing the clutch on a Volkswagen engine, put the engine back together, then found a crucial bearing lying on the floor. I had skipped the step of putting the bearing back in the engine. This incident of skipping a step occurred with a novel procedure, but I occasionally skip steps in familiar procedures as well (for example, driving without releasing the parking brake). In arithmetic dropping a step is a common slip both for students and adults. For instance, a common slip is to forget the borrow-from half of borrowing, as in

$$
\begin{array}{r}
3^14 \\
-1\ 8 \\
\hline
2\ 6
\end{array}
$$

If a student makes a few such slips soon after learning a new subskill and never receives correction, then it is plausible that the slip will become permanent, that is, a bug. In fact there is a bug, Borrow-No-Decrement, that always omits the borrow-from step. Perhaps it was generated by practice without sufficient corrective feedback. On the basis of these anecdotes, it seems plausible that there is some cognitive process that causes unintentional omission of steps (Norman 1981), and another that can cause repetition of such missing-step slips to become permanent.

The next section, presents a set of several bugs, which are called "missing rule" bugs because they seem to be missing a rule, but are otherwise complete procedures. Borrow-No-Decrement is a member of the missing rule bug class. It is plausible that the missing rule bugs are caused by practicing slips, as the story suggests. It could also be that the bugs are caused by some decay or interference process that perturbs the long-term memory structures of the procedure and makes it impossible to retrieve one of its rules. The thrust of this research is to understand and model the acquisition phase of learning and to ignore the memory effects as much as possible, as the latter seem adequately covered by architectural theories such as Act* (Anderson 1983). There are missing rule bugs, however, and because they interact with cognitive process that the theory aims to model, their acquisition must be modeled as well.

Missing rule bugs cannot be generated within the current framework of incremental induction and assimilation. To see why, suppose that the rule that is missing should have been introduced by lesson L_i. The missing rule procedure cannot be a P_i, because those procedures are constrained to be consistent with the examples of L_i, and they would not be if they were missing a rule. So the missing rule procedure must be some P_{i+j}. But the assimilation constraint forbids deleting rules. So P_{i+j} has all the rules of P_i, hence it has the rule that we would like to be missing. So the desired missing rule procedure is not in the set of incomplete procedures. A new way of generating procedures is needed, which can simply be postulated as

The deletion assumption
If P is an incomplete procedure, and R is a rule from a most recently added AND goal, then P without rule R is a procedure in the set of core procedures.

This assumption incorporates two constraints on deletion. The first constraint is that only rules from AND goals are deleted. This is a mere technicality; if other types of rules were deleted, the resulting procedures would function exactly the same as some procedure in the set of incomplete procedure, and we already have a way to generate the incomplete procedures.[11] The more substantive constraint is that only rules from goals that were added most recently to the procedure are subject to deletion. In principle a person could learn all about borrowing, but forget that the answer had to be written down. This would correspond to deleting an old rule long after other AND goals had been learned. Such bugs do not occur and seem like star bugs as well, so their generation is prohibited by the assumption.

4.5 An Overview of the "Observed" Core Procedures

The assumptions introduced in this chapter define a set of generative processes that are intended to define the class of all "possible" procedures that are consistent with the given curriculum. Subsequent chapters formulate constraints on these generators that narrow their output to encompass just the procedures that human students learn. The assumptions made here and in following chapters depend crucially on the analyses presented in the preceding chapters. For instance, some of the assumptions mention rules and subprocedures, which are defined by the assumptions about the representation language. Other assumptions are motivated by the existence of the missing subprocedure bugs and the missing rule bugs; these bug classes are not given to us a priori, but depend on the assumptions about the impasse-repair process. So the learning theory is very much a product of the previous assumptions about the execution and representation of procedures.

Another way to view the development of the theory is to trace the analyses of the data. The data started as raw performances, filled with errors. By studying the pattern of errors a catalog of bugs was developed, and each student's performance was analyzed into a bug set that accounted for most of their error plus a small collection of slips. Reduction of raw performances to bug sets was the first stage of data analysis. In the next stage the bugs were studied, Cartesian product patterns were found, and the existence of impasses and repairs was inferred. At this point each student's performance was further reduced to an underlying core procedure plus the student's choice of repairs at each impasse that occurred.

Approximately 30 distinct core procedures suffice to generate most of the 75 bugs that have been observed (as well as to predict many bugs that have not yet been observed). The details of these derivations is presented in chapter 7 after all the remaining details of the theory have been presented. However, to motivate some of the major assumptions about the learning processes that are responsible for generating these core procedures, this section provides an overview of all the core procedures that have been "observed." The core procedures are grouped into six classes. The classes are called bug classes, highlighting the fact that they actually are a grouping of observed bugs, rather than the core procedures, whose existence can be inferred only in less direct manner.

4.5.1 The Missing Subprocedure Bug Class
Some problems are equivalent in that their correct solution involves exactly the same subskills. For instance, there is a set of problems that do not require borrowing, a set of problems that require borrowing, but not from zero, and a set of problems that require borrowing from zero. The defining characteristic of a bug from the *missing subprocedure bug class* is that the boundary between the problems it answers correctly and those it answers incorrectly falls squarely on the boundary

between adjacent problem sets. Such bugs can be generated by core procedures that are missing subprocedures. The subprocedures that are present are taught in the first several lessons of the curriculum, and the subprocedures that are missing are taught in the remaining lessons.

In point of fact some of our subjects were tested on problems that required subskills that they had not yet been taught. All subjects received roughly the same tests, and the tests contained problems of all types, including complicated borrow-from-zero problems as well as simple nonborrowing problems. Some of the subjects, however, came from the early third grade, and borrowing may not have been taught to them yet. Borrowing from zero is generally not taught until the late third or early fourth grades. So it is likely that some of the students were tested beyond their training.

Having students solve problems that are beyond their training is a common practice in schools. For instance, it is often occurs during placement testing. Also some textbooks routinely include special "advanced" exercises at the end of the lesson so that rapid learners have something to do while the rest of the class works through the normal exercises. Often these advanced exercises are just exercises that require subskills that have not been taught yet. Because solving problems beyond training is common in the schools, it is likely that missing subprocedure bugs exist outside as well as inside our sample. Although our testing may have caused a few students to exhibit bugs that they otherwise would not have exhibited, many of the students probably already had the bugs before they were tested because they had taken similar tests before or had done advanced exercises without adequate supervision. Indeed other studies of systematic errors (Buswell 1926, Cox 1975, Ashlock 1976) have found many of the same subtraction bugs despite the fact that their data were collected with clinical interviews rather than testing.

A list of the fifteen bugs in this class that have actually occurred, along with the four core procedures that generate them, is provided by 4.1.

4.5.2 The Missing Rule Bug Class
The missing rule bugs are best understood in contrast to the missing subprocedure bugs. An example of a missing subprocedure bug is

$$\text{Stop-Borrow-At-Zero} \qquad \begin{array}{r} 3\ 4\ 5 \\ -1\ 0\ 2 \\ \hline 2\ 4\ 3 \end{array} \qquad \begin{array}{r} {}^{3}\\ 3\ \not{4}{}^{1}5 \\ -1\ 2\ 9 \\ \hline 2\ 1\ 6 \end{array} \qquad \begin{array}{r} {}^{2}\\ \not{3}{}^{1}0{}^{1}7 \\ -1\ 6\ 9 \\ \hline 1\ 4\ 8\ \text{X} \end{array} \qquad \begin{array}{r} 3\ 0{}^{1}7 \\ -\quad\ 9 \\ \hline 3\ 0\ 8\ \text{X} \end{array}$$

No Partial Columns: Students do not know how to solve problems that lack a bottom digit. They reach an impasse on the tens and hundreds columns of this exercise.

$$\begin{array}{r} 968 \\ -5 \\ \hline 3 \end{array}$$

Quit-When-Bottom-Blank. Repairs impasse by going on to the next column or the next problem.

$$\begin{array}{r} 968 \\ -5 \\ \hline 413 \end{array}$$

Stutter-Subtract. Repairs impasse by using the last bottom digit as the missing one.

$$\begin{array}{r} 968 \\ -5 \\ \hline 853 \end{array}$$

Sub-One-Over-Blank. Repairs impasse by substituting a one for the missing digit.

No Borrow: Students do not know how to borrow. They reach an impasse in columns where the top digit is less than the bottom digit (for example, the tens column in this exercise).

$$\begin{array}{r} 358 \\ -172 \\ \hline 26 \end{array}$$

Blank-Instead-of-Borrow. Repairs by skipping the column and processing subgoal.

$$\begin{array}{r} 358 \\ -172 \\ \hline 226 \end{array}$$

Smaller-From-Larger. Repairs by reinterpreting Top − Bottom as Larger − Smaller.

$$\begin{array}{r} 358 \\ -172 \\ \hline 206 \end{array}$$

Zero-Instead-of-Borrow. Repairs by writing the smallest number known, zero.

No Borrow From Zero: Students know how to borrow, but not from zeros. They reach an impasse while trying to decrement the zero by one.

$$\begin{array}{r} 30\overset{15}{\cancel{5}} \\ -7 \\ \hline 308 \end{array}$$

Stops-Borrow-At-Zero. Repairs by skipping the stuck subgoal of borrow. Correctly performs other subgoals.

$$\begin{array}{r} \overset{2}{\cancel{3}}0\overset{15}{\cancel{5}} \\ -7 \\ \hline 208 \end{array}$$

Borrow-Across-Zero. Reinterprets the location of the decrement as the nearest nonzero digit in the top row.

$\overset{2\ \ \overset{10\ 15}{}}{\cancel{3}\cancel{0}\cancel{5}}$
$\overset{1}{\ -\ \cancel{2}7}$
298

Borrow-From-Bottom-Instead-of-Zero. Reinterprets the location of the decrement as any nonzero digit in the adjacent column.

$\overset{2\ \ \overset{10}{}}{\cancel{3}\cancel{0}5}$
$-\ 27$
282

Smaller-From-Larger-Instead-of-Borrow-From-Zero. Does an absolute difference instead of borrowing if the borrow is from zero.

No Borrow From Multiple Zeros: Students know how to borrow from one zero, but not from two or more zeros.

$\overset{\overset{15}{}}{300\cancel{5}}$
$-\ \ \ 7$
3008

Stops-Borrow-At-Multiple-Zero. The student attempts to decrement the top digit in the hundreds column, reaches an impasse, and decides to skip the whole decrementing component of borrowing.

$\overset{2\ \ \ \overset{9\ 15}{}}{\cancel{3}0\cancel{0}\cancel{5}}$
$-\ \ \ \ 7$
2098

Stops-Borrow-At-Second-Zero. The student changes the first zero to nine as usual, but reaches an impasse trying to decrement the top digit in the hundreds column. Repairs by reinterpreting the location of the decrement as the next nonzero digit, that is, the thousands column digit in this case.

$\overset{9\ \ \overset{10\ 15}{}}{3\cancel{0}\cancel{0}\cancel{5}}$
$-\ \ 27$
3988

Decrement-Leftmost-Zero-Only. The student skips decrementing the nonzero number (three, in this example) and changes the leftmost zero to nine and the other zeros to ten.

$\overset{2\ 9\ 8\ 15}{\cancel{3}\cancel{0}\cancel{0}\cancel{5}}$
$-\ \ \ 7$
2988

Decrement-Multiple-Zeros-By-Number-To-The-Left. The student changes zeros to nine, eight, seven, and so on as he moves from left to right.

$\overset{2\ 8\ 9\ 15}{\cancel{3}\cancel{0}\cancel{0}\cancel{5}}$
$-\ \ \ 7$
2898

Decrement-Multiple-Zeros-By-Number-To-The-Right. The student changes zeros to nine, eight, seven, and so on as he moves from right to left.

4.1
The 15 missing subprocedures bugs that have occurred, grouped under the four core procedures that generate them. Problems illustrate each bug's work.

The procedure behind this bug does not know how to borrow across zeros. It borrows correctly from nonzero digits, as shown in the second problem. On the third problem it attempts to decrement the zero, hits an impasse, and repairs by skipping the decrement operation entirely (the No-op repair). The point is that this bug has a complete, flawless knowledge of borrowing from nonzero digits, but it knows nothing about borrowing from zero. Precisely at one of the lesson boundaries in the subtraction curriculum, its understanding stops.

Now compare this knowledge state with the one implicated by the following bug:

$$
\begin{array}{lcccc}
 & & \overset{3}{} & \overset{2}{} & \overset{2}{} \\
\text{Don't-Decrement-Zero} & 3\ 4\ 5 & 3\ \cancel{4}^{1}5 & \cancel{3}^{1}0^{1}7 & \cancel{3}^{1}0^{1}7 \\
 & -1\ 0\ 2 & -1\ 2\ 9 & -1\ 6\ 9 & -\quad\ 9 \\
\hline
 & 2\ 4\ 3 & 2\ 1\ 6 & 1\ 4\ 8\ \text{X} & 2\ 1\ 0\ 8\ \text{X}
\end{array}
$$

This bug also misses just the borrow-from-zero problems. Indeed it gets the same answer on the third problem as with the previous bug, Stops-Borrow-At-Zero. However, it solves borrow-from-zero problems in a very different way. Notice the fourth problem. The borrow in the units column caused some but not all of the borrow-from-zero subprocedure to be executed. The following problem state sequence shows the initial problem solving:

$$
\begin{array}{llllllll}
 & \overset{2}{} & & \overset{2}{} & & \overset{2}{} & & \overset{2}{} \\
\text{A.} & \cancel{3}\ 0\ 7 & \text{B.} & \cancel{3}^{1}0\ 7 & \text{C.} & \cancel{3}^{1}0^{1}7 & \text{D.} & \cancel{3}^{1}0^{1}7 \\
 & -\quad\ 9 & & -\quad\ 9 & & -\quad\ 9 & & -\quad\ 9 \\
\hline
 & & & & & & & 8
\end{array}
$$

Most of the borrow-from-zero subprocedure is there. What is missing is its last action, decrementing the ten in the tens column to nine, which should occur between states b and c. Because the bug does some of the borrow-from-zero subprocedure, it is likely that subjects with this bug have been taught borrowing across zero. But it is also clear that they did not acquire all of the subprocedure or else forgot part of it. If the subtraction curriculum was constructed so that teachers first taught half of borrowing across zero and some weeks later taught the other half, then one would be tempted to account for this bug with incomplete learning. But borrowing from zero is in fact always taught as a whole. So some other mechanism (whose existence is assumed by the deletion assumption) is implicated in this bug's generation.

Don't-Decrement-Zero is one of the missing rule bugs. Others are detailed in 4.2. Each bug in 4.2 corresponds to a distinct core procedure because the execution of the core procedures encounters no impasses. However, there are other missing rule core procedures that do reach impasses during execution and thus generate multiple bugs per core procedures. As it happens, none of these bugs have occurred yet in the data.

4.5.3 The Fetch Pattern Bug Class

The bugs in this class seem to do all the right actions, so they are missing neither subprocedures nor rules, but they tend to do the actions in the wrong places. Apparently they come from core procedures whose fetch patterns are not correct. The bug Always-Borrow-Left, which has been mentioned several times in previous chapters is an example of a bug generated by a core procedure with an incorrect fetch pattern. Apparently its pattern is too specific. It seeks a column that is both leftmost and left-adjacent, and the failure to find one causes an impasse. Bugs in the class that have occurred, along with the core procedures that seem to generate them, are enumerated in 4.3.

4.5.4. The Test Pattern Bugs

Like the fetch pattern bugs, the test pattern bugs seem to do all the right actions, so they are missing neither subprocedures nor rules. However, they tend to do the actions at the wrong times. Apparently they come from core procedures whose test patterns are not correct A bug that was mentioned previously, Smaller-From-Larger-When-Borrowed-From, illustrates an incorrect test pattern. Students with this bug take the absolute difference instead of borrowing whenever a borrow column's top digit happens to have been decremented by an earlier borrow, as in the tens column of

$$
\begin{array}{r}
3 \\
3\ \not{4}^15 \\
-1\ 7\ 9 \\
\hline
2\ 4\ 6
\end{array}
$$

Apparently the test pattern is overly specific. It indicates that borrowing should be done only when an *unblemished* column has $T < B$. Bugs in the class that have occurred, along with the core procedures that seem to generate them, are enumerated in 4.4.

4.5.5 The $0 - N$ Bugs

This and the next bug class contain bugs that are not adequately accounted for by the current theory. They have been separated into

Deletion of Borrow-from-Zero Steps: There are several different subprocedures for borrowing from zero. Different bugs come from deleting different steps.

$$\begin{array}{r} \overset{9\ 16}{3\cancel{0}\cancel{6}} \\ -\ 187 \\ \hline 219 \end{array}$$
Borrow-From-Zero. Instead of borrowing across a 0, the student changes the 0 to a 9, but does not continue borrowing from the column to the left.

$$\begin{array}{r} \overset{4\ 10\ 16}{\cancel{5}\cancel{0}\cancel{6}} \\ -\ 318 \\ \hline 198 \end{array}$$
Don't-Decrement-Zero. When borrowing across a 0, the student changes the 0 to 10 instead of 9.

$$\begin{array}{r} \overset{7}{\cancel{8}}\ \overset{10\ 14}{\cancel{9}\cancel{0}4} \\ -\ 237 \\ \hline 577 \end{array}$$
Borrow-Across-Zero. When borrowing across a 0, the student skips over the 0 to borrow from the next column. If this causes him to have to borrow twice, he decrements the same number both times.

$$\begin{array}{r} \overset{10\ 14}{6\cancel{0}4} \\ -\ 235 \\ \hline 479 \end{array}$$
Borrow-From-Zero-Is-Ten. When borrowing across 0, the student changes the 0 to 10 and does not decrement any digit to the left.

$$\begin{array}{r} \overset{9\ 9\ 16}{3\cancel{0}\cancel{0}\cancel{6}} \\ -\ 1807 \\ \hline 2199 \end{array}$$
Borrow-From-All-Zero. Instead of borrowing across zeros, the student changes all the zeros to nines, but does not continue borrowing from the column to the left.

Deletion of Borrowing Steps: Deletion of the borrow-from step leads to the bug below. Deletion of other steps leads to bugs that are plausible, but haven't occurred yet.

$$\begin{array}{r} \overset{12}{6\cancel{2}} \\ -\ 44 \\ \hline 28 \end{array}$$
Borrow-No-Decrement. When borrowing, the student adds 10 correctly, but doesn't change any column to the left.

4.2
The missing rule bugs. Each bug corresponds to a distinct core procedure.

Two-Column Borrows: The student borrows properly only when the borrow is situated in the penultimate column. This procedure is generated by introducing borrows on two-column problems, where the column to be decremented is both leftmost and left-adjacent. The learner induces an overly specific description of where to borrow from. The description causes a reference impasse on all borrows that are not in the penultimate column.

$$\begin{array}{r} \overset{6}{\cancel{7}}\overset{13}{\cancel{3}}\cancel{3} \\ -\ 216 \\ \hline 427 \end{array}$$ Always-Borrow-Left. The student borrows from the left-most digit instead of borrowing from the digit immediately to the left.

$$\begin{array}{r} \overset{5}{\cancel{6}}\overset{12}{\cancel{2}}\overset{12}{\cancel{6}}\cancel{7} \\ -\ 4444 \\ \hline 1828 \end{array}$$ Borrow-No-Decrement-Except-Last. Decrements only in the last column of the problem.

$$\begin{array}{r} 5622 \\ -\ 130 \\ \hline 2 \end{array}$$ Doesn't-Borrow-Except-Last. If the borrow is not into the last column, the student quits.

$$\begin{array}{r} \overset{6}{\cancel{7}}\overset{13}{\cancel{3}}3 \\ -\ 246 \\ \hline 493 \end{array}$$ Smaller-From-Larger-Except-Last. If the borrow is not into the last column, the student does smaller from larger instead.

No Adjacent Borrows: The student has not been trained on problems with adjacent borrows. During the first borrow of a pair of adjacent borrows, the student notices that the decrement will be placed in a column that will later require a borrow. He is not sure if this is right (that is, a reference impasse occurs).

$$\begin{array}{r} \overset{6}{\cancel{7}}\overset{12}{\cancel{3}}\overset{13}{\cancel{3}}\overset{12}{\cancel{7}} \\ -\ 4384 \\ \hline 2958 \end{array}$$ Borrow-Don't-Decrement-Top-Smaller. The student will not decrement a column if the top number is strictly smaller than the bottom number.

$$\begin{array}{r} \overset{6}{\cancel{7}}\overset{13}{\cancel{3}}\overset{12}{\cancel{3}}\cancel{7} \\ -\ 4834 \\ \hline 2508 \end{array}$$ Borrow-Don't-Decrement-Unless-Bottom-Smaller. The student will not decrement a column unless the bottom number is strictly smaller than the top number.

$$\begin{array}{r} 732 \\ -\ 434 \\ \hline 302 \end{array}$$ Smaller-From-Larger-Instead-of-Borrow-Unless-Bottom-Smaller. The student will take the absolute difference in a column if it requires borrowing from a column where the top number is less than or equal to the bottom number.

$$\begin{array}{r} {}^{4\ 11\ 12}_{\not{5}\not{1}\not{3}} \\ -\ 268 \\ \hline 254 \end{array}$$

Borrow-Across-Top-Smaller-Decrementing-To. When decrementing a column in which the top is smaller than the bottom, the student adds 10 to the top digit, decrements the column being borrowed into, and borrows from the next column to the left. Also the student skips any column that has either a 0 over a 0 or a blank in the borrowing process.

$$\begin{array}{r} {}^{8}_{\not{9}2\not{3}}{}^{13} \\ -\ 427 \\ \hline 406 \end{array}$$

Borrow-Skip-Equal. When decrementing, the student skips over columns in which the top digit and the bottom digit are the same.

No Borrows Over Blanks: The student has never had to borrow from a column that has a blank bottom (e.g., 324 − 71). An overly specific description of where to borrow from causes a reference impasse on such problems.

$$\begin{array}{r} 34\overset{17}{\not{7}} \\ -\ \ \ 9 \\ \hline 348 \end{array}$$

Forget-Borrow-Over-Blanks. The student doesn't decrement a number that is over a blank.

Borrow From Zero: Special Columns: The student has seen regular borrow-from-zero problems, such as 306 − 128, but has received no training on problems where the zero is located over blanks or other zeros. Overly specific descriptions cause reference impasses on such problems.

$$\begin{array}{r} {}^{3}_{\not{4}0\not{2}}{}^{12} \\ -\ \ \ 6 \\ \hline 306 \end{array}$$

Borrow-Across-Zero-Over-Blank. When borrowing across a 0 over a blank, the student skips to the next column to decrement.

$$\begin{array}{r} {}^{7}_{\not{8}0\not{2}}{}^{12} \\ -\ 304 \\ \hline 408 \end{array}$$

Borrow-Across-Zero-Over-Zero. Instead of borrowing across a 0 that is over a 0, the student does not change the 0 but decrements the next column to the left instead.

$$\begin{array}{r} 30\overset{15}{\not{5}} \\ -\ \ \ 9 \\ \hline 306 \end{array}$$

Don't-Decrement-Zero-Over-Blank. The student will not borrow across a zero that is over a blank.

$$\begin{array}{r} 30\overset{15}{\not{5}} \\ -\ 107 \\ \hline 208 \end{array}$$

Don't-Decrement-Zero-Over-Zero. The student will not borrow across a zero that is over a zero.

$$\begin{array}{r} \overset{1}{4}\overset{12}{\cancel{0}}\overset{}{\cancel{2}} \\ -\quad 6 \\ \hline 416 \end{array}$$

Increment-Zero-Over-Blank. When borrowing across a 0 over a blank, the student increments the 0 instead of decrementing.

4.3
The incorrect fetch pattern bugs

No Adjacent Borrow—Decision Impasse: The student has not been trained on problems with adjacent borrows. When he comes to a column that needs a borrow but has already been borrowed from, he is unsure whether to borrow (that is, he has a decision impasse).

$$\begin{array}{r} 8\overset{1}{\cancel{2}}\overset{14}{\cancel{4}} \\ -\,157 \\ \hline 747 \end{array}$$

Smaller-From-Larger-When-Borrowed-From. When there are two borrows in a row, the student does the first one correctly but for the second one he does not borrow; instead he subtracts the smaller from the larger digit, regardless of order.

$$\begin{array}{r} 2\overset{2}{\cancel{3}}\overset{14}{\cancel{4}} \\ -\,115 \\ \hline 109 \end{array}$$

X–N = 0-After-Borrow. If a column has been borrowed from, the student writes zero as its answer.

$$\begin{array}{r} 2\overset{2}{\cancel{3}}\overset{14}{\cancel{4}} \\ -\,165 \\ \hline 169 \end{array}$$

X–N = N-After-Borrow. If a column has been borrowed from, the student writes the bottom digit as its answer.

Borrows Only Once: The student has been trained on borrow problems that have more than two columns. However, none of the problems have two or more borrows. So the student induces that one can have at most one borrow per problem.

$$\begin{array}{r} 5\overset{12}{\cancel{3}}\overset{15}{\cancel{5}} \\ -\,278 \\ \hline 357 \end{array}$$

Borrow-Only-Once. When there are several adjacent borrows, the student decrements only with the first borrow.

$$\begin{array}{r} 71\overset{1}{\cancel{2}}\overset{17}{\cancel{7}} \\ -\,2389 \\ \hline 5278 \end{array}$$

Borrow-Once-Then-Smaller-From-Larger. The student will borrow only once per exercise. From then on he subtracts the smaller from the larger digit in each column regardless of their positions.

Overgeneralization: The student has been trained on some number combinations, but not all of them. Numerical predicates, such as $T < B$ or $T = 0$, are overgeneralized.

$$\begin{array}{r} {}^{8\ 15}\llap{\not{9}\not{5}3} \\ -\ \ 152 \\ \hline 7101 \end{array}$$

N–N-Causes-Borrow. Borrows with columns of the form N − N.

$$\begin{array}{r} {}^{7\ 9\ 9\ 13}\llap{\not{8}\not{1}\not{1}\not{3}} \\ -\ \ 568 \\ \hline 7435 \end{array}$$

Borrow-Treat-One-As-Zero. When borrowing from 1, the student treats the 1 as if it were 0; that is, he changes the 1 to 9 and decrements the number to the left of the 1.

$$\begin{array}{r} {}^{9\ 9\ 13}\llap{8\not{1}\not{1}\not{3}} \\ -\ \ 568 \\ \hline 8435 \end{array}$$

Double-Decrement-One. When borrowing from a 1, the student treats the 1 as a 0 (changes the 1 to 9) and continues borrowing to the left unless the column to the left has a blank on the bottom.

$$\begin{array}{r} {}^{2\ 11\ 14}\llap{\not{3}\not{1}\not{4}} \\ -\ \ \ \ 6 \\ \hline 2118 \end{array}$$

Decrement-One-To-Eleven. Instead of decrementing a 1, the student changes the 1 to an 11. According to the bug story, this bug always co-occurs with Don't-Decrement-Zero, which does borrowing from zero by simply changing the 0 to 10. Decrement-One-To-Eleven has only occurred once, and, as predicted, it co-occurred with Don't-Decrement-Zero.

$$\begin{array}{r} {}^{10\ 14}\llap{4\not{1}\not{4}} \\ -\ 277 \\ \hline 237 \end{array}$$

Borrow-From-One-Is-Ten. When borrowing from a 1, the student changes the 1 to 10 instead of to 0. This bug has the same explanation as Decrement-One-To-Eleven, except the co-occurring bug is Borrow-From-Zero-Is-Ten.

$$\begin{array}{r} {}^{9\ 16}\llap{3\not{1}\not{6}} \\ -\ 139 \\ \hline 267 \end{array}$$

Borrow-From-One-Is-Nine. When borrowing from a 1, the student treats the 1 as if it were 10, decrementing it to a 9. This bug has the same explanation as Decrement-One-To-Eleven, except the co-occurring bug is Borrow-From-Zero.

$$\begin{array}{r} 40 \\ -\ 21 \\ \hline 20 \end{array}$$

Diff-0–N = 0. When the student encounters a column of the form 0 − N, he doesn't borrow; instead he writes 0 as the column answer. One possible explanation for this bug is that the student has overgeneralized the rule, "If $B = 0$, then write T in the answer" to become, "If $T = 0$ or $B = 0$, then write T in the answer."

80	Diff-0–N = N. When the student encounters a column of
− 27	the form $0 - N$, he doesn't borrow. Instead he writes N as
67	the answer. One possible explanation for this bug is that

the student has overgeneralized the rule, "If $B = 0$, then
write the other digit in the answer," to become, "If $T = 0$
or $B = 0$, then write the other digit in the answer."

4.4
The test pattern bugs

two classes because the bugs in this class seem closer to being explained than the bugs in the next class.

The $0 - N$ bugs share the characteristic that they incorrectly solve
some columns that have a zero as the top digit. For instance, the bug
Diff-0 $- N = N$ answers all $0 - N$ columns by writing the bottom digit
in the answer. The bug $0 - N = N$-After-Borrow does the same action,
but only for columns whose top zero was generated by decrementing
a one, as in the tens column of

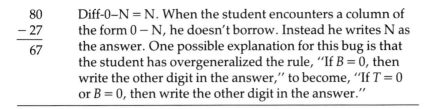

The bug $1 - 1 = 1$-After-Borrow does the same action, but only in columns whose top and bottom digits were originally ones, but whose
top digit has been changed to a zero by an earlier borrow's decrement.

Most $0 - N$ bugs can be generated by appropriately overspecific test
patterns. If the test pattern for borrowing exempts all $0 - N$ columns,
then the bugs Diff-0 $- N = N$ and Diff-0 $- N = 0$ can be generated by
two different repairs to the resulting decision impasse. If the test
pattern exempts $0 - N$ columns whose zero is generated by
decrementing a one, then the bugs $0 - N = N$-After-Borrow and
$0 - N = 0$-After-Borrow can be generated by the same two repairs.
Similarly most of the other bugs can be generated, provided that the
core procedures have exactly the right test patterns.

This bug class could be considered a subclass of the class of test
pattern bugs. However, the current theory has no way of explaining
how these $0 - N$ test patterns are acquired, whereas it can explain
how the other test patterns bugs were acquired. Thus the $0 - N$ bugs

have been allocated a distinct bug class. Bugs in this class, along with the core procedures that generate them, are listed in 4.5.

4.5.6 Miscellaneous Bugs
The remaining observed bugs constitute a class of their own. It is not clear how they are acquired, or even exactly what their core procedures are. They are listed in 4.6.

Top Zero: The following unexplained bugs share the characteristic that they trigger on all columns where the top digit is a zero.

$\begin{array}{r} 30 \\ -\ 4 \\ \hline 39 \end{array}$	Treat-Top-Zero-As-Nine. In a $0 - N$ column the student doesn't borrow. Instead he treats the 0 as if it were a 9.
$\begin{array}{r} 4\overset{10}{\cancel{0}} \\ -27 \\ \hline 23 \end{array}$	Treat-Top-Zero-As-Ten. In a $0 - N$ column the student adds 10 to it correctly, but doesn't change any column to the left.
$\begin{array}{r} 40 \\ -21 \\ \hline 20 \end{array}$	Diff-0–N = 0. When the student encounters a column of the form $0 - N$, he doesn't borrow; instead he writes 0 as the column answer.
$\begin{array}{r} 80 \\ -27 \\ \hline 67 \end{array}$	Diff-0–N = N. When the student encounters a column of the form $0 - N$, he doesn't borrow. Instead he writes N as the column answer.
$\begin{array}{r} \overset{3\ 10}{4\cancel{0}0} \\ -248 \\ \hline 168 \end{array}$	Diff-0–N = N-When-Borrow-From-Zero. When borrowing across a 0 and the borrow is caused by a 0, the student doesn't borrow. Instead he writes the bottom number as the column answer. He will borrow correctly in the next column or in other circumstances.

Top Zero After Borrow: The following unexplained bugs share the characteristic that they trigger on columns that once had a one on top, but the one has been decremented, so a zero is now on top.

$\begin{array}{r} 9\overset{0\ 14}{\cancel{1}4} \\ -486 \\ \hline 508 \end{array}$	0–N = 0-After-Borrow. When a column has a 1 that was changed to a 0 by a previous borrow, the student writes 0 as the answer to that column.

$\begin{matrix} & {}^{0\ 12} \\ & 5\cancel{1}\cancel{2} \\ - & 136 \\ \hline & 436 \end{matrix}$
0–N = N-After-Borrow. When a column has a 1 that was changed to a 0 by a previous borrow, the student writes the bottom digit as the answer to that column.

$\begin{matrix} & {}^{0\ 12} \\ & 8\cancel{1}\cancel{2} \\ - & 518 \\ \hline & 304 \end{matrix}$
1–1 = 0-After-Borrow. If a column starts with 1 in both top and bottom and is borrowed from, the student writes 0 as the answer to that column.

$\begin{matrix} & {}^{0\ 12} \\ & 8\cancel{1}\cancel{2} \\ - & 518 \\ \hline & 314 \end{matrix}$
1–1 = 1-After-Borrow. If a column starts with 1 in both top and bottom and is borrowed from, the student writes 1 as the answer to that column.

Top Zero, Not After Borrow: These bugs trigger only when the column has a zero on top and the zero was there in the original state of the problem.

$\begin{matrix} & {}^{8\ 10\ 15} \\ & \cancel{9}\cancel{1}\cancel{5}0 \\ - & 568 \\ \hline & 8590 \end{matrix}$
0–N = 0-Except-After-Borrow. Thinks $0 - N$ is 0 except when the column has been borrowed from.

$\begin{matrix} & {}^{8\ 10\ 15} \\ & \cancel{9}\cancel{1}\cancel{5}0 \\ - & 568 \\ \hline & 8598 \end{matrix}$
0–N = N-Except-After-Borrow. Thinks $0 - N$ is N except when the column has been borrowed from.

4.5
The top-zero bugs

$\begin{matrix} & 32 \\ - & 15 \\ \hline & 47 \end{matrix}$
Add-Instead-of-Sub. The student adds instead of subtracting.

$\begin{matrix} & {}^{1} \\ & {}^{3\ \cancel{1}\ 1} \\ & \cancel{4}11 \\ - & 215 \\ \hline & 527 \end{matrix}$
Add-LR-Decrement-Answer-Carry-To-Right. Add columns from left to right instead of subtracting. Before processing a column, the top digit is incremented (except in the leftmost column) and decremented (except in the units column).

$\begin{matrix} & {}^{12} \\ & {}^{4\ 11\ 13} \\ & \cancel{5}\cancel{1}\cancel{3} \\ - & 268 \\ \hline & 254 \end{matrix}$
Borrow-Across-Top-Smaller-Decrementing-To. Instead of borrowing across zeros, the student borrows across all columns where the top digit is strictly less than the bottom digit. The student counts the number of columns skipped over and decrements the digit borrowed into by that count.

$$\begin{array}{r} {}^{6}\!\!\not{7}^{10}\!\!\not{1} \\ -\ 38 \\ \hline 32 \end{array}$$

Borrow-Into-One = Ten. When a borrow is caused by a 1, the student changes the 1 to a 10 instead of adding 10 to it.

$$\begin{array}{r} {}^{11}\\ {}^{8}\!\!\not{9}^{7}\!\!\not{2}8^{13}\!\!\not{3} \\ -\ 3566 \\ \hline 5627 \end{array}$$

Borrow-Only-From-Top-Smaller. When borrowing, the student tries to find a column in which the top number is smaller than the bottom. If there is one, he decrements that, otherwise he borrows correctly.

$$\begin{array}{r} {}^{5}\!\!\not{8}^{9}\!\!\not{6} \\ -\ 29 \\ \hline 30 \end{array}$$

Borrow-Unit-Diff. The student borrows the difference between the top digit and the bottom digit of the current column. In other words he borrows just enough to do the subtraction, which then always results in 0.

$$\begin{array}{r} 8 \\ -\ 3 \end{array}$$

Can't-Subtract. The student skips the entire problem.

$$\begin{array}{r} {}^{5}\!\!\not{6}^{9}\!\!\not{0}^{9}\!\!\not{0} \\ -\ 142 \\ \hline 457 \end{array}$$

Decrement-All-On-Multiple-Zero. When borrowing across a 0 and the borrow is caused by a 0, the student changes the right 0 to 9 instead of 10.

$$\begin{array}{r} {}^{8}\!\!\not{4}^{18}\!\!\not{0}1^{13}\!\!\not{3} \\ -\ \ 595 \\ \hline 4398 \end{array}$$

Decrement-Top-Leq-Is-Eight. When borrowing from 0 or 1, changes the 0 or 1 to 8; does not decrement digit to the left of the 0 or 1.

$$\begin{array}{r} 57 \\ -\ 20 \\ \hline 30 \end{array}$$

Diff-N−0 = 0. The student thinks that N − 0 is 0.

$$\begin{array}{r} 83 \\ -\ 13 \\ \hline 73 \end{array}$$

Diff-N−N = N. Whenever there is a column that has the same number on the top and the bottom, the student writes that number as the answer.

$$\begin{array}{r} {}^{4}\!\!\not{5}^{10}\!\!\not{0}^{16}\!\!\not{6} \\ -\ 318 \\ \hline 198 \end{array}$$

Don't-Decrement-Zero-Until-Bottom-Blank. When borrowing from a 0, the student changes the 0 to a 10 instead of a 9 unless the 0 is over a blank, in which case he does the correct thing.

$$\begin{array}{r} 24 \\ -\ 14 \\ \hline 1 \end{array}$$

Don't-Write-Zero. Doesn't write zeros in the answer.

143
− 22
21

Ignore-Leftmost-One-Over-Blank. When the left column of the exercise has a 1 that is over a blank, the student ignores that column.

$\overset{14}{\overset{8\,4\,13}{\cancel{953}}}$
− 147
7106

N–N-After-Borrow-Causes-Borrow. Borrows with column of the form N − N if the column has been borrowed from previously.

$9\overset{3\,14}{\cancel{44}}$
− 348
616

N–N-After-Borrow. If a column had the form N − N and was borrowed from, the student writes 1 as the answer to that column.

348
− 2
126

Simple-Problem-Stutter-Subtract. When the bottom number is a single digit and the top number has two or more digits, the student repeatedly subtracts the single bottom number from each digit in the top number.

$47\overset{5}{\cancel{6}}3$
$− 30\overset{12}{\cancel{2}}5$
9772

Sub-Bottom-From-Top. The student always subtracts the top digit from the bottom digit. If the bottom digit is smaller, he decrements the top digit and adds 10 to the bottom before subtracting. If the bottom digit is zero, however, he writes the top digit in the answer. If the top digit is 1 greater than the bottom digit, he writes 9.

648
− 231
631

Sub-Copy-Least-Bottom-Most-Top. The student does not subtract. Instead he copies digits from the exercise to fill the answer space. He copies the leftmost digit from the top number and the other digits from the bottom number.

4.6
Miscellaneous unexplained bugs

Chapter 5
The Acquisition of Control Structure

The study of procedure acquisition can be conveniently divided up along syntactic lines. This chapter covers constraints on control structure acquisition; the next chapter covers constraints on pattern acquisition. The separation of the discussion is not meant to imply that the two learning processes take place at different times or even that there are separate learning processes for patterns and control structure. However, there are separate sets of constraints for specifying the acquired patterns and control structures, and necessarily so, because the constraints must mention the formats of the items they constrain, and the formats of patterns and control structure are very different. Hence the constraints come out quite differently.

Because this chapter does not deal with patterns, it is helpful to use a simplified notation for procedures that abbreviates the patterns. A rule-based notation is used in this chapter. Here 5.1 shows the same procedure as 3.8, but with the test patterns and fetch patterns abbreviated. The test patterns are shown in a second column to the right of the rule to which they apply. Arguments are indicated by subscripts. The fetch patterns are indicated by computed subscripts, for example, $C + 1$ means fetch the next column to the left. The OR

Subtract $\rightarrow$ Sub1Col$_C$	For each column$_C$
Sub1Col$_C \rightarrow$ Diff$_C$	When Top$_C \geq$ Bottom$_C$
Sub1Col$_C \rightarrow$ BorrowFrom$_{C+1}$ Add10$_C$ Diff$_C$	When Top$_C <$ Bottom$_C$
BorrowFrom$_C \rightarrow$ Decr$_C$	When Top$_C \neq 0$
BorrowFrom$_C \rightarrow$ BorrowFrom$_{C+1}$ Add10$_C$ Decr$_C$	When Top$_C = 0$

5.1
A core procedure written in a rule-based notation

goals and FOREACH goals are implicit; only their rules are shown. The AND goals have become the right sides of rules.

There are minor differences between this rule-based notation and the one given previously. For instance, two rules cannot call exactly the same AND node because there are no AND nodes, but they can approximate this by having identical right sides. However, the constraints on representation only define a class of representations, and both these notations are members of the class. To put it another way, the differences between the two notations do not seem to make any difference in the generative power of the theory.

5.1 The Core Procedures to Be Generated

The preceding chapter listed the core procedures that seem necessary and sufficient for explaining the bug data currently available. There were roughly thirty of them. However, if we ignore differences resulting from patterns, there are far fewer. In particular the core procedures for the test pattern bugs and the fetch pattern bugs have the same control structures as do the core procedures for the missing subprocedure bugs and the missing rule bugs. In fact there are so few of them that most can be displayed in two tables, 5.2 and 5.3. These tables show the major core procedures that seem to underlie the missing subprocedures bug class. Both tables show a complete sequence of procedures, from an initial procedure that can do only single-column subtraction to a procedure that can correctly answer any multi-column subtraction problem. The difference between them stems from how borrowing is structured. Most subtraction textbooks include a lesson on regrouping, wherein students are taught to do the combination of adding ten and decrementing in isolation from the rest of the subtraction procedure. It is not clear whether all teachers use these lessons or even, if they do, whether all students integrate the regrouping procedure they acquire with their subtraction procedure. The odd-numbered core procedures, shown in 5.3, result when regrouping is taught and is integrated into the subtraction procedure. The even-numbered procedures, shown in 5.2, result from not incorporating a special regrouping subprocedure. Notice that the procedure sequence that has the separate regrouping procedures produces a correct subtraction procedure after the first lesson on borrowing from zero, which teaches how to borrow across a single zero. The procedure sequence that lacks a separate regrouping procedure requires an additional lesson to explicitly teach how to borrow across multiple zeros.

-------------------------- Procedure 1 --------------------------

Subtract → $Diff_C$ For each column C

The first lesson in most subtraction curricula teaches how to solve problems that have multiple columns, but no borrowing columns and no partial columns. Thus, this core procedure can solve $56-34$ without an impasse, but $56-3$ causes an impasse in the tens column. Repairs to this impasse generate a bug-free performance as well as the bugs Quit-When-Bottom-Blank, Stutter-Subtract, and Sub-One-Over-Blank.

-------------------------- Procedure 2 --------------------------

Subtract → $Sub1Col_C$ For each column C
$Sub1Col_C$ → $Diff_C$ When $Top_C \geq Bottom_C$
$Sub1Col_C$ $Show_C$ When $Bottom_C$ is blank

The second lesson teaches how to solve problems with partial columns. Thus, $56-3$ is solved correctly and without impasse by this procedure. However, the procedure still does not know how to borrow. Thus, it reaches an impasses on borrow columns. Repairs generate the bugs Blank-Instead-of-Borrow, Smaller-From-Larger, and Zero-Instead-Of-Borrow.

-------------------------- Procedure 4 --------------------------

Subtract → $Sub1Col_C$ For each column C
$Sub1Col_C$ → $Diff_C$ When $Top_C \geq Bottom_C$
$Sub1Col_C$ $Show_C$ When $Bottom_C$ is blank
$Sub1Col_C$ → $Decr_{C+1}$ $Add10_C$ $Diff_C$ When $Top_C < Bottom_C$

This procedure is produced from the first lesson on borrowing (assuming that that the regrouping lesson is either absent or ignored). It can borrow from non-zero digits, but does not know how to borrow across zero. Consequently, they will reach an impasse on problems such as $305-7$. Various repairs generate the bugs Stops-Borrow-At-Zero, Borrow-Across-Zero, and several others.

-------------------------- Procedure 6 --------------------------

Subtract → $Sub1Col_C$ For each column C
$Sub1Col_C$ → $Diff_C$ When $Top_C \geq Bottom_C$
$Sub1Col_C$ $Show_C$ When $Bottom_C$ is blank
$Sub1Col_C$ → $BorrowFrom_{C+1}$ $Add10_C$ $Diff_C$ When $Top_C < Bottom_C$
$BorrowFrom_C$ → $Decr_C$ When $Top_C \neq 0$
$BorrowFrom_C$ → $Decr_{C+1}$ $Add10_C$ $Decr_C$ When $Top_C = 0$

This procedure results from the introductory lesson on borrowing from zero. It can borrow from a single zero, but reaches an impasse on problems such as $3005-7$. Repairs generate the bugs Stops-Borrow-At-Multple-Zero, Stops-Borrow-At-Second-Zero, and several others.

-------------------------- Procedure 8 --------------------------

Subtract → $Sub1Col_C$ For each column C
$Sub1Col_C$ → $Diff_C$ When $Top_C \geq Bottom_C$
$Sub1Col_C$ $Show_C$ When $Bottom_C$ is blank
$Sub1Col_C$ → $BorrowFrom_{C+1}$ $Add10_C$ $Diff_C$ When $Top_C < Bottom_C$
$BorrowFrom_C$ → $Decr_C$ When $Top_C \neq 0$
$BorrowFrom_C$ → $BorrowFrom_{C+1}$ $Add10_C$ $Decr_C$ When $Top_C = 0$

This procedure results from teaching how to borrow from multiple zeros. It is a correct procedure.

-------------------------- Primitives --------------------------

$Diff_C$: Write $Bottom_C$-Top_C in $Answer_C$ $Decr_C$: Overwrite Top_C with Top_C - 1
$Show_C$: Write Top_C in $Answer_C$ $Add10_C$: Overwrite Top_C with Top_C+10

5.2
The major core procedures without separate regrouping subprocedures

---------------------------- Procedure 1 ---------------------------

Subtract $\rightarrow$ Diff$_C$ For each column C

See procedure 1 in table 5-2.

---------------------------- Procedure 2 ---------------------------

Subtract $\rightarrow$ Sub1Col$_C$ For each column C
Sub1Col$_C$ $\rightarrow$ Diff$_C$ When Top$_C \geq$ Bottom$_C$
Sub1Col$_C$ $\rightarrow$ Show$_C$ When Bottom$_C$ is blank

See procedure 2 in table 5-2.

---------------------------- Procedure 3 ---------------------------

Subtract $\rightarrow$ Sub1Col$_C$ For each column C
Subtract $\rightarrow$ Regroup$_{Right\text{-}most\text{-}column}$ When no minus sign
Sub1Col$_C$ $\rightarrow$ Diff$_C$ When Top$_C \geq$ Bottom$_C$
Sub1Col$_C$ $\rightarrow$ Show$_C$ When Bottom$_C$ is blank
Regroup$_C$ $\rightarrow$ Decr$_{C+1}$ Add10$_C$ Always

This procedure results when students are taught regrouping in isolation, and the students choose to incorporate the subprocedure into their subtraction procedure. Although this procedure can regroup, it still reaches impasses on subtraction problems requiring borrowing.

---------------------------- Procedure 5 ---------------------------

Subtract $\rightarrow$ Sub1Col$_C$ For each column C
Subtract $\rightarrow$ Regroup$_{Right\text{-}most\text{-}column}$ When no minus sign
Sub1Col$_C$ $\rightarrow$ Diff$_C$ When Top$_C \geq$ Bottom$_C$
Sub1Col$_C$ $\rightarrow$ Show$_C$ When Bottom$_C$ is blank
Sub1Col$_C$ $\rightarrow$ Regroup$_C$ Diff$_C$ When Top$_C <$ Bottom$_C$
Regroup$_C$ $\rightarrow$ Decr$_{C+1}$ Add10$_C$ Always

This procedures results from teaching students how to use regrouping to answer subtraction problems. Its external behavior, in terms of the impasses and bugs it manifests, is identical to procedure 4 of table 5-2.

---------------------------- Procedure 7 ---------------------------

Subtract $\rightarrow$ Sub1Col$_C$ For each column C
Subtract $\rightarrow$ Regroup$_{Right\text{-}most\text{-}column}$ When no minus sign
Sub1Col$_C$ $\rightarrow$ Diff$_C$ When Top$_C \geq$ Bottom$_C$
Sub1Col$_C$ $\rightarrow$ Show$_C$ When Bottom$_C$ is blank
Sub1Col$_C$ $\rightarrow$ Regroup$_C$ Diff$_C$ When Top$_C <$ Bottom$_C$
Regroup$_C$ $\rightarrow$ BorrowFrom$_{C+1}$ Add10$_C$ Always
BorrowFrom$_C$ $\rightarrow$ Decr$_C$ When Top$_C \neq 0$
BorrowFrom$_C$ $\rightarrow$ Regroup$_C$ Decr$_C$ When Top$_C = 0$

This procedure results from teaching how to borrow from a single zero. It can solve all types of borrowing problems without reaching an impasse.

---------------------------- Primitives ---------------------------

Diff$_C$: Write Bottom$_C$-Top$_C$in Answer$_C$ Decr$_C$: Overwrite Top$_C$ with Top$_C$ - 1
Show$_C$: Write Top$_C$ in Answer$_C$ Add10$_C$: Overwrite Top$_C$ with Top$_C$+10

5.3
The major core procedures with separate regrouping subprocedures

The tables leave out several minor variants of the major core procedures, which are formed by interchanging the order of the elements on the right sides of the borrowing rules. Presumably these procedures are acquired when teachers present the actions of borrowing in a different order.

All the other core procedures presented at the end of the preceding chapter are variations of the eight core procedures shown in the tables (or their variants, with the different borrowing orders). The procedures for the missing rule bugs are formed by deleting right-side elements from selected rules. The procedures for the test pattern bugs and the fetch pattern bugs are generated when specific patterns, including incorrect ones, are used in place of the abbreviations shown in the table. Thus the empirical target for this chapter is to explain why the procedures of 5.2 and 5.3 are acquired.

It is worth reiterating that these particular control structures are only a few of the many possible control structures that could successfully solve subtraction problems or subsets of subtraction problems. For instance, the recursive borrowing routines could be replaced with iterative routines. The reason that these particular control structures are believed to characterize students' procedures is that they make the impasse-repair process generate exactly the right bugs.

5.2 One Subprocedure per Lesson

One can see from 5.2 that very little new material is introduced with each lesson. In fact each lesson introduces just one new subprocedure. To put it more precisely, the new material seems to consist of three types:

1. a new rule that calls a primitive (as in the transition from procedure 1 to procedure 2)
2. a new rule that calls a new AND goal (as in the transitions $2\rightarrow 3$, $2\rightarrow 4$, $3\rightarrow 5$, and $4\rightarrow 6$)
3. The replacement of a call to a subgoal by a call to an OR node that calls that subgoal (as in the transitions $5\rightarrow 7$ and $6\rightarrow 8$)

Sometimes the addition of a new rule necessitates adding an OR goal, as in the transition from procedure 1 to 2. However, this is an artifact of the rule-based notation. In other notations for this kind of procedural representation, this syntactical modification is unnecessary. A network notation of the core procedures of 5.2 is shown in 5.4. In this notation every lesson results in adding a new arc to the network, plus a new level if necessary. Note that the transitions of type 3, where a subgoal call has been replaced, have also become simply the addition of a new arc to the network.

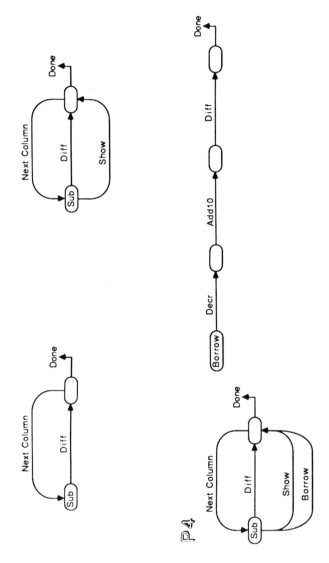

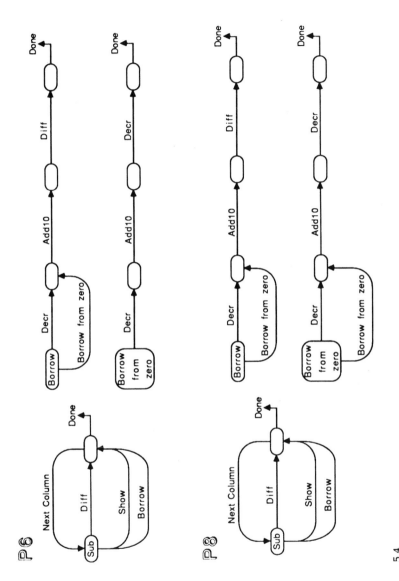

5.4
The core procedures of 5.2 notated as transition networks

The network notation makes it clear that all these transitions are actually of the same type: the addition of a new control path to the procedure and a branch point that attaches it to the old procedure. Moreover the new control path had no branch points in it that were not in the procedure already. Thus the new material introduced by a lesson seems to consist of exactly one branch point plus the control path that it branches to. This observation seems worthy of an assumption, but before it can be stated, we need to name these chunks of new material.

To label these chunks of new material in a notation-independent way, the terminology of logic seems appropriate. A branch point in a procedure corresponds to a disjunction in logic because control can flow one way *or* the other. Thus the material on one side of branch point corresponds to a *disjunct*, which is the logician's name for the constituents of a disjunction. Given this term, the assumption can be stated as

The one disjunct per lesson assumption
If $P_i \epsilon$ Learn (P_{i-1}, L_i), then P_i has the fewest new disjuncts possible, with a maximum of one, while remaining consistent with the positive examples of L_i.

The assumption is written to allow for the possibility that the new lesson does not introduce any new disjuncts. This type of learning does occur. In fact a typical subtraction curriculum has many lessons, most of which are review of drill lessons. The lessons mentioned in connection with 5.2 and 5.3 are interleaved among them. Also there are lessons that broaden the student's skills without adding new subprocedures. For instance, borrowing is initially introduced with two-column problems. A later lesson shows how to do borrowing in three-column problems. A still later lesson shows how to do three-column problems with two borrows in them. These later lessons do not seem to introduce a new subprocedure, but rather they seem to generalize an existing subprocedure. Thus we cannot assume that *all* lessons introduce new disjuncts. When new disjuncts are introduced, however, they are spread across lessons so that only one disjunct is introduced per lesson.

Human learning is notoriously slow, and the one disjunct per lesson assumption could be part of the explanation, but the usual assumption is that the student's memory is the bottleneck. That is, one typically assumes that students can assimilate information from the teacher as fast as the teacher can present it, but that more rapid presentation does not allow time for practice, and practice is essential for fixing the material reliably in memory. Actually this assumption makes just as much sense relative to the core procedure data as the one disjunct per lesson assumption, so let us state it then contrast it with its competitor.

The fewest disjuncts assumption

If $P_i \epsilon$ Learn (P_{i-1}, L_i), then P_i has the fewest new disjuncts possible while remaining consistent with the positive examples of L_i.

This assumption says that people learn as fast as the information can be presented to them. If there are limits on learning rate, they lie outside the knowledge communication aspect of learning (that is, in the practice-driven, knowledge-compilation aspect of learning). This assumption implies that it is an artifact that the core procedure sequence has just one new subprocedure per lesson. To put it more bluntly, the teachers and textbook authors, not the students' cognition, control how many disjuncts per lesson are taught and acquired.

However, the argument runs the other direction just as well. Obviously the teachers and authors do control the pace of lessons, but why would they happen to choose such a slow pace? In fact why not present the whole procedure all in one lesson and spend the rest of the time practicing it? The answer to both questions could be that faster-paced lesson sequences were tried and found to be less effective than the one-disjunct-per-lesson sequences. That is, the curricula in existence now may have been designed by trial and error to fit the cognition of the students. (Clearly this argument applies only to subject matter that has been taught for many generations, but arithmetic is just such a subject matter.)

Laboratory studies of learning point toward the importance of a curriculum organized as one disjunct per lesson. Anderson, for example, has found that students tend to answer exercise problems by finding a similar exercise in the book that has been solved already, then mapping the solution over to their problem (Anderson, Farrell, and Saurers 1984). Similar phenomena have been found by other investigators (Chi, Bassok, Lewis, Reimann, and Glaser 1989). If this learning process is the one in use for arithmetic, then a curriculum that puts two or more disjuncts in a lesson is going make the students' task harder. They will have two types of solved exercises in the lesson, and they will have to decide which to use as the source for their analogical problem solving. If they decide incorrectly, they could develop serious misconceptions. On the other hand if all lessons have just one disjunct in them, then the students do not have to make a choice. They simply refer to any of the solved examples in the lesson. Crucially they must *know* that they do not have to make a choice to reap the benefits of this organization. Thus if the analogy-driven learning account holds for classrooms as well as laboratories, then optimization of the learning process could have caused the curriculum to evolve a one-disjunct-per-lesson format, and more important it could cause students to evolve an expectation that lessons would teach just one disjunct.

If we take seriously the idea that learning is communication of information combined with practice-driven compilation, then as a type of communication between humans, instruction should have conventions that govern it, because all other forms of communications between people seem to. The fact that the students and teachers do not have conscious access to the rules governing the communication between them is not an argument that such rules do not exist. In fact it is circumstantial evidence that such rules *do* exist, because most rules of human communication are not available to conscious access. In honor of some famous tacit conventions on natural-language conversation, Austin's (1962) *felicity conditions*, the conjecture that there might be tacit conventions governing instruction is called the *felicity conditions conjecture*.

The one disjunct per lesson assumption, if it is a correct characterization of how people learn, could be explained by the felicity conditions conjecture. The basic idea is that by the time students reach the third grade, they have experienced enough instruction that they believe that all lessons introduce at most one new disjunct. If the teacher needs to introduce several ideas, the students reason, then surely the teacher would announce that and probably would organize the time as a series of quick minilessons, one for each disjunct. Thus if the teacher has made no such announcement, then there is no use in looking for multiple disjuncts in the material.

There are some formal results in learning theory that indicate the value of felicity conditions and the one-disjunct-per-lesson constraint in particular. Currently Valiant's (1984) criterion is held to be an excellent definition of what it means to learn a concept from examples in a reasonable amount of time. Although the field has not yet addressed concepts as complex as procedure, there are already some negative results with simpler concepts, such as boolean functions, that bear on induction of procedures. Valiant (1984) presents strong evidence of the intractability of learning arbitrary boolean functions (a boolean function is an arbitrarily nested expression in propositional logic, containing just AND, OR, and NOT). The class of procedures subsumes the class of boolean functions (because a sequence of actions is like an AND expression and a conditional branch is like an OR expression). So Valiant's evidence implies that procedure learning is also intractable.

However, Valiant concludes, "If the class of learnable concepts is as severely limited as suggested by our results, then it would follow that the only way of teaching more complicated concepts is to build them up from such simple ones. Thus a good teacher would have to identify, name, and sequence these intermediate concepts in the manner of a programmer." (Valiant 1984, p. 1135) Rivest and Sloan (1988) pointed out that having the teacher actually identify, name, and sequence the subconcepts makes learning trivial, but it places a great burden on the teacher. They presented an algorithm that eases the load on the teacher, but still ensures successful learning. The algorithm can learn any concept representable as a boolean function, with the help of a teacher who breaks the concept into subconcepts and teaches one subconcept per lesson, where a subconcept corresponds to a conjunction or disjuncton in the boolean expression. This is based of course on a type of felicity condition that is quite similar to the one disjunct per lesson assumption.

In summary both the fewest disjuncts assumption and the one disjunct per lesson assumption have deep roots in cognitive science. The view that memory is the bottleneck supports the fewest disjuncts assumption. The felicity conditions view and the computation learning theory support the one disjunct per lesson assumption. The appropriate way to settle the argument is to teach some students a curriculum that has two disjuncts per lesson and see what they do. That experiment is in progress, and I hope to report the results in the near future.

Fortunately there is no difference between the two assumptions with respect to the theories' predictions, because the curricula used in arithmetic uniformly obey the convention that they teach at most one disjunct per lesson. As a consequence we can merely refer to the two assumptions together as the *disjuncts* assumption and differentiate them only when necessary.

5.3 *The Space of All Possible Procedures*

The disjuncts assumption puts extremely strong constraints on the output of the Learn function. This section begins by developing a technique for constructing the total output of the Learn function then showing how the disjuncts assumption reduces that set of manageable levels. In the process an algorithm is developed for generating the output of the Learn function.

In the rule-based notation a procedure looks much like a context-free grammar. Instead of S→ NP VP we have Sub1Col→ Decr Add-

10 Diff. The major difference is the arguments, which context-free grammars do not have. Because the instantiation assumption puts such strong constraints on the use of arguments, however, many of the algorithms from the grammar literature can be used with only minor modifications.[12]

In particular, just as a grammar can be used to parse a string, a procedure can be used to parse an action sequence, which is merely a string of actions. Moreover, just as one can express the result of parsing a sentence with a parse tree, one can capture the result of parsing an example with a parse tree as well. The parse tree in 5.5 results when the procedure of 5.1 is used in parsing the solution of a subtraction problem.

Using the notions of parsing and parse trees, the set of all possible procedures (ignoring patterns, of course) can be constructed as follows: Given a procedure P_{i-1} and a lesson L_i, we want to find all possible procedures P_i that are consistent with the positive examples of L_i (by the examples assumption), reduced with respect to them (by the reducedness assumption), and that include the rules of P_{i-1} as a subset (by the assimilation assumption). A procedure is consistent with an example only if it parses it. So consistency implies that P_i parses every positive example in L_i. Reducedness means that the new rules of P_i appear somewhere in some parse tree of the examples of L_i. If we knew what the parse trees of P_i were, we could take the union of the rules exhibited by them. By reducedness these rules, when added to the rules of P_{i-1}, would be exactly P_i. Thus to find all possible P_i,

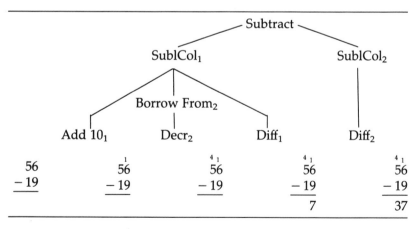

5.5
A parse tree for the procedure of 5.1

We need to find all possible sets of parse trees for the examples of L_i. Each set of parse trees can be easily converted into a P_i.

We face now the subtask of generating all possible sets of parse trees. The key to this task is the idea that a parse tree is a labelled tree. The labels are goal types (plus arguments, which we ignore). To generate all possible sets of parse trees, we first generate all possible sets of *unlabelled* trees then generate all possible labellings of them. When this construction technique is applied to context-free grammars, it generates a well-defined set of grammars, called the derivational version space (VanLehn and Ball 1987).[13]

One of the properties of the derivational version space is that it can be generated by an easily implemented algorithm called *parse completion* (VanLehn 1987a, Nowlan 1987). This is the algorithm used by Sierra to generate control structures. It is presented here because it makes a good framework for stating further constraints on the Learn function.

The parse completion algorithm processes examples serially, one at a time. It is called with the sequence of actions that constitutes an example and the top-level goal type (for example, Subtract). It begins by forming all possible partitions of the example. Thus if the example consists of the string of actions "ABC," then there are four possible partitions:

1. [A][BC]
2. [AB][C]
3. [A][B][C]
4. [ABC]

If there are N actions in the sequence, there are 2^{N-1} possible partitions. For each partition the algorithm chooses labels for the subsequences that make up the partition. The labels can be existing goal types or new ones. It labels the subsequences in all possible ways, and for each labelling it first generates a rule then calls itself recursively, once for each labelled subsequence. The left side of the rule consists of the goal type that the algorithm is called with; the right side consists of the goal types that are used to label the subsequences. Thus if it is passed "Subtract" and the algorithm chooses the partition [A][BC] with the labels "Sub1Col" and "Subtract," then it generates the rule Subtract → Sub1Col Subtract before recursing. The first recursive call would be passed "Sub1Col" and [A]. The second call would be passed "Subtract" and [BC].

As the algorithm recurses, it saves all the rules that it creates. Some of the rules may be in P_i, and some may be new. If the algorithm is constrained to always choose labels in such a way that the rules it creates are in P_i, then the algorithm is merely performing a top-down parse of the action sequence.

If the algorithm is unconstrained, then when it finishes, it will have tried all possible partitionings at each level, and all possible labelings of the partitions. Thus it generates a very large collection of rule sets. And this is only from the first example. For each rule set the algorithm is called on the second example. The rules generated by the second example are added to the rules in the initial rule set, thus creating an even larger collection of rule sets. Although this process eventually halts, having produced a finite collection of rule sets, the collection is very large (see Nowlan 1987 for an upper bound estimate). This collection is the space of all possible procedures that Learn generates if it is bounded only by the examples, reducedness, and assimilation assumptions.[14]

The effect of the disjuncts assumption is profound. The fewest disjuncts assumption means that the choices of partitionings and labelings are constrained in such a way that only existing rules are used unless it proves impossible to parse the example. Thus the first pass at the example is merely a top-down parse. If that succeeds, then the algorithm goes on to the next example. If that fails, then it makes a second pass, allowing only one new rule to be introduced. If this succeeds, then it goes on to the next example. If it fails, then it makes a third pass, allowing two new rules, and so on until it finally is able to parse the example. Thus the algorithm searches for the smallest set of rules that allows it to parse all the examples.

The one disjunct per lesson assumption is even more constraining. If it cannot find a parse after two passes (that is, up to one new rule), it gives up. Because the examples require more than one disjunct, it cannot learn from them.

The multipass organization of the search is not particularly efficient or perspicuous. An easier way to think of the parse completion algorithm, particularly the one-disjunct-per-lesson version, is to visualize a parser trying to parse an example and failing. It comes down from the top as far as possible, but cannot reach all the primitives in the example. So it tries to parse bottom-up as far as possible. This too fails. But the parse can be completed if only some rule existed that would connect the incomplete top-down parse with the incomplete bottom-up parse. Any rule or set of rules that would complete the parse is a candidate for learning. The set of all possible candidates is the algorithm's output. Thus the algorithm is named parse completion.

5.4 *Biases for the Parse Completion Algorithm*

In general there are many ways to complete a parse, and thus there are many possible rules that could be learned. To illustrate this and to lead up to some constraints, consider the transition from core procedure 5 to 7 (see 5.3). Procedure 5 has a regrouping procedure, and it knows how to borrow, but it does not know how to borrow from zero. Suppose Learn is given the example $507 - 128$. The parse tree that procedure 7 would generate is shown in 5.6, but of course procedure 5 cannot generate that parse because it lacks the rules for borrowing across zero. Three different incomplete parses are illustrated in 5.7, 5.8, and 5.9. If rules are invented to fill in the gaps, then three different rules will be invented. The gap of 5.7 causes the correct rule to be generated (that is, the one that turns procedure 5 into procedure 7). The other gaps generate rules that engender other procedures, and apparently these other procedures do not correspond to ones that students learn. The theory needs to block their generation.

Sierra is built to generate all possible gaps consistent with the one disjunct per lesson assumption. Gaps are displayed in a convenient menu-driven way, and the user is allowed to pick an interesting one. This mechanism allowed me to explore a variety of constraints on gaps. It was discovered that the gaps that lead to good core procedures are the smallest. This constraint is quite salient when the gaps are displayed as in 5.7, 5.8, and 5.9 because the smallest gaps occupy the fewest square inches of the figure. However, a proper definition requires a more complicated definition.

The smallest skeleton assumption
In the parse completion algorithm implementation of Learn, if more than one site for parse completion is possible, then choose the one that has the lowest parent, fewest kids, and highest kids, in that order.

This assumption uses some new terminology. The site of the parse completion is characterized topologically by the top-down node above it, which is called the *parent*, and the list of bottom-up nodes below it, which are called the *kids*. A pair consisting of a parent and kids is called a *skeleton*. To implement this assumption, skeletons are first filtered by their parents. If two skeletons, A and B, are such that A's parent is above B's, then skeleton A is discarded. For instance, the skeleton of 5.9 has a parent that is above the skeleton of 5.7 so it would be eliminated. Next the skeletons are filtered by the number of kids that they have. If A has more kids than B, then A is discarded. Last the skeletons are filtered by the height of the kids. If A's kids are

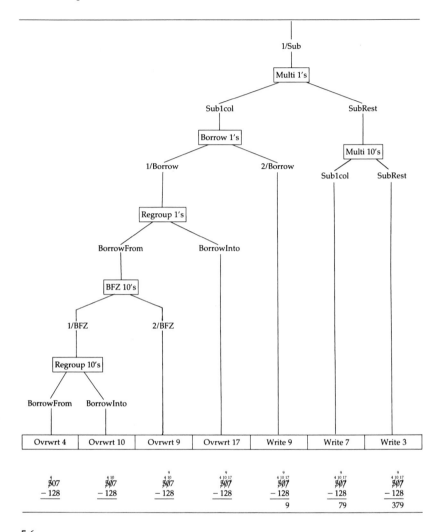

5.6
Parse tree for the solution of a Borrow-From-Zero problem

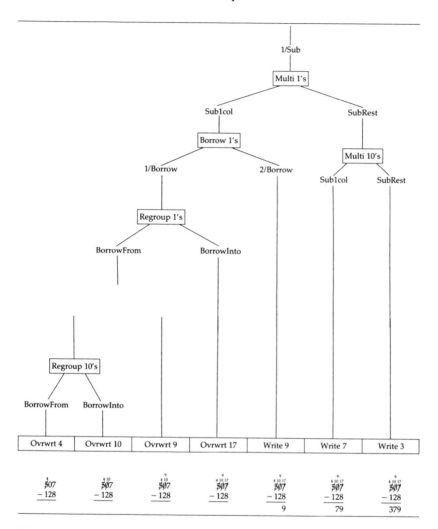

5.7
A skeleton corresponds to a gap in the parse tree.

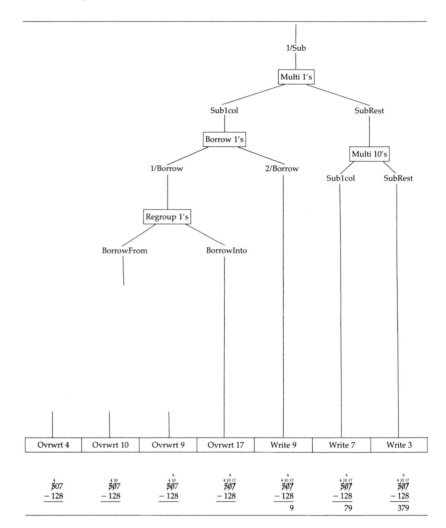

5.8
The kids of a skeleton can be lower.

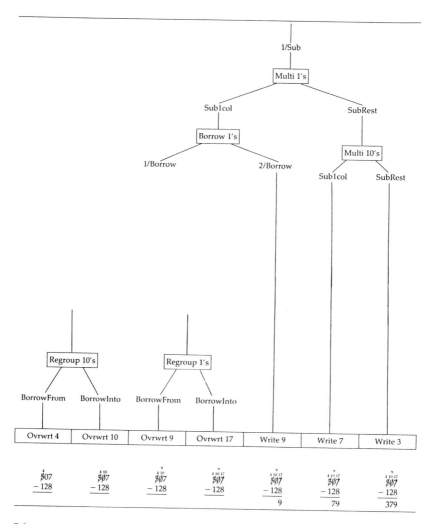

5.9
The parents of a skeleton can be higher.

below B's kids, then A is discarded. The skeleton in 5.8 would be eliminated this way because 5.7 has a skeleton whose kids are higher.

Although this seems like an incredibly finicky assumption, each part of it is indeed necessary to block certain core procedures that would otherwise be generated. Those core procedures usually do not do any immediate harm; the bugs they generate are either the same as the bugs generated by the good core procedures or small variations. The next time Learn is run, however, they are input along with the good core procedures. The resulting procedures can be even stranger. Eventually star bugs are generated. For instance, dropping the fewest-kids constraints creates procedures that can borrow from two zeros but not from three or more. Dropping the lowest-parent constraint creates a procedure that does subtraction in two passes. Its first pass consists of borrowing from zero in the units column, if necessary. Its second pass does the regular column processing, including ordinary borrowing, if necessary.

Another kind of bias is needed to block certain star bugs involving the main loop across columns. As mentioned in the chapter on representation, the FOREACH goal type is not logically necessary. The iteration of Sub1Col across columns can be expressed as a tail recursion instead. A tail recursive implementation, however, would cause star bugs when the Back-up repair is applied to certain impasses. Thus the tail recursive implementation does not appear to be the way the students represent the main loop. This argument motivated including a FOREACH goal type in the representation. However, a second assumption is needed to block these star bugs:

The FOREACH bias assumption
If the skeleton has two or more kids that have the same goal type, then do not form an AND goal, but use a FOREACH goal instead.

This assumption prevents the formation of a tail recursion. Without it both the FOREACH version and the tail recursion would be generated by parse completion.

This assumption also blocks the formation of several other star bugs. It turns out that many curricula introduce multicolumn subtraction using only two-column examples. Without this assumption the parse completion algorithm would generate a rule of the form

Subtract → Sub1Col(units)   Sub1Col(tens)

This rule is unable to correctly answer problems with three or more columns. The resulting bugs are all star bugs (see VanLehn 1983c, pp. 52–53, for a description of the star bugs). Apparently students infer that all columns are answered via Sub1Col even though they have only seen examples with two columns. The FOREACH bias assumption explains this regularity.

5.5 Impasse-Driven Learning

What these constraints mean in terms of a process theory of learning is an open question. The FOREACH bias assumption could perhaps be explained by assuming some sort of visually driven problem solving by analogy. The student might reason, "Because that thing looks like the units column, which I know how to solve, then I'll solve it in the same way I solve the units column." This analogy would cause the student to execute similar procedures whenever the objects they apply to are similar, and that is one way of explaining the preference for FOREACH loops over ANDs.

It is more difficult to see how to explain the other assumption, which concern lowest parents and the like. One conjecture that has been advanced explains the lowest-parent constraint by assuming that learning is *impasse-driven* (VanLehn 1988). Impasse-driven learning assumes that the same mechanism that executes procedures is also responsible for learning them. When the execution process reaches an impasse, however, it does not repair, as it would if the student were in test-taking situation. Rather the student seeks help. The help may come from a teacher, a textbook, or some other source. For instance, the student might look through the textbook for an example similar to the exercise that he or she is working on. The student traces through the example, comparing it to the exercise, until the impasse point is reached. The next few actions in the textbook's example are adapted to the exercise and executed. These actions allow the student to get past the impasse. More important, they show the student what subsequence of actions are correct at this impasse. If the student merely incorporates these actions into a new rule, then learning can take place. Thus impasse-driven learning may underlie the many instances of exercise-example analogy that are reported in the literature (Anderson, Farrell, and Saurers 1984, Pirolli and Anderson 1985, Chi, Bassok, Lewis, Reimann, and Glaser 1989).

If the impasses of Sierra and Soar are the same (see the discussion at the end of chapter 3), and Soar is an accurate model of the human cognitive architecture, then impasse-driven learning is the natural result of a rational, help-seeking solution to the problem of being stuck at an impasse, because Soar learns a chunk at each impasse, and the chunk records the results of the problem solving done there (Laird, Rosenbloom, and Newell 1986, Newell 1990).

Impasse-driven learning might explain an interesting result about skill acquisition: the two-sigma effect. Bloom (1984) found that students who learned a skill in tutorial situations scored two standard deviations above students who learned in normal classroom situations. The impasse-driven learning hypothesis explains this by noting that in tutorial situations it is much easier to get help. In particular the tutor can solve the only hard problem left for a student; when does the subsequence of actions that fixes the impasse end? The tutor can simply say, "OK, now you can do the rest." When the student is learning by analogy from a textbook, this information is not available, so the student must guess. Thus tutorial learning can be expected to be much more effective.

More to the point of the present theory, impasse-driven learning also explains the lowest-parent constraint. Impasses must occur at the lowest possible point in a procedure (see VanLehn 1988 for a proof). If the new rule is attached to the goal where the impasse occurred, then it is necessarily attached to a lowest parent. Assuming that learning is impasse-driven explains why the lowest-parent constraint holds for the present data. Similarly the fewest-kids and the highest-kids constraints can be explained, although the impasse-driven learning hypothesis must be augmented with some assumptions about how examples are perceived in order to do so.

Chapter 6
The Acquisition of Patterns

This chapter's topic is the acquisition of patterns. Several assumptions and technical terms were introduced previously, so it is appropriate to begin by reviewing them.

It was assumed that there are two kinds of patterns: *test patterns* and *fetch patterns*. Fetch patterns, which are attached to rules beneath AND goals and FOREACH goals, describe either objects in the *situation* (that is, an interpreted version of the external world) or the results of mathematical functions. Matching a fetch pattern causes the described objects or results to be referenced. If the pattern fails to uniquely specify an object (that is, it refers to two or more objects, or it refers to no objects), a *reference impasse* occurs. A test pattern is used to make decisions about which rule of an OR goal to take. Each OR goal rule has a test pattern as its condition. If a rule's test pattern does not match, it may not be chosen for execution. If more than one rule has a test pattern that matches, or no rule has a test pattern that matches, then a *decision impasse* occurs. The assumption that there are two kinds of patterns was made in chapter 3, but the argument for it has been saved for this chapter and is presented in section 6.5.

The *pattern assumption* is that interfaces with situations and mathematical facts are represented by expressions in predicate calculus or some equivalent formalism with a basically Tarksian semantics. The intended effect of this assumption is to make pattern matching a binary-outcome event. A pattern either matches or it does not. The "hard edges" of the expressions in predicate calculus are what enable the definition of decision and reference impasses. A "fuzzy-edged" representation of interfaces would make it more difficult to define such impasses.

The *examples assumption* is another important assumption for this discussion because it implies that patterns are learned by induction from examples. Thus the acquisition of patterns is a kind of concept induction. It will be helpful to have some standard terminology from the concept induction literature defined. For test patterns a situation is a *positive instance* if the pattern to be acquired is true of it and a *negative instance* if the pattern to be acquired is false (that is, it does not match). For fetch patterns truth and falsehood do not matter. What matters is the objects fetched from the situations. Thus an instance of fetch pattern consists of a situation plus an object. Thus a positive instance is a situation and an object such that the pattern to be acquired would retrieve that object in that situation. A negative instance is an object and a situation such that the pattern to be acquired would *not* retrieve that object in that situation.

In a standard concept formation experiment, subjects are just given an instance and told whether it is positive or negative. In learning a procedure the subjects are not so fortunate — they must isolate relevant instances and infer whether they are positive or negative. This can be achieved by many means, depending on whether the student is using a textbook, a tutor, or some other source of examples.[15] For the purposes of studying the constraints on learning, independent of the processes, it is assumed that the subjects correctly assign a positive or negative label to the instances.

The general approach to describing learning used throughout this theory is to find the space of all "conceivable" representations consistent with the examples then narrow in on the ones learned by people and describe this subset with constraints. In the discussion of control structure acquisition, the parse completion algorithm was the generator of all "conceivable" control structures. For patterns a standard technique from the machine learning literature can be used for the same purpose. Given a set containing positive instances and possibly some negative instances as well, the set of all patterns consistent with the given instances is called the *version space* (Mitchell 1980). It is easily shown that any version space is partially ordered by the relation "A is a generalization of B," which is true whenever the denotation of A is a superset of the denotation of B, where the denotation of a pattern is the set of all instances that the pattern matches. With a few extra assumptions it can also be shown that a version space has a well-defined subset of patterns that are minimal, in that every other pattern in the version space is a generalization of at least one of these minimally general patterns. This set is traditionally called the S set, because it consists of maximally *specific* patterns. Similarly any version space has a subset of patterns that are generalizations of all other patterns in the space. This set is called the G set, because it consists of maximally *general* patterns. It can be shown that a pattern X is in the version space if and only if X is a generalization of some pattern in S and some pattern in G is a generalization of X. This means that the version space, which is usually a very large set, can be compactly represented by the pair <S, G>. For some representation languages for patterns, there are algorithms that can calculate S and G directly from the set of given instances, rather than first calculating the whole version space then finding the appropriate subsets for S and G. If patterns are represented in propositional calculus, for instance, then S and G can be directly computed. If patterns are represented in unconstrained predicate calculus, then S and G are probably not effectively computable.[16]

The examples assumption and the pattern assumption imply that the set of all "conceivable" patterns is exactly the version space for the given examples. This chapter investigates several specific cases of pattern acquisition and determines from the bug data which subsets of the version space correspond to the patterns that students acquire. It adopts assumptions that constrain induction to generate those patterns and exclude most of the other patterns in the version space. The general argument is to show that students' patterns are maximally specific, that is, they are members of the S set, but only if the representation language for patterns is strongly constrained by permitting patterns to have only conjunction as a logical connective. Disjunction, negation, and universal quantification are barred from use in patterns. These assumptions capture the main trends in the data. Some important technical details remain, however, such as justifying the distinction between test patterns and fetch patterns. These details are discussed toward the end of this chapter.

6.1 The Acquisition of Fetch Patterns

This section covers fetch patterns, and the next section covers test patterns. I begin by surveying the data and finding the general trends then making appropriate assumptions to formalize those regularities.

6.1.1 The Fetch Patterns Are Overly Specific

Much can be discovered about the induction of fetch patterns by looking at its results. Of course we cannot directly inspect fetch patterns, but we can determine a little about their contents by examining the impasses that they cause.

A basic pattern emerges from studying the fetch patterns: the fetch patterns that cause bugs tend to be overly specific. The easiest way to explain what this means is with the aid of a by-now-familiar example. The bug Always-Borrow-Left places its decrements in the leftmost column of the problem. This means that the fetch pattern must have the descriptor "leftmost" in it. The pattern might have other descriptors in it, or it might not. If it has only the "leftmost" descriptor in it, then a form of pattern acquisition that is sometimes called "discrimination" learning (Langley 1987) is implicated in its acquisition. The student would seem to have picked a pattern that is as general as possible yet still sufficient to discriminate the leftmost column from all the other potential columns in the problem for placing a borrow. On the other hand if the fetch pattern includes descriptors other than "leftmost," then discrimination is not a good model of fetch pattern acquisition because the pattern is more specific than necessary for discriminating one column from the others. Thus the issue of what kind of learning underlies this fetch pattern's acquisition hinges on whether the pattern has "leftmost" alone or in combination with other descriptors.

This issue can be determined by seeing if the fetch pattern causes impasses. If the fetch pattern mentions both "leftmost" and "left-adjacent" in its fetch pattern, then reference impasses will occur whenever the borrow is located in such a way that there is no column that is both adjacent to it and on the far left end of the problem. On the other hand if the fetch pattern mentions *only* "leftmost" in its description, it will always uniquely refer to the leftmost column, regardless of where the borrow originated from, and thus it would never cause an impasse. As argued in connection with column two of 2.1, among other places, there is indeed an impasse caused by this fetch pattern. This can be established with the aid of a Cartesian product pattern or with bug migrations. (The relevant bugs are Borrow-No-Decrement-Except-Last, which is caused by a No-op repair to the impasse, and Smaller-From-Larger-Except-Last, which is caused by a Back-up repair.) Explaining these regularities in the data seems to require postulating an impasse, and that in turn seems to require using an overly specific fetch pattern.

All the other fetch bugs seem also to require overly specific fetch patterns. The following lists these patterns and the bugs that each explains:

- If the fetch pattern is "Leftmost and left-adjacent," then the bugs are Always-Borrow-Left (via Barge-on), Borrow-No-Decrement-Except-Last (via No-op), Smaller-From-Larger-Except-Last (via Back-up), and Dosen't-Borrow-Except-Last (via Back-up twice).
- If the fetch pattern is "$T < B$ and left-adjacent," then the bugs are Borrow-Don't-Decrement-Unless-Bottom-Smaller (via No-op) and Smaller-From-Larger-Unless-Bottom-Smaller (via Back-up).
- If the fetch pattern is "$T \leq B$ and left-adjacent," then the bug is Borrow-Don't-Decrement-Top-Smaller (via No-op).

- If the fetch pattern is "$T \neq B$ and left-adjacent," then the bug is Borrow-Skip-Equal (via No-op).
- If the fetch pattern is "Bottom-not-blank and left-adjacent," then the bug is Forget-Borrow-Over-Blank (via No-op).
- If the fetch pattern is "$T \neq 0$ and left-adjacent," then the bugs are Borrow-Across-Zero (via Barge-on), Stops-Borrow-At-Zero (via No-op), Smaller-From-Large-Instead-of-Borrow-From-Zero (via Back-up), and Borrow-From-Bottom-Instead-of-Zero (via Barge-on).

Explaining how these fetch patterns are acquired is the chief goal in the next section.

6.1.2 Constraints on the Acquisition of Fetch Patterns
It does not work to simply state that the fetch patterns acquired are the most specific ones possible. When the representation language is unconstrained, it can describe each positive instance precisely, and it can describe any set of positive instances precisely by forming a large disjunction whose disjuncts are precise descriptions of each instance in the set. Such a pattern would be maximally specific because it matches exactly that set of instances and no other instances. Thus requiring that fetch pattern be maximally specific predicts that a fetch pattern is a huge disjunction that matches *only* the positive instances that have been presented. If other situations are presented, it may fail to match at all and thereby cause an impasse. For instance, if the given situation requires decrementing a 5, and no training problem happens to have required decrementing a 5, then an impasse may result. No such hyperspecific impasse has been found, although the brevity of the tests would make them difficult to detect even if they did occur.

The underlying problem is that an unconstrained bias toward specificity leads to the untenable position that the student remembers every detail of every training situation. This is clearly not plausible psychologically, nor is it necessary for explaining the fetch bugs. Some lower limit on specificity needs to be found and stated as constraints on pattern induction. A simple way to do so is to reduce the expressive power of the representation language in such a way that the patterns induced are the most specific ones possible, given the impoverished expressive abilities of the language. This leads to the following two assumptions:

The conjunctive patterns assumption
The representation language for patterns contains only conjunction as a logical connective and only existential quantification as a

variable binder. Disjunction, negation, and universal quantification do not appear in patterns.

The fetch pattern bias assumption
Fetch patterns are the most specific patterns consistent with the positive training instances.

The effect of these two assumptions is that fetch patterns consist of only the *common features* of the training instances. That is, if all the training instances have "leftmost" in their descriptions, then "leftmost" occurs in the fetch pattern. If any are missing "leftmost," then it does not appear.

From a technical point of view these two assumptions mean that fetch patterns are in the S set of a version space whose members consist only of conjunctive patterns. The constraint that patterns be conjunctive is extremely powerful. If can be shown that it makes the version space finite. More important for the implementation of Sierra, there is a fast algorithm for calculating S and G directly from the instances when patterns are restricted to conjunctive patterns (VanLehn 1989). Sierra uses this algorithm to generate the whole version space (as represented by the pair <S,G>) and allows its user to explore which patterns cause impasses of the right kinds. Using this facility, it was discovered that members of the S set sufficed for generating the references impasses. It was also found that there are patterns in the S set that *do not* generate appropriate impasses, so the two constraints are not sufficient. A subsequent section deals with additional constraints that appear necessary for accurate prediction of students' fetch patterns.

The conjunctive pattern assumption is written so as to apply to test patterns as well as fetch patterns. This generality is as yet unmotivated, except by theoretical simplicity and parsimony. It will turn out that test patterns also tend to be overly specific, however, so they also need a bound on their specificity, just as the fetch patterns do. The conjunctive pattern assumption seems to specify the right sort of bound for test patterns as well as fetch patterns.

6.2 Constraints on the Acquisition of Test Patterns

There seem to be two distinct groups of test pattern bugs. One seems to be caused by overly specific test patterns and one by overly general test patterns. The bugs in each group are discussed, then a few ideas on removing the apparent contradiction are presented.

The overly specific test pattern bugs have derivations that are similar to the derivations of the fetch pattern bugs. As an illustratory case consider the bug Smaller-From-Larger-When-Borrowed-From. This bug takes the absolute difference in a column that requires borrowing if that column has a decrement in it from previous borrowing activities. Thus A below is solved correctly, but B is not because the tens column of B is borrowed from incorrectly:

$$
\text{A.} \quad \begin{array}{r} 2 \\ \cancel{3}^{1}4\ 5 \\ -1\ 8\ 2 \\ \hline 1\ 6\ 3 \end{array} \qquad \text{B.} \quad \begin{array}{r} 3 \\ 3\ \cancel{4}^{1}5 \\ -1\ 8\ 7 \\ \hline 2\ 5\ 8 \end{array}
$$

Two other bugs also answered borrowed-from columns incorrectly, $X - N = 0$-After-Borrow and $X - N = N$-After-Borrow. All these bugs can be derived if there is a decision impasse at columns that have been borrowed from. That is, when a column has been borrowed from, students get stuck because they cannot decide whether this column needs a borrow. For there to be a decision impasse, either no rule or more than one rule is applicable. The latter case implies that more than one rule's test pattern is true. It is difficult to see how this could occur in this case. Because the person successfully differentiates borrowing from nonborrowing columns most of the time, their test patterns must include $T < B$ or its converse, so both test patterns cannot be true at the same time on columns in question, because in those columns $T < B$. So the other alternative is assumed to hold, that is, that no rule's test pattern is true.

Because borrowing happens correctly on most columns, we can infer that the test pattern for borrowing has $T < B$ in it. However, the test pattern is false on borrowed-from columns, so it must have some additional conjunct in it that is not matched by borrowed-from columns. That is, the test pattern must include something like

. . . (Digit T) & (Value-of T TV) & (Value-of B BV) & (LessThan TV BV). . . .

where the primitive predicate Digit is true if the cell has just a digit in it and false if it has some scratch marks in it as well. This pattern causes an impasse at just the right places to generate the three bugs. Because the test pattern has the predicate Digit in it, it has more information in it than is logically necessary to differentiate borrow from nonborrow problems. Thus it is overly specific.

Some other bugs with similar derivations include the following:

• For the borrow versus no-borrow decision, the test pattern "no-scratch-marks and $T < B$" generates the bugs Smaller-From-

Larger-When-Borrowed-From (via Barge-on), $X - N = 0$-After-Borrow (via Barge-on), and $X - N = N$-After-Borrow (via Barge-on).

- For the borrow versus no-borrow decision, the test pattern "never-borrowed and $T < B$" generates the bugs Borrow-Once-Then-Smaller-From-Larger (via Barge-on) and Borrow-Only-Once (via mystery repair).

- For the borrow-from-zero versus regular-borrow decision, the test pattern "Bottom-not-blank and $T = 0$" generates the bugs Don't-Decrement-Zero-Over-Blank (via No-op), Increment-Zero-Over-Blank (via Barge-on), and Borrow-Across-Zero-Over-Blank (via Barge-on).

- For the borrow-from-zero versus regular-borrow decision, the test pattern "$B \neq 0$ and $T = 0$" generates the bugs Don't-Decrement-Zero-Over-Zero (via No-op) and Borrow-Across-Zero-Over-Zero (via Barge-on).

All these bugs seem to be caused by test patterns that are overly specific. Notice that they can be expressed as a conjunction of primitive predicates. This justifies putting a lower bound on their specificity, as the conjunctive pattern constraint did. The conjunctive pattern constraint plus the following assumption formalize the student's bias in acquiring test patterns:

The test pattern bias assumption
Test patterns are the maximally specific patterns consistent with the examples.

6.2.1 Overly General Test Patterns

Unfortunately the test pattern bias assumption fails to predict a certain group of bugs that seem to be generated by overly general patterns. This subsection presents those bugs and an explanation of them within the framework of the bias toward overly specific test patterns.

An illustrative member of this class of bugs is $N - N$-Causes-Borrow. This bug borrows whenever $T \leq B$. There does not seem to be an impasse; if there were an impasse, bugs like $X - N = N$-When-$N - N$ and $X - N = 0$-When-$N - N$ would be generated by using the same repair strategies as were used to generate bugs of similar names in the overspecific bugs group. Such bugs have not been found, however, so it seems there is no impasse (further data may falsify this assumption, of course). The lack of an impasse means that the test pattern for the borrowing rule contains $T \leq B$ instead of $T < B$.[17] This predicate makes the test pattern more general than it should be; it is true of more columns than the correct test pattern.

Bugs that seem to be caused by overly general test patterns include the following:

- If the test pattern for the borrowing rule has $T \le B$, then the bug N − N-Causes-Borrow is generated.
- If the test pattern for when to borrow-from-zero is $T \in \{1,0\}$, then the bug Borrow-Treat-One-As-Zero is generated.
- If the core procedure for the bug Don't-Decrement-Zero (which is generated by deletion of the rule that decrements the ten to a nine) has the BFZ (borrow from zero) test pattern of $T \in \{1,0\}$, then a compound bug (Don't-Decrement-Zero and Decrement-One-To-Eleven) is generated. This procedure adds ten to either the one or the zero, generating eleven or ten, respectively.
- If the core procedure for the bug Borrow-From-Zero (which is generated by deletion of the recursive call to borrow-from) has the BFZ test pattern $T \in \{1,0\}$, then the compound bug (Borrow-From-Zero and Borrow-From-One-Is-Nine) is generated. The student merely overwrites the one or the zero with nine.
- If the core procedure for the bug Borrow-From-Zero-Is-Ten (which is generated by deletion of all but the Add-ten from BFZ) has $T \in \{1,0\}$ as the BFZ test pattern, then the bug compound (Borrow-From-Zero-Is-Ten and Borrow-From-One-Is Ten) is generated. The bug's BFZ consists merely of changing the zero or one to ten.

It is noteworthy that several compound bugs are predicted by a combination of overly general test patterns and deletion. Decrement-One-To-Eleven is predicted to occur only with Don't-Decrement-Zero. It has appeared only once, and it did indeed appear with Don't-Decrement-Zero. Borrow-From-One-Is-Nine has appeared only twice, both times with Borrow-From-Zero, as predicted. Borrow-From-One-Is-Ten has appeared once, as part of a compound bug with Borrow-From-Zero-Is-Ten, as predicted. This remarkable prediction of some compound bug data came as a total surprise to me. It shows how independently motivated sources of bugs can sometimes work together to produce new predictions successfully.

One shared characteristic of the overly general test patterns is that the overgeneralization involves numerical predicates. The predicate $T < B$ was generalized to $T \le B$, and the predicate $T = 1$ was generalized to $T \in \{1,0\}$. Moreover both of the overly general predicates make sense as primitives. Suppose we simply include them in the vocabulary of primitive numerical predicates and use the standard induction of maximally specific patterns. Will this generate overly general test patterns? No, because the patterns will contain both the overly general predicates and the correct predicates, for example,

> . . . (Value-of T TV) & (Value-of B BV) & ($TV < BV$) & ($TV \le BV$). . . .

Such patterns will not generate the bugs. To generate the bugs, the correct primitives must be *replaced* by the incorrect ones. This suggests that the patterns contain an ambiguous primitive, for example,

> . . . (Value-of T TV) & (Value-of B BV) & (LessThan TV BV) . . .

which is interpreted as $T < B$ by some subjects and $T \le B$ by others. Similarly (IdentityElement TV) could mean different things to different subjects. This motivates

The ambiguous primitives assumption
Test pattern primitives for accessing mathematical predicates are ambiguous. In particular (LessThan x y) can mean either $T < B$ or $T \le B$, and (IdentityElement x) can mean either $T = 1$ or $T \in \{1,0\}$.

It is possible that such ambiguous primitives come from the natural-language explanations that accompany examples. If the student hears "You have to borrow if the top number is less than the bottom number," then "less than" might simply be stored in its partially interpreted form in the pattern. The vagueness in its interpretation is not noticed until a column with $T = B$ is attempted. If this occurs during a test or when help is not available, the student could choose the overly general interpretation and wind up with a bug.[18]

6.2.2 More on Misunderstanding Natural Language
This last comment brings in a new idea for how to generate bugs, namely, by misunderstanding natural language. This is a derivational method that could potentially generate a great number of bugs. In particular it might be able to account for a rather large group of bugs involving borrowing columns whose top digits are zero (see 4.5). Suppose that when students are taught how to borrow across zero, they are told "You can't borrow from zero," and they overgeneralize this phrase to mean "You can't borrow from *or into* zero." This means they reach an impasse on columns that require a borrow but have a top zero. A Barge-on repair causes either $0 - N = N$ or $0 - N = 0$. This explains the bugs Diff-0 $- N = N$ and Diff-0 $- N = N$.

Many other bugs might be explained by combining this misunder-

Occurrences—with Recursive Borrow Bug (plus others, in some cases)

15	Borrow-Across-Zero
17	Stops-Borrow-Across-Zero
3	Smaller-From-Larger-Instead-of-Borrow-From-Zero
1	Borrow-From-Bottom-Instead-of-Zero
36	total

Occurrences—with Nonrecursive Bug (plus others, in some cases)

7	Borrow-No-Decrement
4	Smaller-From-Larger
1	Diff-N–0 = 0
1	Blank-Instead-of-Borrow
1	Borrow-From-Zero
14	total

6.1
Occurrence of Diff-0 −N = 0 and Diff-0 − N = N in compound bugs

standing mechanism with the ordinary test pattern induction mechanisms that tend to generate overly specific patterns. For instance, the bug pair $0 - N = $ N-After-Borrow and $0 - N = 0$-After-Borrow can be generated by combining the descriptor "not-borrowed-from" from the ordinary test pattern induction mechanism with the "not zero" descriptor from the natural-language misunderstander.

If this explanation is correct, then we should find that most of the top-zero bugs occur after borrowing from zero has been learned. Although accurate records on the student's position in the curriculum are not available, a rough estimate of where they are can be derived by examining the core procedure that the top-zero bugs were found in. If the core procedure has a borrow-from-zero subprocedure, then chances are better that the top-zero bug was generated after the subprocedure was taught and that "Can't borrow from zero" is the source of the bug. Fortunately the two bugs Diff-0 − N = N and Diff-$0 - N = 0$ are common enough that we can get a reliable estimate of their time of generation via this technique, as shown in 6.1.

These occurrence frequencies seem to show that there are two mechanisms responsible for the bugs. One is the misunderstanding of zero; it is the major mechanism because it accounts for 72 percent

(36 of 50) of the occurrences of the bugs. The other mechanism seems to operate early in the lessons sequence. It might be a simple over-generalization of the rule "If one of the numbers in a column is zero, then the answer is the other number." The next step in the development of the theory should probably be to incorporate such misunderstanding processes into the model and see if they could be made to cooperate with the other generative mechanisms.

6.3 *Where Does the Variety Come From?*

The acquisition of both test patterns and fetch patterns has been constrained so that only the most specific patterns are produced. Experiments with Sierra indicate that almost invariably a unique, maximally specific pattern is produced from a given set of positive instances (modulo the ambiguity produced by LessThan and IdentityElement). But the subjects seem to have a variety of overly specific patterns. Where does this variety come from?

Most of it can be accounted for by the fact that different students were tested between different lessons in the lesson sequence. For instance, one textbook's lesson sequence has the following lessons on borrowing: (1) two-column problems, (2) three-column problems with a borrow in the units column, (3) three-column problems with a borrow in either the units or tens column, but not both, and (4) three-column problems with two borrows. The maximally specific fetch pattern for borrow-from after lesson 1 contains leftmost, never-borrowed, $T > B$, $T \neq 0$ and other predicates. This fetch pattern causes Always-Borrow-Left and its companions. After lesson 3 the fetch pattern has lost the "leftmost" descriptor, but retained the others. If all of them are present, impasses occur whenever there is a second borrow, regardless of whether that borrow is adjacent to the first borrow. If the descriptor "never-borrowed" is missing, then second borrows cause impasses only if they are adjacent to the first borrow. After lesson 4 only borrowing from zero causes an impasse (as it did before lesson 4). In short much of the variety can be accounted for by incomplete training.

Some of the observed variety, however, cannot be as easily explained as resulting from incomplete training. One such case is the alternation between reaching an impasse on all second borrows or only on adjacent borrows. Explaining this impasse as the result of incomplete training is possible, but only by postulating a lesson sequence that does not correspond to the lesson sequence of the students' textbooks. In particular this impasse can be explained by postulating that the student worked some four-column problems that had two nonadjacent problems in them. This could cause the "never-borrowed" descriptor to be dropped from the pattern, but leave the "$T > B$" descriptor intact. Similarly other patterns can be explained by postulating lesson material that does not appear in the textbooks. It is possible that some variety is indeed caused by teachers, parent, or peers who teach outside the lesson sequence prescribed by the book.

However, it is likely to be the case that when detailed longitudinal studies are conducted, students' conceptions are not so neatly tied to their position in the curriculum. The patterns they use are necessarily held in memory and thus are susceptible to forgetting and biased reconstruction. A finer-grained account of where the variety in patterns comes from would probably have to include a model of long-term memory.

6.4 The Pattern Focus Assumption

As mentioned, the job of putting a lower bound on the specificity of the fetch patterns is not yet complete. The S set of the version space sometimes contains patterns that do not lead to observed impasses. The same problem occurs with test patterns. Their S sets are also too large on occasion. This section presents the problem for fetch patterns and a plausible solution. However, no plausible solution for the equivalent problem with test patterns is known.

6.4.1 Pattern Focusing for Fetch Patterns

In principle, the situation encompasses not just the column where the fetch needs to occur or even just the problem. The situation could include the whole problem set or even the desk on which it lies, and so on. Taken literally, the assumption that fetch patterns be as specific as possible implies that patterns mention not only the column's position in the current problem but also the problem's position in the current page, the page's position on the desk, and so forth. In principle fetch patterns could be infinite. Clearly this is not what people do. A constraint is needed to limit the size of the fetch patterns to the relevant areas of the situation. The constraint is called the *pattern focus* hypothesis.

A precise formulation of the pattern focus hypothesis can be obtained by examining the bug Always-Borrow-Left. A previous section presented its derivation from two-column borrowing problems. The discussion centered on the fetch pattern for borrow-*from*. The fetch pattern for borrow-*into* is equally interesting. The following illustrates a typical example of problem states just before each of the two actions:

$$
\text{A.} \quad \begin{array}{r} 5\,3 \\ -1\,9 \\ \hline \end{array}
\qquad
\text{B.} \quad \begin{array}{r} \overset{4}{\cancel{5}}\,3 \\ -1\,9 \\ \hline \end{array}
$$

Problem state A is just before the borrow-from action. The learner induces the fetch pattern for borrow-from from states like state A. Problem state B is the sort of state used for inducing borrow-into's fetch pattern. A previous section showed that borrow-from's fetch pattern is often specific enough to cause impasses on three-column problems. The essential problem was that the pattern's induction from two-column problems led to incorporating the fact that the borrow-from column is the leftmost column of the problem, and it is also adjacent to the column that originated the borrow. If the induction of the fetch pattern for borrow-*into* is similarly biased, then it too should cause impasses because it expects two-column problems. But no such impasses occur. Borrow-into seems not to have the over-specific pattern that borrow-from has. This is a key piece of evidence for the pattern focus hypothesis.

The two fetch patterns in question before applying the focus pattern hypothesis are shown in 6.2. Part-whole trees are used for legibility. A part-whole tree is a way of displaying patterns that emphasizes Part-of relationships of the pattern by drawing them as links in a tree. Pattern variables are shown as tree nodes. The node label is the variable's name along with the unary predicates on that variable. For instance, AC2 is the variable for the whole units column. Variable C1 matches the top cell of the tens column, which is either a digit (in part A of 6.2) or an overwritten digit (in part B). Variable C6 matches the units column's answer cell. A little bit of focusing has already been applied in that the two patterns have been pruned to mention only the columns of the current problem. With no focusing at all, the patterns would be infinite. The pattern variables that the input/output variables are boxed. By input/ouput variable I mean that the variable is either of the following:

1. An *input* variable to the fetch pattern: The variable is an argument of the goal that this pattern's rule is under. Thus this variable is bound before pattern matching begins.
2. An *output* variable of the fetch pattern: The variable is used by the action of the rule that the fetch pattern is in. The whole point of the fetch pattern is to get its output variables bound.

That is, if a fetch pattern is thought of as a function for retrieving objects from the problem state, then the input/output variables are the function's inputs and outputs. There are essentially just three

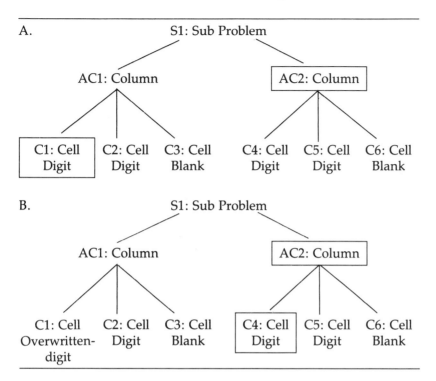

6.2
Part-whole trees displaying patterns for borrow-from (A) and borrow-into (B)

input/output variables in 6.2. Variable AC2 is an input variable because it is the argument of the goal Borrow in both patterns, and these patterns are on rules beneath the Borrow goal. This variable matches the whole units column. In 6.2A the Borrow-from subgoal is passed the output variable C1 as an argument. The variable matches the top digit in the tens column in problem state A. In 6.2B the subgoal Borrow-into is passed the output variable C4 as an argument. It matches the top digit of the units column in problem state B.

The only major difference between the two patterns of 6.2 is where the input/output variables are located. This provides the distinction that is needed to state

The pattern focus assumption
A fetch pattern has the smallest part-whole tree that will span its input/output variables.

The focused fetch pattern for 6.2A is the pattern corresponding to the tree headed by S1. The focused fetch pattern for 6.2B corresponds to the tree headed by AC2.

When the borrow-into pattern is focused this way, it mentions only the units column. Hence it is not as specific as the borrow-from pattern, which mentions both columns. In particular the overspecificity of the borrow-from pattern is absent in the borrow-into pattern. The borrow-from pattern insists that the two columns be both adjacent and boundary columns (that is, leftmost and rightmost, respectively). The borrow-into pattern does not care about adjacency because it mentions only one of the two columns. Whereas the overspecificity of the borrow-from pattern causes an impasse, the borrow-into pattern is now general enough that it can match without causing an impasse. This explains why there are no bugs that the equivalent of Always-Borrow-Left for borrow-into patterns. The focus pattern hypothesis has removed most of the overspecificity of the borrow-into patterns.

This formulation of the focus hypothesis makes intuitive sense. The focus of attention is no larger than the problem solver needs to discriminate among various bindings of the output variables. If the focused pattern of 6.2B were larger, say, including the tens column as well as the units (that is, the focused pattern tree headed by S1), then the tens column could potentially match several different ways without having any effect at all on the bindings of the units column section of the pattern. These matches are superfluous, given that all the solver has to do is choose the top digit of the current column, which is the units column. It is pointless to look at the tens column to figure out how to match the units.

6.4.2 Pattern Focusing for Test Patterns

Test patterns are subject to the same problems as fetch patterns in that they could in principle mention the position of the problem on the page, the position of the page on the desk, and so on. The solution used for fetch patterns might not work for test patterns, however, because test patterns have no output variables.

My intuition is that test pattern induction is driven by natural-language phrases, such as "You can't borrow from zero." The primitives corresponding to these phrases are placed in the test patterns, and the variables that occur in these critical primitives act as the output variables in the fetch patterns, in that test patterns are pruned to use only the variables necessary to connect these "output" variables to the goal's arguments. Thus the basic approach of the pattern focus assumption could be extended to cover test patterns. Unfortunately this intuition has not been tested with Sierra, although it could be. It is not known whether it will work. (In the present version of Sierra test patterns are focused ad hoc by limiting the description of situations to include only the problem and not the position of the problem on the page, and so forth. This means that test patterns only mention objects in the current problem—an ad hoc focusing of them.)

6.5 The Patterns and Fetch Patterns Are Distinct

So far no evidence has been presented that fetch patterns and test patterns are distinct types of patterns. Although it was assumed that they were different so that the syntax of the representation could be defined in chapter 3, that assumption needs to be backed up. This section does just that.

A competing hypothesis is that there is no difference between test and fetch patterns. It could be that a single pattern is used for two conceptually distinct purposes, but that the distinction is not reflected in the actual procedural representation. This single-pattern approach is the one most often used in production systems. The condition side of a production rule has patterns that serve both functions simultaneously. If the pattern matches, the rule may be run. As a byproduct of the match, variables are bound for use in the action side of the rule. So production rules (and many other pattern-invocation formalisms, such as Microplanner; Sussman et al. 1971) use one pattern for both testing and fetching. There is fairly clear evidence, however, that two distinct patterns are needed to cover the bug data.

Suppose that the fetch patterns for the bugs listed in subsection 6.1.1 double as predicates for when to borrow. When patterns are used as predicates, a failure to match is equated with falsehood. As the preceding sections showed, the fetch patterns fail to match on the columns that exhibit the bugs' characteristic behaviors. Thus they would be false there. For instance, the fetch pattern for Always-Borrow-Left would be false if the borrow originated in the units column of a three-column problem. But this means that borrow would not be chosen for execution on those columns. Consequently the fetch patterns would never be executed, and the bugs could not be generated. This argument shows that test patterns and fetch patterns must be distinct.

The two patterns assumption
Test patterns and fetch patterns are different expressions in the procedural representation language.

The argument shows not only that test patterns are distinct from fetch patterns, it also shows that test patterns tend to focus on different parts of the problem. Because both types of patterns are assumed to be overly specific, it must be the focusing that causes them to be distinct. As an illustration take the case of Always-Borrow-Left. Its fetch pattern's focus includes two columns—the column originating the borrow and the column to be decremented—whereas its test pattern seems to mention only the column originating the borrow. If both patterns were focused so as to mention both columns, then the learning mechanism would produce patterns that are equivalent to each other because the mechanism for test and fetch patterns obeys the same bias toward maximal specificity. Thus the main difference between the content of test and fetch patterns appears to be due to how they are focused.

6.6 Some Details about Repairs

The repair strategies mentioned througout the book have never been precisely defined because the requisite parts of the representation language have not been defined until now. This section explicates how the three major repair strategies work. As a whole the following comments constitute the *repair strategies assumption*, for future reference.

The Back-up repair strategy is simply popping the goal stack. A pop of one stack frame is equivalent to the No-op repair. A pop of more than one stack frame is what has generally been called a Back-up repair. These two were named differently because the two repair strategies occur with different frequencies (see sub-section 2.3.5).

The Barge-on repair strategy is more complicated. Its actions depend on the type of impasse being repaired. A reference impasse occurs when a fetch pattern fails to uniquely specify the values of output variables. There are two cases:

1. There is more than one way to give values to the output variables. In this case Barge-on merely chooses one.
2. There is no way to give values to the output variables. In this case Barge-on finds a minimal subset of the fetch pattern's primitives such that ignoring those primitives allows the pattern to match (this is sometimes called pattern relaxation, or closest matching, in AI). If there is more than one such minimal subset, then Barge-on merely chooses one.

The techniques generate values for the output variables, but those values do not necessarily fix the impasse. Thus the Barge-on repair strategy must search among the possible values for one that allows execution to continue. This highlights the idea that repair strategies are in fact problem-solving strategies, and as such they may need to search to achieve their goal of getting past the impasse.

A decision impasse occurs when the test patterns do not uniquely specify with rule to choose. Again there are two cases that Barge-on deals with:

1. If two or more rules' test patterns match, then Barge-on chooses one.

2. If no test patterns match, then Barge-on chooses one of the rules arbitrarily. Often this leads later to more impasses.

A primitive impasse occurs when some primitive cannot be executed, such as trying to write into a place that already has something written in it. What happens at these impasses is not easily circumscribed. The impasses and repairs to primitives summarize processes that occur at a finer grain-size, at the level of the implementation of the primitive rather than the level of the theory's unit of analysis. In general the Barge-on repair strategy is used as a catch-all category for these repairs.

The Back-up and Barge-on repair strategies are not claimed to be the only possible repair strategies. Indeed evidence of a few others is sprinkled throughout the bugs. For instance, some repair strategy causes carrying to be the repair for an impasse that occurs when the student attempts to write a two-digit number as the answer to a subtraction column. In tasks from outside the domain of arithmetic, repair strategies can be very elaborate. As mentioned in the context of an anecdote about assembling a barbecue grill, one repair involved disassembling the grill. So Back-up and Barge-on are not the only repair strategies, although they may be the only ones that change the interpretation of procedures without changing either the procedure or the situation.

Chapter 7
Sierra and Observational Adequacy

This chapter concerns the model, a computer program named Sierra, and the accuracy of the predictions it makes. The term "model" is used in a narrow way to mean an artifact whose structure and performance is similar in certain ways to the cognition under study. Under this usage "model" is not synonymous with "theory." The model is a thing, the cognition is a thing, and the theory asserts how the two things relate. In physics a model is usually a system of equations that the theory relates to the physical system being studied. A physical theory might say, for instance, which variables in the model are measurable, which equations represent natural laws, and which equations represent boundary conditions that are idiosyncratic to particular experiments. Theories include much more than a model and assertions about it. This theory includes, for instance, a tacit set of distinctions or ways of analyzing the cognition. It includes an analysis of how the data and the model's performance relate. It includes of course the hypotheses and the competitive arguments that support them. Indeed everything in this book is included in the theory. This chapter, however, covers merely the model and its performance.

Computer simulation models are plagued with a methodological problem that occurs in mathematical models as well, although it is less severe there. A typical mathematical model has parameters whose values are chosen by the experimenter in such a way that the model's predictions fit the data as closely as possible. Certain parameters, sometimes called *task* parameters, encode features of the experimental task (for example, what kind of stimulus material is used). Other parameters, called *subject* parameters, encode aspects of individual subjects' cognition or performance. There are other kinds of parameters as well. The difference between the parameters lies in how they are used in fitting the model's predictions to the data. Subject parameters may be given a different value for each subject. Task parameters get a difference value for each experimental task, but that value is not permitted to vary across individual subjects. When AI-based models have been used for cognitive simulations, there has often been considerable obscurity in the boundary between what is meant to be true of all subjects and what is meant to be true of a particular subject. Often the same knowledge base (rule set or whatever) is used for both subject parameters and task parameters. Yet it is critical that theories, even if they use nonnumeric parameters, identify which of the model's components and principles are universal, which are task specific, and which may be tailored to the individual.

But this is just the beginning of the problem. Even if the kinds of tailoring have been clearly delineated as universal, task, subject, or whatever, there remains the difficult issue of determining how much influence the theorist can exert over the model's predictions by manipulating the parameters' values. In a mathematical model such power is often measured by counting degrees of freedom or performing a sensitivity analysis. For models whose "parameters" are knowledge bases or rule sets, there is as yet no equivalent measure of tailorability. It is crucial, however, that the tailorability of such models be better understood. A model whose fit to the data depends on the cleverness of the theorist writing the rules does not really tell us much of interest. Understanding Sierra's tailorability *and reducing it* have been major concerns in developing this theory. Reduced tailorability is as much a goal for the theory as empirical fidelity. Many of the assumptions that are presented in preceding chapters were adopted just because they reduce the tailorability of the model.

In addition to describing the model, this chapter covers its empirical accuracy in the context of one particular experiment, called the *Southbay experiment*, in which 1,147 students studying subtraction were tested. As Sierra is described, its various parameters are illustrated by mentioning the values that they are given in tailoring it to fit the Southbay data. This chapter is the only place in the book where empirical accuracy is actually measured, and for good reason. There is no "Null" model against which this model should be judged, so there is no standard threshold that the model's predictions should exceed to warrant our belief in it. Fortunately there is another model for the bug data, proposed by Richard Young and Tim O'Shea (Young and O'Shea 1981). Although it is a little unfair to compare this model to theirs, for reasons to be explained, that comparison at least provides a ballpark estimate of how well this model does. The major value of measuring empirical accuracy is to compare the current theory against proposed revisions to it as a way of evaluating those proposals. Many of the proposals concern major assumptions, however, and it simply is not feasible to reimplement Sierra to test each of them. Consequently the informal argumentation style used in the preceding chapters has proved superior to actually measuring empirical accuracy. Nonetheless it is interesting to see how much of the data can be accounted for in the absolute sense, and so that measurement was conducted (at great computational cost) and is presented here.

7.1 An Overview

Sierra generates the theory's predictions about a certain class of experiments. To understand the way Sierra makes predictions, it helps to review the experimental method. For each school district the experimenter ascertains what textbooks are used in teaching the given skill and when it is scheduled to be taught. In the case of the Southbay experiment, multicolumn subtraction was taught from the middle of the second grade to the end of the fourth grade. Classrooms and testing dates are selected so as to sample this time span fairly evenly. Next the experimenter meets with the participating teachers to brief them and to give them blank test forms, such as the one in 7.1. Soon thereafter the teachers hand out the test sheets to their students who work them alone with no time limit. The teacher collects the test sheets and mails them to the experimenter for analysis. An important point to notice is the temporal relationship between the administration of the test and the episodes of lesson learning. Suppose that a certain curriculum has ten lessons: $L_1, L_2, L_3, \ldots, L_{10}$. Some of the students have taken only lesson L_1 at the time they are tested, whereas other students have taken L_1 and L_2, and so forth. Although a few students have taken the whole lesson sequence at the time they are tested, many data come from students who have traversed only a prefix of the lesson sequence.

This motivates the top-level design of Sierra. Sierra's major components are called the *learner* and the *solver*. Sierra's learner is given a lesson L_1 and an initial procedure P_0. The learner produces a set of new procedures, $\{P_1^1, P_1^2, P_1^3, \ldots, P_1^k\}$. The subscripts indicate that the procedures were generated by the first lesson, and the superscripts differentiate one procedure from another. Generally the superscripts are left off, so P_1 refers to any of the P_1^i. Each P_1 is given to the learner along with L_2, and again the learner produces a set of procedures, one for each P_1. For convenience all these procedures are designated by P_2, indicating that they were produced from the second lesson. This process continues, generating a tree of procedures (such a tree is discussed in a following section—see 7.8 for a preview).

To generate predictions about students who have taken lessons only up to L_i, each P_i is given to Sierra's solver along with a diagnostic

Subtraction Test

Name _____

Teacher _____

```
   6 4 7        8 8 5        8 3        8 3 0 5
 -   4 5      - 2 0 5      - 4 4      -       3
 _____     _____     _____     _____


     5 0        5 6 2        7 4 2        1 0 6
   - 2 3      -     3      - 1 3 6      -   7 0
   _____     _____     _____     _____


   7 1 6      1 5 6 4      6 5 9 1        3 1 1
 - 5 9 8      -   8 8 7    - 2 6 9 7    - 2 1 4
 _____     _____   _____   _____


   1 8 1 3      1 0 2        9 0 0 7      4 0 1 5
 -   2 1 5    -   3 9      - 6 8 8 0    -   6 0 7
 _____   _____       _____   _____


   7 0 2      2 0 0 6      1 0 0 1 2      8 0 0 1
 - 1 0 8    -     4 2    -     2 1 4    -     4 3
 _____     _____     _____    _____
```

7.1
One of the test forms used to collect the subtraction data

test such as the one in 7.1. For each P_i, the solver produces at least one solved test. If the procedure reaches an impasse, then each of the applicable repairs is applied, producing different solutions to the test. So sometimes a single P_i produces multiple solved tests. The union of solved tests for each P_i is formed, and the resulting set of solved tests, T_i, represents a testable prediction about the results of testing students who have only completed the first i lessons.

The model's predictions are the sets of solved tests, the T_i. In principle they could be compared directly with observed test solutions, the ones mailed in by the teachers. For several mundane reasons this is not practical. Several test forms are used in the schools to thwart students who look at their neighbor's paper. If the T_i were to be compared directly with the observed test solutions, Sierra would have to be run many times, each with a different test form. Also direct comparison of test solutions would have to deal with the slips that students make. A single facts error (for example, $7 - 5 = 3$) would prevent an observed test solution from matching a predicted test solution. Some model of slip-based "noise" would have to be applied in the matching process. Even if such a slip model were quite rudimentary, it would have to be carefully and objectively parameterized lest it cause Sierra to be unfairly evaluated.

Debuggy is used to solve these problems. Debuggy is equipped to deal with multiple test forms and slip-based noise (Burton 1982). Its slip model, which was developed long before this theory, has been carefully honed in the process of analyzing thousands of students' work. Debuggy is used to analyze both predicted and observed test solutions. When Debuggy analyzes a solved test, it redescribes the test solution as a set of bugs. Sometimes the set is a singleton, but often a test solution, even one generated by the model, requires several bugs to accurately describe its answers. Given these bug sets, matching is simple. A predicted test solution matches an observed test solution if Debuggy converts both to the same set of bugs.

This way of comparing test solutions has an added benefit. It affords a natural definition of partial matching: two test solutions partially match if the intersection of their bug sets is nonempty. Partial matching is a useful investigative tool. For instance, if the model generates a test solution whose bug set is {A B}, and there is a test solution in the data whose bug set is {A B C}, then partial matching allows one to discover that the model is accounting for most of the student's behavior, but the student has a bug C that the model does not generate. If the two solved tests were compared directly, they would not match at all (say), yielding the experimenter no clue as to what is wrong. So comparing solved tests via Debuggy not only handles multiple test forms and noise, it promotes a deeper understanding of the empirical qualities of the model.

Sierra has a natural internal chronology. P_2 is necessarily produced after P_1. Perhaps this chronology makes true temporal predictions. In the Southbay experiment, for instance, the testing dates and the textbooks are known, so the approximate locations of each student in the lesson sequence can be inferred. It would be remarkable if a T_i matched only the test solutions of students between the lessons corresponding to L_i and L_{i+1}. Longitudinal data could even be predicted, provided that the model is changed slightly.[19] Given that a student's test solution matched a solved test in T_i, one could predict that a subsequent test solution would have matched some test in T_j for $j \geq i$. In fact one may be able to predict that the second test would have to match certain tests of the T_j, because only those test solutions derive from the knowledge state P_i that the student seemed to have at the time of the first test. Although not designed for it, Sierra can make predictions about the chronology of skill acquisition.

Even a cursory examination of the data reveals that such chronological predictions would turn out rather poorly. Partly this is because the experiments did not carefully assess chronological factors. Although the general locations of students in the curricula were recorded, there is no way to know an individual's case history in any detail. In the Southbay experiment, for instance, some young students who had taken only the first few subtraction lessons could already subtract perfectly. Perhaps they learned at home or with special tutoring from the teacher. Keeping careful track of how much instruction students actually receive is of course a major problem in any longitudinal study. That is why I have concentrated on nonchronological account of skill acquisition.

Even if excellent longitudinal data were available, I doubt that Sierra's prediction of them would be anywhere near the mark. Basically this theory attacks only half of schoolhouse learning: knowledge communication. Knowledge compilation is the other half. It deals with changes in the memory of the skill that occur with practice and seems to be adequately accounted for by models such as Act* (Anderson 1983), Soar (Laird, Rosenbloom, and Newell 1986), and other similar models. Knowledge compilation undoubtedly affects the chronology of skill acquisition. Because Sierra does not model practice effects, it would be inappropriate to take its chronology seriously as a reflection of the chronology of human learning.

The model's empirical quality is measured nonchronologically. All the T_i are simply unioned. This creates a large set of predicted solved tests—call it PT. Similarly the observed solved tests are collected together into a large set—call it OT—without regard to when the students were tested. The solved tests in both PT and OT are redescribed as bug sets using Debuggy. Empirical quality is measured by their overlap:

> $OT \cap PT$ is the set of confirmed predictions. It should be large.
>
> $OT - PT$ is the set of observed behaviors that the model does not account for. It should be small.
>
> $PT - OT$ is the set of predictions that are not confirmed by the data. Some of these predictions will be absurd: star bugs. There should be very few of these. The rest are outstanding predictions. Further data may verify them. It does not matter how large the set of outstanding predictions is, as long as its members are all plausible predictions.

In linguistics this overlap-based measure is traditionally called *observational adequacy*. It is the only empirical measure that is used in validating the present theory.

This section has covered the way that the main parts of the model—the learner, the solver, the P_i, the L_i, and the T_i—hook together. It also covered the way that the theory's observational adequacy is assessed. With these frameworks in hand it is time to plunge into a detailed description of the model. In section 7.2 the input to the learner and the solver, namely, the L_i and the diagnostic tests are described. Section 7.3 presents the core procedures produced by the learner when it was run over the lesson sequence of the Southbay study. Section 7.4 presents the bugs generated by impasses and repairs from these core procedures. In section 7.5 the observational adequacy is measured by calculating the overlap between predictions and observations. In section 7.6 this degree of observational adequacy is compared with that of Young and O'Shea's model.

One major caveat is that the results presented here come from the model that corresponds to the 1983 version of the theory, which is described in VanLehn 1983a,b. Three major changes have occurred since then. (1) The FOREACH execution type was added to the representation language for procedures. (2) The set of repair strategies was simplified. (3) The bias for inducing test patterns was changed. Because I have not fully implemented the new version or the model, the older results are presented here, with comments indicating how they would be different if the model were brought up to date.

7.2 The Representation of Observables: Lessons and Diagnostic Tests

As mentioned, Sierra takes three inputs: (1) a lesson sequence L_i, (2) a diagnostic test, and (3) a student's initial knowledge state P_0. Sierra's output is a large set of solved tests, the T_i. Although the theorist must guess what the initial student knowledge state is, the other inputs and outputs represent observable quantities. Sierra's accuracy as a model depends somewhat on how these observable quantities are formalized. This section covers the representations used for the observables: lessons, tests, and solved tests. The formal definitions are tediously simple:

- A *problem state* is a set of symbol-position pairs, where a symbol's position is represented by the Cartesian coordinates of the symbol's lower-left corner and its upper-right corner.
- An *exercise* is a single problem state.
- An *example* is a sequence of problem states.
- A *lesson* is a pair: it is a list of examples followed by a list of exercises.
- A *lesson sequence* is a list of lessons.
- A *test* is a list of exercises.
- A *solved* test is a list of examples.

These definitions all depend on the representation of problem states, so it is worth a moment to examine that definition in detail. In 7.2 problem state A represents B, and C represents D. The formal representations A and C, are sets of pairs. Each pair represents an instance of a symbol at a place. The first element of the pair is the symbol, usually an alphanumeric character or a special symbol like HBAR, which stands for a horizontal bar. The second element of the pair is a tuple of four Cartesian coordinates that represent the symbol's position. The details of representing the symbol's position do not matter. The point is only that a problem state is little more than a picture of a piece of paper or a chalkboard. It is not an interpretation or parsing of the symbols. For instance, the problem state does not force the model to treat $507 - 29$ as two rows, or as three columns, or as rows and columns at all. How the problem state is parsed is determined by a component of the student's knowledge state, called the grammar. Grammars are described in subsection 3.7.1.

How faithful are these formal representations to real curricula and real diagnostic tests? Faithfulness of tests is easy to obtain. In 7.1 a copy of one of the diagnostic tests was presented. It can be quite faithfully represented as a sequence of exercises (problem states). However, accurately representing a lesson is not so simple. The illus-

A. ((HBAR (12 17 20 17))
    (– (12 17 14 19))
    (5 (14 19 16 21))
    (0 (16 19 18 21))
    (7 (18 19 20 21))
    (2 (16 17 18 19))
    (9 (18 17 20 19)))

B.   507
   – 29
   ――――

D. 5x + 1

C. ((5 (12 10 14 12))
    (x (14 10 16 12))
    (+ (16 10 18 12))
    (1 (18 10 20 12)))

7.2
The representation of problem states

tration in 7.3 is a black-and-white rendering of a page from a third-grade textbook. It is the first page of two-page lesson that introduces borrowing across zero. The lesson leads off by posing a word problem. It is followed by an example, 304 − 126. The example consists of four problem states. (In the textbook the four problem states are differentiated by four lightly colored boxes, which are not reproduced here.) The rest of the page contains exercises. However, the teacher undoubtedly works the first few exercises on the chalkboard. In effect this converts the first few exercises into examples. The second page of the lesson contains more exercises and a few word problems.

Sierra's lessons differ from real lessons in several ways. In keeping with the assumption that learning, in this domain, is driven mostly by examples, Sierra's examples lack the English commentary that the real examples have. Its lessons also omit word problems, pictures, and analogies with concrete objects like coins or blocks. They have only examples and exercises. In 7.4 the formal lesson corresponding to the real lesson of 7.3 is summarized. The problem state sequence that represents the first example is shown at the top of 7.4. On the assumption that the teacher would work this example on the board, the intermediate problem states that are not pictured in the textbook are shown in the formal version of the example. A summary of the whole lesson is depicted at the bottom of 7.4. The formal lesson is considerably shorter than the real lesson: it has fewer examples (probably) and much fewer exercises. Because Sierra is slow, I have kept the lessons as short as possible.

A curriculum is formalized as a sequence of lessons. Some of the tacit issues behind formalizing curricula are best discussed in the context of specific cases. Two textbooks were used by the schools that participated in the Southbay experiment: the 1975 edition of Scott-Foresman's *Mathematics Around Us* and the 1975 edition of Heath's *Heath Elementary Mathematics*. From these textbooks three formal

...ding Hundreds First

There are 304 birds at the Lincoln Zoo.
126 birds are from North America.
How many birds are from other places?

304 − 126 = ■

Need more ones? *Yes.* But no tens to trade. Need more tens.	Trade 1 hundred for 10 tens.	Trade 1 ten for 10 ones.	Subtract the ones. Subtract the tens. Subtract the hundreds.
3 0 4 − 1 2 6	2 10 3̸ 0̸ 4 − 1 2 6	9 2 10 14 3̸ 0̸ 4̸ − 1 2 6	9 2 10 14 3̸ 0̸ 4̸ − 1 2 6 1 7 8

304 − 126 = 178   178 birds are from other places.

Subtract.

1. 401 − 182	2. 205 − 77	3. 300 − 151	4. 102 − 4	5. 406 − 28
6. 700 − 513	7. 608 − 39	8. 503 − 304	9. 900 − 28	10. 802 − 9
11. 806 − 747	12. 500 − 439	13. 407 − 8	14. 904 − 676	15. 600 − 89
16. 100 − 56	17. 306 − 197	18. 204 − 7	19. 600 − 29	20. 508 − 429

21. 402 − 16   22. 700 − 8   23. 900 − 101

7.3

A page from a third-grade mathematics textbook (Bitter, G. G., Greenes, C. E., Sobel, M. A., Hill, S. A., Maletsky, E. M., Shufelt, G., Schulman, L., and Kaplan, J. 1981. *McGraw-Hill Mathematics*. New York: McGraw-Hill. Reproduced with permission.)

A.
304
− 126

B.
²304
− 126

C.
²·¹⁰304
− 126

D.
⁹ ²·¹⁰304
− 126

E.
⁹ ²·¹⁰·¹⁴304
− 126

F.
⁹ ²·¹⁰·¹⁴304
− 126
‾‾‾‾‾
8

G.
⁹ ²·¹⁰·¹⁴304
− 126
‾‾‾‾‾
78

H.
⁹ ²·¹⁰·¹⁴304
− 126
‾‾‾‾‾
178

A.
⁹ ²·¹⁰·¹⁴304
− 126
‾‾‾‾‾
178

B.
¹¹ ⁷·¹·¹⁴824
− 358
‾‾‾‾‾
466

C.
⁹ ⁶·¹⁰·¹⁷707
− 28
‾‾‾‾‾
679

D.
804
− 356

E.
304
− 166

F.
800
− 44

7.4
(Top) The first example of the lesson as a problem state sequence (omitting crossing-out actions). (Bottom)A summary of the three examples and three exercises that constitute the formal lesson.

A. 3 tens 7 ones
−   5 ones
‾‾‾‾‾‾‾‾‾‾‾‾‾‾‾‾‾
__ tens __ ones

B.

tens	units
3	7
−	5
3	2

C. 37
− 2

7.5
Problems notated in special ways

lesson sequences were eventually derived. (This development is interesting partly because it is a clear case of tailoring.) Some curricular features that at first seemed important turned out not to be. In particular both textbooks introduce multicolumn subtraction using special notational devices that emphasize the columns and their names. Scott-Foresman labels the digits as in 7.5a, then switches to column labels as in 7.5b, then finally to standard notation as in 7.5c. Heath starts with 7.5b then switches to 7.5c. Generally the textbooks would stick with their first notation until the second lesson on borrowing. Then they would shift to the next notation and teach the last few lessons over again using the new notation. The original formal version of this lesson sequence copied these notational excursions faithfully—lines, words, and all. It was found that these extra markings made no significant difference in Sierra's predictions. When the extra markings were omitted from the examples, the resulting core procedures generated the same bugs. This finding suggests that the extra markings are included in the examples because they help students learn a grammar for subtraction notation. Sierra is given a grammar instead of learning it, so it receives no benefit from the extra markings. The lesson sequences that were ultimately arrived at use only the standard notation (type c in 7.5). This makes them shorter, saving Sierra time.

There is no guarantee that the lesson sequence printed in a textbook is the lesson sequence that the teachers actually used, although the teachers and administrators I have spoken with claim that math is the one subject where teachers tend to "stick to the book" the most. To investigate this potential ambiguity in what lessons were actually presented, some textbooks' lesson sequences were formalized in more than one way, and the model's performance on the alternative formal sequences was studied. The lesson sequences for Heath (H) and for Scott-Foresman (SF) are shown in 7.6. Note that both H and SF involve a special lesson on regrouping. (In the McGraw-Hill lesson of 7.3, this subskill is called "trading" instead of "regrouping.") The regrouping lesson is L_3 in H and L_1 in SF. The regrouping lesson does not teach how to answer subtraction problems per se. It teaches how to do a subprocedure, regrouping, that is later incorporated into the subtraction procedure. It is possible that teachers did not use this lesson or, even if they did, that students may not understand that this regrouping lesson has anything to do with subtraction. After all, students are being taught many other skills (for example, addition) as they are taught subtraction, yet few develop subtraction bugs by mistakenly incorporating lessons from addition or other skills. To explore these possibilities, a third lesson sequence was constructed by delet-

L1.
```
      8 11
  29      9̸1̸
- 15
----
  14
```

L2.
```
  37
-  4
----
  33
```

L3.
```
  8 11
  9̸1̸
```

L4.
```
  8 12
  9̸2̸
- 44
----
  48
```

L5.
```
   257
 - 123
 -----
   134
```

L6.
```
  437
-   6
-----
  431
```

L7.
```
   2 14
   3̸4̸8
 - 151
 -----
   197
```

L8.
```
      13
   4 3 12
   5̸4̸2̸
 -   68
 -----
   474
```

L9.
```
        9
     2 10 14
    3̸0̸4̸
  - 126
  -----
    178
```

L10.
```
      9 9
    7 10 10 14
    8̸0̸0̸4̸
  - 129
  ------
   7875
```

L1. Solving two columns.
L2. Handling partial columns.
L3. Regrouping.
L4. Simple borrowing.
L5. Solving three columns without borrowing.

L6. Handling nonfinal partial columns.
L7. One borrow in three columns.
L8. Two adjacent borrows (3 columns).
L9. Borrowing from zero (3 columns).
L10. Borrowing from multiple zeros.

L1.
```
  8 11
  9̸1̸
```

L2.
```
  2 14
  3̸7̸
-  8
----
  29
```

L3.
```
  35
-  4
----
  31
```

L4.
```
  4 13
  5̸3̸
- 39
----
  14
```

L5.
```
  29
- 15
----
  14
```

L6.
```
   2 14
   3̸4̸8
 - 151
 -----
   197
```

L7.
```
      10
   7 0 17
   8̸1̸7̸6
 - 593
 -----
   7583
```

L8.
```
       9
    7 10 14
   8̸8̸0̸4̸
 - 3356
 ------
   5448
```

L9.
```
    9 9
  7 10 10 14
  8̸0̸0̸4̸
- 129
------
 7875
```

L_1. Regrouping.

L_2. Borrowing in 3-digit problem.

L_3. Nonborrowing in 3-digit problem.

L_4. Borrowing in 4-digit problem.

L_5. Nonborrowing in 4-digit problem.

L_6. Solving 3-columns, with one borrow.

L_7. Adjacent borrows, in 4-column problem.

L_8. Borrowing from zero (4 columns).

L_9. Borrowing from multiple zero.

7.6

(Top) The H lesson sequence. (Bottom) The SF lesson sequence. Topics are listed below sample problems.

ing the regrouping lesson from H. This lesson sequence, HB, turned out to be quite productive. It generated eight observed bugs that would not otherwise have been generated.[20] So it seems that some students take regrouping to be a part of subtraction, and some do not, or that some teachers omit the regrouping lesson. Lesson sequence HB is included with the other two in generating the Southbay predictions.

Of the three inputs to the model—the initial knowledge state P_0, the diagnostic test, and the lesson sequence L_i—the one that has the most effect on the model's predictions is the lesson sequence. In fact for the Southbay experiment only three runs of Sierra were used, one for each of H, SF, and HB. The same P_0 and diagnostic test were used with each run.

7.3 Core Procedure Trees for the Southbay Experiment

To illustrate the way the learner works and to start the discussion of observational adequacy, this section illustrates the inducer's performance when given a particular subtraction lesson sequence, the one called H in 7.6. Because the model is older than the theory, the procedures it constructs differ slightly from the ones discussed in previous chapters. One of the procedures produced by the learner from the H lesson sequence is shown in 7.7. Notice that it uses a tail recursion for the loop across columns. This is caused by the lack of FOREACH goal type. Also there are two rules, numbers 6 and 9, for answering columns with blank bottoms. This too is caused by the lack of a FOREACH type.

Sierra's inducer may produce more than one output procedure from a single input procedure and a lesson. This comes out clearly in

1. $Sub_P \rightarrow Diff_C$	When P has just one column, C.
2. $Sub_P \rightarrow$ $Multi_{RightmostColumn(P)}$	When P has more than one column
3. $Sub_P \rightarrow$ $Regroup_{RightmostColumn(P)}$	When P is a two-digit row
4. $Multi_C \rightarrow Sub1Col_C$ $SubRest_{C+1}$	Always
5. $SubRest_C \rightarrow Multi_C$	When C is not leftmost
6. $SubRest_C \rightarrow Show_C$	When C is leftmost and B_C is blank
7. $SubRest_C \rightarrow Diff_C$	When C is leftmost & B_C is not blank
8. $Sub1Col_C \rightarrow Diff_C$	When $T \geq B$ and B_C is not blank
9. $Sub1Col_C \rightarrow Show_C$	When B_C is blank
10. $Sub1Col_C \rightarrow Regroup_C \ Diff_C$	When $T < B$ & B_C not blank
11. $Regroup_C \rightarrow BorrowFrom_{C+1}$ $Add10_C$	Always
12. $BorrowFrom_C \rightarrow Decr_C$	When $T_C \neq 0$
13. $BorrowFrom_C \rightarrow Regroup_C$ $Decr_C$	When $T_C \neq 0$

7.7
A procedure learned from the H lesson sequence

7.8, which shows the *core procedure tree* for the learner. The core procedure tree shows which procedures are derived from which other procedures. The initial procedure is at the top. It is called 1c because it can only do one-column problems. The links in the core procedure tree are labelled with the lesson names. Thus lesson L_1 produces procedure 2c-full. The remainder of this section is a walk down the core procedure tree. The procedure labelled "ok" is the procedure shown in 7.7. The procedures in the core procedure tree are described by listing the subset of the rules of 7.3 that they correspond to most closely.

The first lesson, L_1, teaches how to solve problems of the form NN-NN. The resulting procedure, 2c-full, can do two-column problems, where both columns are full. It corresponds to rules 1, 2, 7, and 8 of 7.3. Lesson L_2 teaches how to solve incomplete tens columns, producing a procedure called 2c that can do any two-column problem that does not require borrowing. This corresponds to adding rule 6. Les-

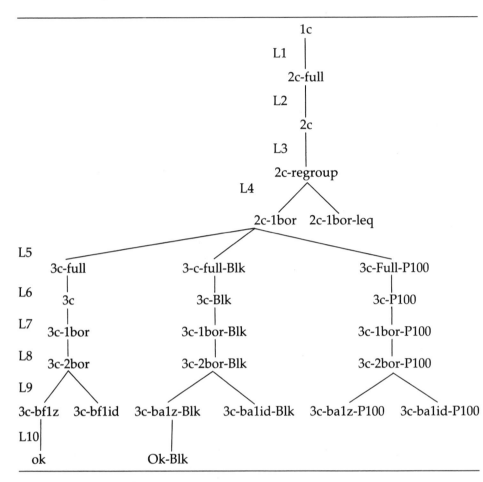

7.8
The core procedure tree of lesson sequence H, with lesson labels on the left

son L_3 introduces regrouping offline, so to speak. It uses examples that are not subtraction problems. The subtraction procedure that results (add in rules 3, 11, and 12) from this lesson, 2c-regroup, can do both regrouping exercises and two-column subtraction problems, but it cannot do two-column subtraction problems that require borrowing. That capability is taught in lesson L_4. Lesson L_4 integrates regrouping into the column-traversal algorithm (add in rule 10).

Notice that there are two output procedures: 2c-1bor and 2c-1bor-leq. Part of what lesson L_4 teaches is when to borrow. It uses examples like $34 - 18$ to show when to borrow and examples like $34 - 13$ to show when not to borrow.[21] However, Lesson L_4 does not include examples like $34 - 14$, where the units column's digits are equal. Hence the learner has no way to tell whether the test for borrowing should be $T < B$ or $T \leq B$. Sierra's learner thus produces two procedures: procedure 2c-1bor borrows when $T < B$, and procedure 2c-1bor-leq borrows when $T \leq B$. This constitutes a prediction that some students will borrow when $T = B$, as in $34 - 14$. This is a correct prediction. The corresponding bug, which is called $N - N$-Causes-Borrow, has been observed.

Lesson L_5 teaches how to solve three-column problems (add in rule 5). It produces three new procedures. If the representation language had a FOREACH goal type, this lesson would not produce any new procedures. The old procedure would suffice to handle three-column problems. Procedures 3c-full and 3c-full-Blk are almost identical. The only difference is the test pattern that they use to tell when to recurse. For procedure 3c-full, the test is whether the current column is the leftmost column in the problem; if it is not, then the procedure recurses. For 3c-full-Blk, the test is whether there are any unanswered columns left. Both procedures lead ultimately to correct subtraction procedures (the ones labelled "ok" and "ok-Blk"). The intermediate Blk procedures, however, generate star bugs. Certain repairs, which attempt to omit answering a column, cause these Blk procedures to go into an infinite loop trying to answer the column that was left blank. This whole branch of Blk procedures should not be generated. This is one of the arguments for including a FOREACH goal type in the representation language.

The third procedure output from lesson L_5, 3c-full-P100, passes arguments to the recursive call a little strangely. Whereas both 3c-full and 3c-full-Blk pass the rightmost unanswered column through the recursion, 3c-full-P100 passes the leftmost column (hence its suffix, P100, which abbreviates "passing the hundreds column"). This only works correctly for three-column problems. Procedure 3c-full-P100 gets stuck if it is given a four-column problem. In fact it and all its descendants are star procedures because of the strange ways that they answer problems with four or more columns. This branch of the core procedure tree should not be generated. The lack of FOREACH goal type forces the learner to build a recursion to traverse columns, and this causes the Blk and P100 groups of star bugs.

Lesson L_6 teaches how to solve three-column problems of the form NNN-N (add in rule 9). This lesson is a fabrication. At about this point in the Heath textbook, NNN-N problems start appearing in the practice exercises, but there is no specific lesson on the subskill. Lesson L_6 has been included in the lesson sequence to get around the missing FOREACH loop problem. If column traversal were structured around a FOREACH loop, then the lesson that teaches how to solve NN-N problems (lesson L_2) would suffice to teach how to do a partial column that occurs anywhere in the problem. Because there is no FOREACH loop in the current knowledge representation language, omitting L_6 from the lesson sequence means that all the procedures generated from H will be unable to solve NNN-N problems. In particular the learner will be unable to generate a correct subtraction procedure. This is yet another argument for the necessity of a FORE-ACH goal type. Because the representation lacks one, L_6 was added to H.

Lesson L_7 teaches how to solve three-column problems when one of the columns (but only one) requires borrowing. This lesson refines the fetch pattern that determines where to do the decrement during borrowing. Before L_7 the fetch pattern would return both the left-adjacent (tens) column and the leftmost (hundreds) column for borrows that originate in the units column (compare with the discussion of the bug Always-Borrow-Left in chapter 6). This lesson modifies the fetch pattern so that only the left-adjacent column is fetched. All the previous lessons have added new subprocedures; lesson L_7 does not. It only modifies existing material.

Lesson L_8 is similar. It teaches how to do problems with two adjacent borrows. It does not add a new subprocedure, but only adjusts some fetch patterns. It produces a procedure 3c-2bor (or 3c-2bor-Blk or 3c-2bor-P100) that can correctly solve any three-column problem that does not involve borrowing from zero.

Lesson L_9 teaches how to borrow from zero (add in rule 13). It produces two procedures that are identical except for their test patterns. The test for 3c-bf1z (or 3c-bf1z-Blk and the like) is $T = 0$, which causes the procedure to borrow from zero if the digit to be decremented is a zero. The test pattern for 3c-bf1id is $T \in \{1,0\}$, which makes the procedure borrow across zeros and ones. Procedure 3c-bf1id corresponds to an observed bug, Borrow-Treat-One-As-Zero. The reason the learner produces two procedures is that the lesson is missing a crucial example, one where the digit to be borrowed from is a one (for example, $514 - 9$). Without this example the learner cannot discriminate which of the two possible test patterns is right. This illustrates one of the few ways in which the set of primitives has been tailored to improve the theory's predictions. If $T \epsilon \{1,0\}$ were taken out, then this bug could not be generated.

The learner finishes up by taking lesson L_{10}, which teaches how to borrow across multiple zeros. This lesson has no effect on 3c-bf1z because the procedure can already do that.

The core procedure tree has two two-way branches and one three-way branch. It could have as many as $2 \times 2 \times 3 = 12$ final procedures. In fact there are just two. The other branches are pruned when the learner is unable to assimilate the next lesson. For instance, the branch for $T \leq B$ as the test for borrowing (that is, procedure 2c-1bor-leq) is terminated at lesson L_5 because one of the examples in that lesson is

$$
\begin{array}{r}
9\ 8\ 5 \\
-\ 6\ 2\ 5 \\
\hline
3\ 6\ 0
\end{array}
$$

The procedure expects the units column to have a borrow, but the example does not have a borrow there. The learner could install a new subprocedure that would avoid borrowing whenever $T = B$. However, lesson L_5 is already introducing a new subprocedure. The learner cannot introduce two subprocedures in one lesson because that would violate the one disjunct per lesson assumption. So this branch of the core procedure tree is pruned. Intuitively such pruning represents remediation.

It might seem that the model is doing a very poor job of explaining where students' bugs come from. It seems to explain only two bugs: N − N-Causes-Borrow and Borrow-Treat-One-As-Zero. The real test of the learner, however, is not what bugs it produces *directly* but what structures it assigns to the procedures that it produces. A procedure's structure has a direct effect on deletion and the impasse-repair process. By examining the bugs produced by deletion and the solver, one can ascertain whether the procedure's structures are plausible.

The deletion component is assumed to delete only rules from the most recently added AND goals. Thus only some of the procedures in the core procedure tree generate further core procedures. The results are shown in 7.9, again referring to the rules of 7.7. For each of the "mainline" procedures in the core procedure tree, it shows the effects

Procedure	Rule : Action	Bugs
2c-full	4 : 1	*Only-Do-Tens-Column . . .
2c-full	4 : 2	*Only-Do-Units-Column . . .
2c	4 : 1	*Only-Do-Tens-Column . . .
2c	4 : 2	*Only-Do-Units-Column . . .
2c-Regroup	11 : 1	In regrouping exercises, only do the Add10 . . .
2c-Regroup	11 : 2	In regrouping exercises, only do the decrement . . .
2c-1bor	11 : 1	Borrow-No-Decrement . . .
2c-1bor	11 : 2	Smaller-From-Larger-With-Borrow . . . Top-With-Borrow . . . Zero-With-Borrow . . .
2c-1bor-leq	11 : 1	Borrow-No-Decrement . . .
2c-1bor-leq	11 : 2	Smaller-From-Larger-With-Borrow . . . Top-With-Borrow . . . Zero-With-Borrow . . .
3c-full	11 : 1	Borrow-No-Decrement . . .
3c-full	11 : 2	Smaller-From-Larger-With-Borrow . . . Top-With-Borrow . . . Zero-With-Borrow . . .
3c	11 : 1	Borrow-No-Decrement . . .
3c	11 : 2	Smaller-From-Larger-With-Borrow . . . Top-With-Borrow . . . Zero-With-Borrow . . .
3c-1bor	11 : 1	Borrow-No-Decrement . . .
3c-1bor	11 : 2	Smaller-From-Larger-With-Borrow . . . Top-With-Borrow . . . Zero-With-Borrow . . .
3c-1bor	11 : 1	Borrow-No-Decrement . . .
3c-1bor	11 : 2	Smaller-From-Larger-With-Borrow . . . Top-With-Borrow . . . Zero-With-Borrow . . .

3c-2bor	11 : 1	Borrow-No-Decrement . . .
3c-2bor	11 : 2	Smaller-From-Larger-With-Borrow . . .
		Top-With-Borrow . . .
		Zero-With-Borrow . . .
3c-bf1z	13 : 1	The decrement-zero bugs
3c-bf1z	13 : 2	Don't-Decrement-Zero
3c-bf1id	13 : 1	The decrement-zero bugs
3c-bf1id	13 : 2	Don't-Decrement-Zero & Decrement-One-To-Eleven
ok	13 : 1	The decrement-zero bugs
ok	13 : 2	Don't-Decrement-Zero

7.9
Bugs generated by deletion from the procedure of 7.3. Ellipses indicate bugs that would be generated by the procedure before its rules were deleted. An asterisk indicates a star bug.

of all possible deletions. Usually the deletion bugs occur together with the bugs that the procedure would normally generate. For instance, if the procedure does not know how to borrow from zero before deletion, then deleting a rule generally causes a deletion bug that occurs together with one of the decrement-zero bugs. These extra bugs are indicated with ellipses in 7.9.

The deletion operator is not very productive for this core procedure tree. It is a little more productive for the core procedure tree of the HB sequence, which is missing the regroup procedure. This allows it to generate the bugs Borrow-From-Zero, Borrow-From-Zero-Is-Ten, and Borrow-Across-Zero, and the bug compounds corresponding to these that come from the core procedure 3c-bf1id, which borrows across ones as well as across zeros.

7.4 The Impasse-Repair Process

Each of the procedures output by the learner is given, one by one, to the solver. The solver takes a diagnostic test by applying the procedure to solve each problem on the test. The solver has two parts: the *interpreter* and the *local problem solver*. The interpreter executes the procedure. The local problem solver executes repairs whenever the interpreter's execution is halted by an impasse. When the interpreter reaches an impasse, the local problem solver selects one of a set of repairs. Applying the selected repair changes the internal state of the interpreter in such a way that when the interpreter resumes, it is no longer stuck. The local problem solver may (or may not) create a patch, which will cause the same repair to be chosen if that impasse ever occurs again. Stable bugs are accounted for by creating and retaining patches for long periods; bug migrations result from short-term patch retention. By systematically varying the choice of repairs and the use of patches during repeated traversals of the test, the set of all predictions that can be generated from the given procedure can be collected.

When Sierra is given a diagnostic test and a procedure, it generates solved tests corresponding to all possible combinations of repairs to the impasses it encounters. This varying of repairs to impasses is a prolific source of predictions. This is displayed in 7.10 by sketching the impasse-repair tree for the core procedure 3c-2bor when it takes the diagnostic test shown in 7.1. The repairs and the impasses do not correspond exactly to those presented in the preceding chapters, so a complete description would be confusing and, as it turns out, unnecessary as well, for a general impression of the impasse-repair process will suffice for following the remaining discussion.

This procedure does not know how to borrow across zeros. The solver reaches its first impasse on the test's fourteenth problem, $102 - 39$, which is the first problem that requires borrowing from a zero. Each of the leftmost branches in the tree corresponds to a different way to repair this impasse. The six nodes are labelled with the impasse "Pcv: Sub1 Zero?" Which identifies it as a precondition violation impasse, where SUB1's error test, ZERO?, is true when SUB1 is called. The letter following the impasse identification is a code for the repair that is applied: Q for Quit, B for Back-up, F for Force, N for No-op, and R for Refocus. (In the current terminology Q and B are instances of the Back-up repair strategy, whereas F and R are instances of the Barge-on repair strategy.) There are always at least five branches for each impasse because there are five repairs. There may be more because some repairs can apply more than one way. Notice that there are two nodes labelled with R among the first six branches. These correspond to two ways to apply the Refocus repair. If a repair is not applicable to a certain impasse, or the repair fails to fix the impasse when it is applied, then the corresponding node has F, for filtered, as a prefix.

Some of the repairs lead to further impasses. When this happens, the node has a subtree to its right (for example, the Back-up repair to this impasse). On the other hand if the test can be completed without further local problem solving, the node is a leaf of the tree, and it has a number as its prefix. The number is an index into the table in figure 7.10. For instance, solved test 1 has exactly the answers produced by the bug Borrow-Won't-Recurse. Solved test 2 generates exactly the answers produced by a set of three bugs. (Actually the "bugs" with exclamation points in their names are called *coercions* and are explained in the appendix.)

Sierra's solver has a switch that controls whether it generates bug migrations or not. The impasse-repair tree is generated by turning off bug migration. This causes the solver to use patches so that whenever an impasse occurs that has occurred before on the test, the solver applies the same repair that it chose before. If bug migration is left on, then the solver generates a huge number of solved tests. Essentially each occurrence of the original impasse (that is, the borrow-from-zero impasse in this case) yields an impasse-repair tree. There are seven borrow-from-zero columns on the diagnostic test. Hence Sierra would generate approximately 20^7 solved tests if bug migration were left on. Most of these probably would be identical, but still Sierra would have to generate them all, if observational adequacy were to be thoroughly assessed. Needless to say, this is not what is done. For practical reasons observational adequacy is assessed only with respect to bugs, not bug migrations.

7.5 Observational Adequacy

In principle the following simple procedure is used to test the observational adequacy of the theory:

1. Administer diagnostic tests to a large number of students.
2. Collect the test sheets and code the answers into machine-readable form.
3. Analyze each test solution with Debuggy, thus redescribing it as a set of bugs.
4. Call the set of all test solutions (represented as bug sets) *OT*—the observed test solutions.
5. Formalize the textbooks used by the students, producing several lesson sequences.
6. Formalize an initial state of knowledge, P_0.
7. Run Sierra's learner over each lesson sequence. This produces one core procedure tree per lesson sequence.
8. Formalize a diagnostic test form.
9. For each procedure in each core procedure tree, run Sierra's solver over the diagnostic test. This produces one impasse-repair tree per core procedure.

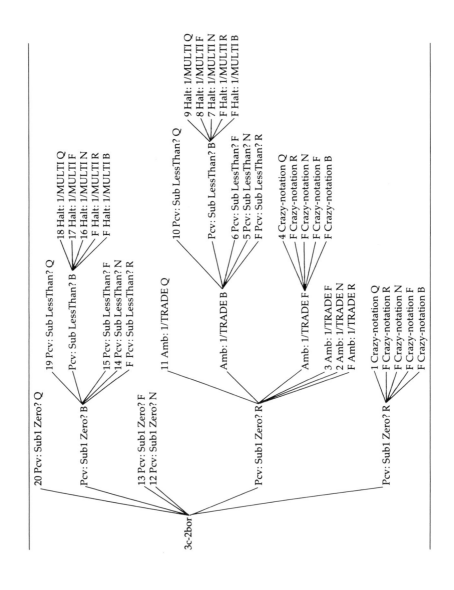

1. {Borrow-Won't-Recurse}
2. {Borrow-Across-Zero !Touched-Zero-Is-Ten !Touched-Double-Zero-Is-Quit}
3. {Borrow-Across-Zero !Touched-Double-Zero-Is-Quit}
4. {Borrow-Across-Zero !Touched-0-Is-Quit}
5. {Borrow-Across-Zero !Touched-0−N = Blank !Touched-Double-Zero-Is-Quit}
6. {Borrow-Across-Zero !Touched-0−N = N !Touched-Double-Zero-Is-Quit}
7. {Borrow-Across-Zero !Touched-0−N = Blank !Touched-Double-Zero-Is-Quit}
8. {Borrow-Across-Zero !Touched-0−N = 0 !Touched-Double-Zero-Is-Quit}
9. {Borrow-Across-Zero !Touched-0-Is-Quit}
10. {Borrow-Across-Zero !Touched-0-Is-Quit}
11. {Borrow-Across-Zero !Touched-0-Is-Quit}
12. {Stops-Borrow-At-Zero}
13. {Borrow-Add-Decrement-Instead-of-Zero}
14. {Blank-Instead-of-Borrow-From-Zero}
15. {Smaller-From-Larger-Instead-of-Borrow-From-Zero}
16. {Blank-Instead-of-Borrow-From-Zero}
17. {Top-Instead-of-Borrow-From-Zero}
18. {Borrow-Won't-Recurse}
19. {Borrow-Won't-Recurse}
20. {Borrow-Won't-Recurse}

7.10
(a) Impasse-repair tree for the core procedure 3c-2bor. (b) Debuggy's analysis of each of the 20 predicted test solutions

10. For each leaf of each impasse-repair tree (except the leaves representing filtered repairs), analyze the leaf's solved test with Debuggy. This produces one bug set per solved test.
11. Call the set of all such bug sets PT—the predicted solved tests.
12. Calculate $OT \cap PT$, $OT - PT$, and $PT - OT$.
13. Separate the star bugs, if any, from $PT - OT$.

In practice things are more complex. Steps 5 and 6 involve tailoring. Trying different lesson sequences led to the discovery that omitting the regrouping lesson causes the model to generate several new, valid predictions. In principle the initial knowledge state P_0 should be a rich source of variation because it is likely that not all students have the same initial understanding. In the Southbay experiment just one P_0 was used. Two others were tried briefly, but they produced almost the same observation adequacy as the chosen P_0.[22]

The steps that involve Debuggy, steps 3 and 10, are actually quite a bit more complex than the description so far. In fact most of the rest of this section is concerned with the practical aspects of using bug-based observational adequacy. First, the reality of step 3, analyzing the observed test solutions, is described. Then the reality of step 10, analyzing the test solutions generated by Sierra, is described. Finally, the Southbay numbers for $OT \cap PT$, $OT - PT$, and $PT - OT$ is presented.

7.5.1 The Southbay Data

The main data come from a study conducted by Jamesine Friend, Richard Burton, Beth Berg, and me. During the school year of 1979–1980, we tested about one thousand students in two school districts located in the southern part of the San Francisco Bay area. The study is called the Southbay study to differentiate it from five similar studies done in Nicaragua; New York City; Oakland, California; Wellesley, Massachusetts; and in the Philippines. Only the Southbay data are discussed here because they were collected under our direct control and have been analyzed more thoroughly than the data from the other studies. The results of the Southbay study are similar qualitatively and quantitatively to the other studies' results. For a complete discussion of the bug data, see VanLehn 1982.

Subjects and Methods   Two school districts agreed to participate. Both school districts were heterogeneous mixtures of social classes and races, although the majority of the children came from white, English-speaking families. Standardized test scores from the two districts show that one is slightly above the national norm, and the other is at the seventieth percentile. The district offices solicited volunteers, and 33 teachers from the third, fourth, and fifth grades agreed to participate. Although the teachers were self-selected, we have no reason to believe their students are unrepresentative of their grade level's population.

Teachers administered a written test to their whole class. These tests were carefully designed to be able to detect and to differentiate all logically possible combinations of the bugs known to us at that time. Designing these tests was one of the most difficult aspects of the study (see VanLehn 1982 and Burton 1982 for discussion). A copy of one such test is shown in 7.1. The teachers were asked not to impose a time limit on the students. Teachers reported that the test typically took fifteen minutes to complete, but there were some students who finished it in five minutes, and some who took a half hour. Teachers were also asked to instruct the students to respond to every item even if they were not sure how to do it.

Three classrooms were tested a second time two days after the first testing session, with no subtraction instruction in between. This allowed us to see if students' bugs were stable in the short term. To study the long-term stability of students' bugs, students in fourteen classrooms were tested two to six months after the first testing session.

Data Analysis   The data were analyzed with the aid of Debuggy, Burton's automated diagnosis program (Burton 1982). Debuggy cannot invent new bugs. Its inventiveness is limited to finding a set of bugs that fits the given student's test answers. Finding such compound bugs, as they are called, can be quite difficult because bugs can interact with each other in complex ways. After Debuggy analyzed a test, its analysis was always checked by at least one of the Southbay investigators to see if the student had a bug that was not in Debuggy's bug library. If so, the new bug was added to the bug library. Bugs were also added to the library when intuition or the theory suggested that they might exist. This strategy loaded Debuggy's library with all the bugs that might plausibly exist so that if a student was tested who had any bug, Debuggy would detect the bug.[23]

Debuggy has complicated criteria for measuring the degree of fit between a student's answers and the answers predicted by a bug set. The fit is measured relative to an explicit, cognitive model of slips (that is, unintentional actions, such as off-by-one errors in arithmetic facts). This assures a much better measure of fit than criteria based on standard models of errors (for example, chi square). In several studies Debuggy's diagnoses were found to be just as good or better than a human diagnostician's judgments (VanLehn 1982).

Category	Grade 3	Grade 4	Grade 5
Buggy	237 (49%)	87 (27%)	13 (13%)
Bug-free	96 (20%)	125 (40%)	60 (61%)
Undiagnosed	148 (31%)	104 (33%)	25 (26%)
Totals	481 (100%)	316 (100%)	98 (100%)

7.11
Students in each Debuggy category, by grade level

Proportion of Subjects with Bugs   Debuggy puts students' tests into one of three diagnostic categories:

- *Bug-free*   The student's answers are correct or nearly correct.
- *Buggy*   The student's answers closely match the answers generated by a bug or a combination of bugs.
- *Undiagnosed*   The student's answers closely match neither the correct answers nor any known combination of bugs.

The numbers of students assigned to each category are listed by grade level in 7.11. The proportion of students assigned to the category varied with the amount or training the students had received. Earlier grades had fewer bug-free students and more buggy students. As mentioned, all students were given the same test, regardless of grade level, so naturally the proportion of bug-free students would be lower for the earlier grades because these students had not yet been taught the skills required by some of the test problems.

The "undiagnosed" category stayed constant at about one-third of the students. This suggests that membership in the category was caused by some cognitive process that does not change across grade levels. To find out what it is, some of the undiagnosed students were studied in more detail by using the two-test data from the short-term study. It was discovered that these undiagnosed students were behaving systematically (either executing a buggy procedure or a correct one), but they made so many slips that Debuggy could not assign them to the appropriate category. It was shown that if the tests had been twice as long (that is, the same number of items as the two-test data), the number of undiagnosed students would be reduced by a factor of four (VanLehn 1982). Thus it seems that the cognitive process that was constant across grade levels was the putative "noise" in the human information processor. About one-third of the students in all grades made enough slips (that is, they had enough noise in their

	Occurs	Bug Set
1.	103	(Smaller-From-Larger)
2.	34	(Stops-Borrow-At-Zero)
3.	13	(Borrow-Across-Zero)
4.	10	(Borrow-From-Zero)
5.	10	(Borrow-No-Decrement)
6.	7	(Stops-Borrow-At-Zero Diff-0–N = N)
7.	6	(Always-Borrow-Left)
8.	6	(Borrow-Across-Zero !Touched-0-Is-Ten)
9.	6	(Borrow-Across-Zero Diff-0–N = N)
10.	6	(Borrow-Across-Zero-Over-Zero Borrow-Across-Zero-Over-Blank)
11.	6	(Stops-Borrow-At-Zero Borrow-Once-Then-Smaller-From-Larger Diff-0–N = N)

7.12
The eleven most common bug sets

processors) that the short tests used in the experiment were not sufficient for diagnosing them.

An Overview of the Bugs that Occurred   Debuggy assigned each student in the "buggy" category a set of bugs. Often there was just one bug in the set. However, 36 percent of the buggy students had more than one bug. Chapter 10 lists all the bug sets that occurred, and 7.12 lists the eleven most common bug sets.

Bug Migrations   Bug migration is the phenomenon of a student switching from one bug set to another. For instance, a student might exhibit one set of bugs during one testing session and another set during a subsequent testing section. Or they might even switch during a single test.

Debuggy was designed before we knew bug migration existed, so it was not designed to detect bug migration during a test. However, it can find cases of bug migration that occur between tests by analyzing each test individually and comparing the bug sets. Debuggy found several cases of such intertest bug migration during its analysis of the short-term data. This prompted us to reanalyze the short-term data by hand, looking for cases where students switched among bugs dur-

12	(38%)	Bug migrations explainable as different repairs to same impasse
12	(38%)	Other bug migrations
3	(9%)	Stable bugs
5	(15%)	Unanalyzable
32	(100%)	Total non-bug-free students

7.13
Bug migration among students from short-term experiment, excluding bug-free students

ing a testing session (*intra*test bug migration). The results as shown in 7.13. Although these data came from a rather small sample, it appears that bug migration is much more common than expected and stable bugs are much less common.

Although more research is needed to verify these proportions, it is clear that Debuggy and other diagnostic instruments must be designed to diagnose bug migrations as well as bugs, even if they occur within a test. Because this dramatically increases the space of potential diagnostic hypotheses, tests would have to double or triple in length to achieve good fits.

This section has presented the set of observed bugs, *OT*, and how it was obtained. The next section presents the set of predicted bugs, *PT*.

7.5.2 Generating and Analyzing the Predicted Test Solutions
To generate the Southbay predictions, Sierra's learner traversed lesson sequences H, SF, and HB, producing three core procedure trees. In principle all core procedures in all three core procedure trees would be submitted individually to Sierra's solver, along with the appropriate deletion-generated core procedures. This would be 63 core procedures, for the trees just given. However, many of the core procedures are quite similar. Others are known to be "star" core procedures in that all the solved tests that they generate are marred by star bugs (for example, the P100 branch of H's tree is a "star" branch. It would be blocked by adding a FOREACH loop to the knowledge representation language). Running these redundant or star core procedures through the solver would only generate more instances of already generable bugs, not bugs that could not be generated some other way. Consequently a subset of the 63 core procedures was selected and run through the solver.[24] Thirty core procedures were submitted to Sierra's solver, generating 30 impasse-repair trees. The

trees' leaves yielded 893 solved tests, which were analyzed by Debuggy.

The analysis of predicted test solutions has to be more stringent than analysis of observed test solutions. Basically a predicted test solution counts as analyzed only if Debuggy's bug set for it *exactly matches* its answers. Inexact analyses do not make sense, because Sierra does not make slips nor did it do bug migration (bug migration is turned off in the solver when generating the impasse-repair trees). Exact matching, however turned out to be too stringent a criterion. In Debuggy's versions of certain bugs, there is special code inserted to handle rare cases, such as the bug running off the left edge of the problem while borrowing. In Sierra such cases are handled automatically by the usual local problem-solving mechanism. However, the special case code in Debuggy's bugs occasionally would not correspond to any of the various impasse-repair combinations that Sierra generated. The net effect was that none of Sierra's solved tests would *exactly* match Debuggy's bug's performance. In almost all cases the analysis was off by one problem. That is, Debuggy's analysis would match 19 out of 20 answers on a solved test, but the 20th problem's answer would not match exactly (although the rightmost few digits would often be the same). Consequently the analyses were divided into two classes: perfect and almost perfect. The latter class includes the off-by-one analyses.

At first Debuggy's data base of bugs was insufficient to analyze very many of the solved tests. Only 1 percent of the tests could be perfectly or almost perfectly analyzed. To solve this problem, Debuggy's data base was expanded from 103 bugs to 147 bugs. The 44 added bugs included star bugs as well as bugs that could plausibly be observed bugs. Any bug was added that would get more of the solved tests analyzed. However, a point of diminishing returns was reached. The number of solved tests at the point where I stopped adding bugs to the data base is shown in 7.14. The solved tests are separated into two groups that correspond to two groups of core procedures. The "good" group (the left column of 7.14) contains solved tests from core procedures that know how to loop across columns. These would presumably be roughly the same when the FOREACH loop problem is fixed. The other group (middle column) comes from core procedures that suffer the effects of not being able to process multicolumn problems. I tended to add few bugs to the data base in the service of their analysis because I expected that they would not be with us much longer. The figures reflect this. Enough bugs were added to the data base to analyze 95 percent of the good solved tests,

	Good	Proc's	Star	Proc's	All	Proc's
No errors	2	(1%)	0	(0%)	2	(0%)
Perfect	209	(83%)	289	(46%)	498	(56%)
Almost perfect	28	(11%)	91	(14%)	119	(13%)
Unanalyzable	12	(5%)	256	(40%)	274	(31%)
Total	251	(100%)	636	(100%)	893	(100%)

7.14
The 893 solved tests generated by Sierra, categorized by how well Debuggy's analysis matched

but only 60 percent of the solved tests were analyzable from the other set of solved tests.

After the 44 bugs were added to Debuggy's data base to Sierra, the Southbay data were reanalyzed. Six of the 45 bugs turned up in the analyses.[25] Two of them even occurred rather frequently—seven times each. This was quite a surprise.

7.5.3 Results

Debuggy's analysis of the 1,147 observed test solutions yielded bug sets for 375 of them. However, many of these bug sets were identical (compare with 7.12). There were only 134 distinct bug sets. So *OT* has 134 members. Similarly the analysis of predicted test solutions yielded a *PT* containing 119 distinct bug sets. Unfortunately measuring the observational adequacy with respect to bug sets yielded rather unimpressive numbers (see 7.15).

This evaluation measure underrates the goodness of the theory. For instance, the present theory can generate all the bugs mentioned in 7.12 except Diff-0 − N = N and Borrow-Once-Then-Smaller-From-Larger. The bug Diff-0 − N = N, however, occurs in three distinct bug sets, for example, {Stops-Borrow-At-Zero Diff-0 − N = N}. Because the theory cannot generate one bug, the whole bug set fails to count. This is unfair, especially given that many of the bugs most difficult to generate—those that argue decisively for hypotheses—occur only in bug sets with pesky Diff-0 − N = N and its ilk (see subsection 4.5.5 for more on this bug class and why the model does not generate it). To take another case, the most common bug in the data is Smaller-From-Larger, but it appears in *PT* only in bug sets such as {Smaller-From-Larger *Only-Do-First} that contain a star bug caused by the missing FOREACH goal type. Needless to say, this predicted bug set does not match any observed bug set. Thus the theory is unfairly penalized, as if it had not generated Smaller-From-Larger at all.

$OT \cap PT$	11 bug sets
$OT - PT$	113 bug sets
$PT - OT$	118 bug sets, of which 53 bug sets contain star bugs.

7.15
Observational adequacy with respect to bug sets

To put it more sharply, suppose that all the bugs occur in pairs. Let x be the probability that the first bug of an observed pair is generable by the theory, and let y be the probability that the second bug of the pair is generable by the theory. Let us also assume that $0 < x,y < 1.0$ and that x is approximately equal to y. Under these conditions it would be fair to say that the theory is generating about $100x$ percent of the bugs. However, if one only counts bug sets as generable by the theory if *both* bugs are generable by the theory, then the theory is generating only $100xy$ percent of the bugs, which is considerably less than $100x$. If the bugs occur in triples, then it is approximately $100x^3$ percent. Clearly the multiple occurrence of bugs makes counting bug sets an unfair evaluation.

These remarks indicate that a fairer evaluation of the theory can be had by measuring observational adequacy with respect to individual bugs rather than sets of bugs. Let us define OB to be the set of individual bugs that occurred (that is, the union over the set of OT) and PT to be the set of predicted bugs. Then observational adequacy can be measured by calculating $OB \cap PB$, $OB - PB$, and $PB - OB$.

Overall 75 individual bugs occurred (that is, OB has 75 members). A few bugs occurred quite often. The most common bug by far was Smaller-From-Larger. (This bug never borrows, but instead simply takes the absolute difference in each column.) The bug appeared 106 times alone and 18 times as part of a multibug diagnosis. From there the frequency fell off rapidly, with the next five most common bugs coming in at 67, 51, 40, 22, and 19 occurrences (see appendix 2). About half the bugs (32) were quite rare, occurring only once or twice. This marked skew in the frequencies of occurrence explains the impression left by less formal studies (Buswell 1926, Cox 1975, Ashlock 1976) that there are only a dozen or so systematic errors. In fact there are many more, but it took precision analysis of thousands of students to find them.

PB, the set of individual bugs that are predicted by Sierra (see appendix 2), has 49 members. At last the observational adequacy can be calculated. It is shown at the top of 7.16. Also shown are the figures with the four bugs that can be generated by varying P_0 (mid-

1983 version of the theory

$OB \cap PT$	25 bugs
$OB - PT$	50 bugs
$PB - OB$	17 non-star bugs and 7 star bugs

1983 version of the theory, varying P_0

$OB \cap PT$	28 bugs
$OB - PT$	47 bugs
$PB - OB$	19 non-star bugs and 7 star bugs

Present version of the theory (estimated)

$OB \cap PT$	39 bugs
$OB - PT$	36 bugs
$PB - OB$	21 non-star bugs, and 0 star bugs

7.16
Observational adequacy with respect to individual bugs

dle of 7.16). Hand simulation indicates that bringing Sierra up to date (that is, giving it a FOREACH goal type and changing the way test patterns are generated) would account for an additional 11 bugs, yielding the observational adequacy shown at the bottom of the table.[26] Essentially the latter figures say that 65 percent of the theory's predictions are confirmed (39 of the 61 bugs are observed), and 35 percent of the predictions stand as targets for future observation. Of the 75 observed bugs, the current theory accounts for 52 percent, leaving 36 bugs (48 percent) unexplained. Perusal of chapter 9 indicates that most of the 36 unexplained bugs belong to the class of top-zero bugs (see subsection 4.5.5) and thus could be explained if the learning theory could cause an impasse to occur when $T = 0$ in a column that needs borrowing. Thus most of the 36 bugs are close to being explained. Of the remainder (see 4.6) most are not very common and could be the result of a misanalysis of a student's tests (that is, the pattern of errors could be caused by slips and not the putative bug).

7.6 A Comparison with Other Generative Theories of Bugs

The numbers presented in 7.16 are difficult to understand without some point of reference. Two such points are provided by earlier generative theories of subtraction bugs. An early version of Repair theory has been documented by Brown and VanLehn (1980). Its empirical adequacy can be compared with that of the present theory (Sierra's theory). Clearly Sierra's theory does better because it includes the ideas of its predecessor. Another generative theory of subtraction bugs was developed by Richard Young and Tim O'Shea (1981). They constructed a production system for subtraction such that deleting certain of its rules (or adding certain other rules in some cases) would generate observed bugs. They showed that these mutations of the production system could generate many of the bugs described in the original Buggy report (Brown and Burton 1978). It is important to note that some of the 75 currently known subtraction bugs had not yet been observed back then. One can assume that their model would generate more bugs than the ones reported by Young and O'Shea (1981).

A chart comparing the results of the three theories (using the predicted bugs from the 1983 version of the theory rather than the estimates of the present theory's result) are presented as 7.17. Observed bugs that no theory generates are not listed, nor are bugs that have not been observed. (The figures in Brown and VanLehn 1980 count bugs differently than the way they are counted here. That report counts combinations of bugs with coercions as distinct bugs—see the note on coercions in chapter 9.) The chart shows that the present theory generates more bugs, which is not surprising because it embeds many of the earlier theories' ideas. What is perhaps a little surprising is that there are a few bugs that the previous theories generate but the present theory does not. These bugs deserve a closer look. Repair theory generates a bug called Stutter-Subtract that Sierra's theory does not generate:

Stutter-Subtract:
$$\begin{array}{ccc} 3\,4\,5 & 3\,4\,5 & 8\,9\,7 \\ -\quad\ \ 2 & -2\,2\,2 & -\ \ 6\,7 \\ \hline 1\,2\,3\,\text{X} & 1\,2\,3 & 2\,3\,0 \end{array}$$

This bug does not know how to handle one-digit columns. It impasses when it tries to do such a column. Repair theory used a repair called Refocus Right to fix the impasse. It would cause the column difference operations to use the nearest digit in the botton row instead of the blank. Thus the second column in the first problem is answered with $4 - 2$.

Sierra has a nondirectional Refocus repair. It finds the fetch pattern responsible for the current focus of attention and rematches the pattern. It finds the closest match than gets the procedure past the impasse. In this case there is no such match because of the way the grammar structures the subtraction problem. To obtain the equivalent

YO	RT	ST	Occurs	Bug
		+	6	Always-Borrow-Left
		+	1	Blank-Instead-of-Borrow
		+	7	Borrow-Across-Second-Zero
+	+	+	41	Borrow-Across-Zero
		+	4	Borrow-Don't-Decrement-Unless-Bottom-Smaller
		+	2	Borrow-From-One-Is-Nine
		+	1	Borrow-From-One-Is-Ten
+	+	+	14	Borrow-From-Zero
+			1	Borrow-From-All-Zero
	+	+	2	Borrow-From-Zero-Is-Ten
	+	+	18	Borrow-No-Decrement
		+	6	Borrow-No-Decrement-Except-Last
		+	1	Borrow-Treat-One-As-Zero
	+		1	Can't-Subtract
		+	1	Doesn't-Borrow-Except-Last
+			15	Diff-0–N = 0
+			43	Diff-0–N = N
+			1	Diff-N–N = N
+			6	Diff-N–0 = 0
		+	7	Don't-Decrement-Zero
		+	4	Forget-Borrow-Over-Blanks
		+	2	N–N-Causes-Borrow
		+	1	Only-Do-Units
	+	+	5	Quit-When-Bottom-Blank
+	+	+	115	Smaller-From-Larger
		+	3	Smaller-From-Larger-Except-Last
	+	+	5	Smaller-From-Larger-Instead-of-Borrow-From-Zero
		+	7	Smaller-From-Larger-Instead-of-Borrow-Unless-Bottom-Smaller
		+	3	Stops-Borrow-At-Multiple-Zero
+	+	+	64	Stops-Borrow-At-Zero
	+		4	Stutter-Subtract
	+	+	1	Top-Instead-of-Borrow-From-Zero
+	+		5	Zero-Instead-of-Borrow
10	12	25		Totals

7.17
Comparison of observed bugs generated by three theories: YO = Young and O'Shea; RT = Brown and VanLehn's repair theory; ST = Sierra's theory.

of Refocus Right would require a grammar that views the problem as three multidigit rows instead of a list of three-place columns. Such a grammar would probably generate Stutter-Subtract, but might generate some star bugs as well.

The point behind Stutter-Subtract is that Repair theory has some notational knowledge embedded in its repairs. It has several Refocus repairs, and they are specialized for the gridlike notation of subtraction. In Sierra's theory all knowledge about notation is embedded in the grammar. The Refocus repair is general. It does not know about any particular notation. In Repair theory it is stated that the repairs are *specializations* of weak, general-purpose methods. They are tailored for subtraction. In Sierra's theory the repairs actually *are* general-purpose methods, not specializations.

Young and O'Shea's model generates a class of bugs called pattern errors. At that time four bugs were included in this class:

1. Diff-0 − N = N   If the top of a column is 0, write the bottom as the answer.
2. Diff-0 − N = 0   If the top of a column is 0, write zero as the answer.
3. Diff-N − 0 = 0   If the bottom of a column is 0, write the zero as the answer.
4. Diff-N − N = N   If the top and bottom are equal, write one of them as the answer.

Young and O'Shea derived all four bugs the same way. Each bug is represented by a production rule, and the rule is simply added to the production system that models the student's behavior. Put differently, they derived the bugs formally by stipulating them then explaining the stipulation informally. Their explanations are (Young and O'Shea 1981, p. 163):

> The zero-pattern errors are also easily accounted for, since particular pattern-sensitive rules fit naturally into the framework of the existing production system. For example, from his earlier work on additon, the child may well have learned two rules sensitive to zero. NZN and ZNN [two rules that mean $N \pm 0 = N$ and $0 \pm N = N$]. Included in a production system for subtraction, the first, NZN, will do no harm, but rule ZNN will give rise to errors of the "$0 − N = N$" type. Similar rules would account for the other zero-pattern errors. If the child remembers from addition just that zero is a special case, and that if a zero is present then one copies down as the answer one of the numbers given, then he may well have rules such as NZZ or ZNZ [the rules for the bugs Diff-N − 0 = 0 and Diff-0 − N = 0]. . . . Rule NNN [the

rule for the bug Diff-N − N = N] covers the cases where a child
asked for the difference between a digit and itself writes down
that same digit. It is clearly another instance of a "pattern" rule.

The informal explanations, especially the one for Diff-0 − N = N, are
plausible. To treat them fully, one would have to explain why only
the zero rules and not the other addition rules, are transferred from
additions.

The point is that one can have as much empirical adequacy as one
wishes if the theory is not required to explain its stipulations in a
rigorous, formal manner. The present theory could generate the same
pattern bugs as in Young and O'Shea's model simply by adding the
appropriate rules to the core procedures and reiterating their informal
derivation (or tell any other story that seems right intuitively). This
would not be an explanation of the bugs but only a restatement of the
data embroidered by interesting speculation. This approach does not
yield a theory with explanatory value. In short there is a trade-off
between empirical adequacy and explanatory adequacy. If the model
is too easily tailored, then it is the theorist and not the theory that is
doing the explaining. The theory per se has little explanatory value.
So tailorability and explanatory adequacy in general are key issues in
evaluating the adequacy of the theory.

7.7 Summary: Hillclimbing in the Sierras

It would be foolish to claim that Sierra's theory is wonderful because
two-thirds of its predictions about the Southbay experiment were
confirmed. It would be equally foolish to assert that the theory is in
desperate need of improvement because it models only two-thirds of
the bugs in the Southbay sample. The observational adequacy figures
are meaningless in isolation. As an absolute measure of theoretical
quality, observational adequacy is nearly useless. It is excellent, however, as a relative measure of theoretical quality. One takes two
theories and compares their observational adequacy over the same
data, taking care to study their tailorability as well.

Observational adequacy is particularly useful in comparing a new
version of the theory with an older version. This allows one to determine whether the new version improves the empirical quality or
hurts it. Indeed this is how the present theory arrived at its current
form. To put it in the language of heuristic search (which some claim
is a good metaphor for scientific discovery), observational adequacy
has been used to hillclimb—to find a maximum in the space of possible theories. The claim therefore is not that the theory's current
degree of observational adequacy is good or bad in an absolute sense

but rather that it is the best that any existing theory can do, given the same data and the same objectives.

There is a well-known problem with hillclimbing. One can get trapped at a local maximum that is not a global maximum. A common solution to this problem is to begin with a gross representation of the landscape so that the search can find the general lay of the land and thereby determine approximately where the global maxima will be. This done, hillclimbing can be done at the original level of detail, but remaining in the limited area where any local maxima are likely to be global maxima as well. The same strategy has been used in this research (or at least one can reconstruct the actual research history this way). There are three levels of hypotheses (which are also the three levels of organization of the preceding chapters). The most general level, where impasses, repairs, and general assumptions about procedural knowledge are discussed, is a gross representation of the cognitive landscape. Hillclimbing at this level yields several hypotheses that define the theory in a nondetailed way. The next lower level of detail is the representation level. It searches through a thicket of knowledge representations issues, for example, whether procedures should be hierarchical. The third level is the last stage of hillclimbing. It finds assumptions about inductive biases that optimize the fit between the model's predictions and the data. Because the arguments for assumptions are structured into gross, medium, and fine levels of detail, one can be somewhat assured that the hillclimbing implicit in this strategy has brought the theory to a global maximum.

It bears reiterating that empirical quality is not the only measure of theoretical validity. It must be balanced against explanatory adequacy—does the theory really explain the phenomena or does it just recapitulate them, perhaps because they have been tailored into the model's parameter settings? This theory is quite strong in the explanatory department. The model takes only three inputs, and these inputs are such that the theorist has little ability to tailor the predictions to the data. This implies that the predictions are determined by the structure of the model, which is in turn determined by the hypotheses of the theory. So the competitive argumentation that fills the preceding chapters can be construed as a hillclimbing adventure where the measure of progress is a combination of increasing observational adequacy and decreasing tailorability.

Chapter 8
Dependencies among Assumptions

One of the objectives of this research is methodological: to find out if a computational theory could be supported by competitive argumentation for each of its assumptions. It was discovered that such support is much more difficult to construct than had been anticipated. The problem is that assumptions depend on one another in complex ways. This makes it impossible to simply remove one, substitute a new assumption for it, and run the theory to find out which leads to better predictions. Substituting one assumption for another often necessitates changing many other assumptions that depended on the original assumption. This chapter reviews the types of interassumption dependencies that exist in the present theory.

8.1 A Classification of Dependencies

There seem to be three classes of assertions in the theory. One class consists of the assumptions. A second class consists of assertions that integrate a set of assumptions into one assertion. An example of such an assertion is the summarization of the assumptions about representation in the form of a specific language for notating procedures. Another example is the assertion that parse completion generates all control structures that are possible according to the assumptions about learning and representation. These assertions are not meant to introduce new hypotheses, but rather are meant to be mere logical implications of assumptions that have been made already. So it is appropriate to call these assertions *theorems* even though they are not backed up by proofs. The third class of assertions state *issues* that the theory must address. For instance the examples assumption implies that the missing rule bugs cannot be generated, thus raising the issue that "the missing rules bugs must be generated somehow." Another instance of an issues assertion is "the procedural representations must have an interface with the situation." Of course these assertions—assumptions, theorems, and issues—are not the only assertions that have been made in this book. However, they seem like a reasonable basis for explicating the structure of the arguments.

Connecting these assertions are several classes of dependencies. The most prominent is the *competitive argument*, which connects an issue to some assumptions. One assumption is made to resolve the issue. Other possible assumptions are rejected as being less valuable to the theory as a way of resolving the issue. Another class of dependencies connects a set of assumptions to a theorem. The theorem is meant to summarize the assumptions and be a logical implication of them. Thus the dependencies are called *implications*. A third class of dependencies connects assumptions to issues. An assumption often raises a new issue. For instance, the assumption that people are following procedures raises the issue of how the procedure is mentally represented. It also raises the issue of what happens when the procedure cannot be followed (that is, what happens at impasses). This class seems intuitively to contain a heterogeneous set of dependencies, so a bland name is given to them—*raisings*, as in an assumption raising an issue. The fourth type of dependency connects an issue to a set of issues. Such dependencies occur when one issue is decomposed into smaller issues, as when the issue of how to represent control structure was divided into the serial versus parallel issue, the variables versus variable-free issue, the control regime issue, and the data flow regime issue. Such dependencies are called *decompositions*. A fifth type of dependency is a *justification*, which is used to indicate when one assumption has been used in justifying another assumption. The five dependency types are summarized in 8.1.

Given these types of dependencies, the argumentation structure of the theory can be presented. The presentation is broken into three parts, corresponding to the three stages of argumentation used in the preceding chapters.

Dependency Type	Source Type	Destination Type
competitive argumentation	issue	assumption
implication	assumption	theorem
raising	assumption	issue
decomposition	issue	issue
justification	assumption	assumption

8.1
Types of dependencies between theoretical assertions

8.1.1 What Is Procedural Knowledge and How Is it Used?

The argumentation structure of the first stage is displayed in 8.2, which presents what procedural knowledge consists of in this domain and how it is used to solve problems. This illustration and the others that display argument structures use the following conventions: Assumptions are indicated by boxing their label with a light line. Theorems are boxed with a heavy line. Issues have no boxes around their labels. The dependencies between assertions are shown as labeled arrows: R means raising, CA means competitive argumentation, I means implication, D means decomposition, and J means justification.

The procedure following assumption is that subjects in this task domain solve problems by following a procedure rather than searching for a goal state. It immediately raises the issue of what happens at an impasse, which is defined to be a point in time when the procedure cannot be followed. There are several ways that subjects could handle impasses, including, for instance, always taking the same default action, such as quitting. The bug data show clearly that most subjects handle impasses by changing their interpretation of the procedure locally, that is, by modifying the control state of the interpreter, to put it metaphorically. This conclusion is bolstered by the ateleological assumption, which asserts that most subjects do not understand the design of the procedure and are thus insufficiently equipped to handle the impasse in any way other than to assume that they just misunderstood the procedure. This competitive argument ends with the impasse-repair assumption as the winner.

The impasse-repair assumption immediately raises two issues: what types of states count as impasses and what repair strategies are typically used by students. These issues are not answered until much later, when the representation is fully worked out. Nonetheless they are intimately a part of the definition of how subjects use procedures, so they are discussed here. The "What is an impasse?" issue is resolved when the impasse assumption is formulated. The "What is a repair?" issue is settled by the repair strategies assumption. Enroute we adopted an auxiliary hypothesis, the common knowledge assumption, which was used to test the impasse-repair hypothesis by predicting a Cartesian product pattern. Because this assumption was later instantiated as the repair strategies assumption, it is not shown in 8.2.

A further issue is raised by the fact that the impasse-repair assumption seems to predict that bugs always migrate, which puts it at variance with the fact that there are many cases of bugs remaining stable for months or years. The "Stable bugs?" issue is resolved,

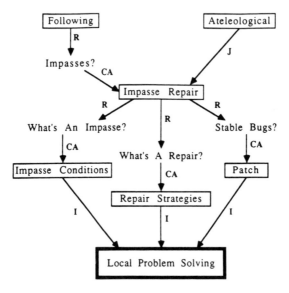

8.2
Argument structure for the execution stage

somewhat unsatisfactorily unfortunately, by the adoption of the patch assumption.

The conjunction of the assumptions about how procedures are used implies a theorem-type assertion, which is labeled "local problem solving" in 8.2. This theorem is not really stated anywhere in the text (but see Brown and VanLehn 1980). If it were, it would describe the local problem-solver module of Sierra.

8.1.2 What is the Representation of Procedures?

The second stage of the argument concerns the issue of how procedures are represented. The structure of this stage's arguments is shown in 8.3. The procedure-following assumption mentions "procedures" as the information that people are following, so it naturally raises the issue of how procedures are represented. This gigantic issue is decomposed first into the issue of control structures and interfaces. This decomposition is so important that it is also the subject of the decomposition assumption, which is not shown in 8.3. Like all decompositions this one is based on a divide-and-conquer strategy, that is, that the subissues can be solved separately in such a way that their solutions can be combined into a solution to the overall issue. This strategy may fail, and if it does, it is unlikely to be noticeable in the results, for the combinations of solutions to the subissues always

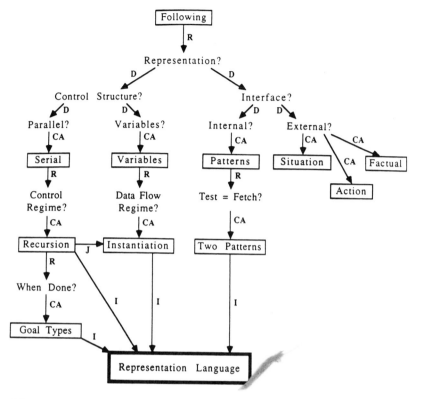

8.3
Argument structure of the representation stage

yield *some* solution, but it just may not be the best one. Consequently making a particular decomposition is really making some kind of assumption. Thus the particular decomposition made here was allocated an assumption of its own. Perhaps all decompositions should be recorded as assumptions.

The control structure issue decomposes into two subissues: The first is whether procedures in this domain are serial or parallel; they are assumed to be serial. The second subissue is whether procedures have variables. Variable-free procedures, which were once popular with associationists, are making a comeback in the hands of the connectionists. The bug data, however, indicate that it is safe to assume that procedures in this domain have variables (the variables assumption).

The next issue is the control regime issue, which contrasts recursive with nonrecursive control regimes. Although this issue is indicated in

8.3 as being raised by the serial assumption, I am not entirely happy with this classification of its dependency. It seems that the control regime issue is really more basic. It can be posed for parallel as well as serial computations. Similarly the data flow regime is shown as being raised by the variables assumption. However, the data flow issue is to provide facilities for storing and moving information that refers to objects external to the computation (that is, data). That issue is surely germane to parallel systems and even to variable-free systems. It seems that this section of the argument structure relies on concepts and distinctions from traditional, serial computer science, but those distinctions are rapidly changing as parallel computer science, especially connectionism, develops. This illustrates the often-voiced complaint that scientific theories depend on the vocabulary used to formulate them. In this case we clearly need more investigation into the foundations of computing to have a better set of distinctions to work with.

The issue of which control regime and which data flow regime is used in the subjects' representation of procedures is settled by reference to the Back-up repair. The control regime competitive argument is won by the recursion assumption. The competitive argument over data flow is won by the instantiation assumption, which is justified by the recursion assumption as well as the bug data.

When a procedure is hierarchical, as the recursion assumption claims this domain's procedures are, each individual subprocedure in the hierarchy must eventually return control to the subprocedure that called it. This raises the issue of how a subprocedure knows when it is done. Supported by bug data, the goal types assumption was adopted.

The other half of the top-level decomposition concerns the issue of how to represent the interface between procedures and information in the external world (the situation) or in long-term declarative memory (the mathematical facts). This issue can be decomposed into two subissues: how to represent the procedure's side of the interface and how to represent the external side of the interface. The theory is concerned only with representing the procedure; the situation and declarative knowledge are represented only because the procedure has to have something to interface to. The issue of how to represent the procedure's side of the interface is resolved by adopting the patterns assumption, which asserts that the procedure uses expressions in predicate calculus to refer to objects or to test properties. This assumption is refined by the two-pattern assumptions, which assumes that fetch patterns and test patterns are distinct. The argument supporting this assumption is in the learning section, because it depends on knowing what contents the patterns have.

The issue of how to represent the external side of the interface is handled by three assumptions: the situation assumption, the action assumption, and the factual primitives assumption.

The implications of all these assumptions (except the last three) is summarized by a theorem that describes the representation language. Actually the theorem is not stated precisely but instead a particular representation language is given at the end of chapter 3 as an exemplar of the whole class of representation languages admissible by the assumptions.

8.1.3 What Constraints Govern Procedure Acquisition?

The third stage of argumentation, whose structure is shown in 8.4, aims to discover constraints obeyed by the processes that learn procedures. The initial assumption is that learning is incremental and that the intermediate products of learning as well as the final products appear in the bug data. This assumption decomposes the learning issue into two subissues: (1) What is the relation between a procedure and its immediate precursor? (2) What is the relation between a procedure and the lesson that produced it from its precursor? The first problem can be solved by merely assuming that procedures grow by accretion rather than radical restructuring (the assimilation assumption). The relation between procedures and the instructional material is much more difficult to resolve. Based on a number of arguments involving both the bug data and results from laboratory experiments, it seems that procedural skill acquisition is driven by examples rather than verbal or textual explanations (the examples assumption).

The examples assumption raises two issues: The first issue stems from the finding that some bugs exist that are not consistent with the examples. These missing rule bugs motivated the deletion assumption. The second issue is the philosopher's problem that unconstrained induction can generate totally irrelevant generalizations. This issue is solved by adopting the reducedness constraint.

Reducedness, assimilation, and the assumptions about control structure allow the formulation of the theorem that all possible control structures admissible by the assumptions can be generated by the parse completion algorithm. Similarly reducedness, assimilation, and the assumptions about interface representations imply that all possible interface expressions can be generated by the version space algorithm (in principle). Of course both algorithms overgenerate wildly, producing many more procedures than the observed core proce-

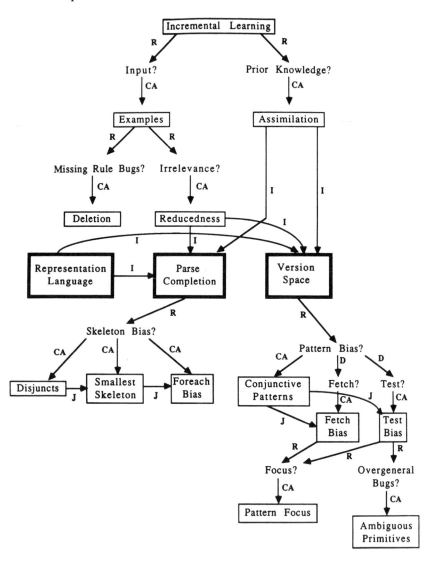

8.4
The structure of the acquisition stage's arguments

dures. The rest of the discussion of learning concerns biases on these algorithms.

Parse completion can induce dozens of new rules per example. Examination of the putative core procedure sequence shows that only one is induced *per lesson*. This motivates two assumptions: the fewest disjuncts assumption and the one disjunct per lesson assumption. They both assert that students minimize the number of rules they learn. The one disjunct per lesson assumption also assumes that students cannot learn more than one disjunct per lesson. The two assumptions cannot be discriminated by the data on hand, so they must be left as a single combined assumption, called the disjuncts assumption. The disjuncts assumption does not constrain parse completion enough, so a second assumption is required—the smallest skeleton assumption. This assumption works in that it constrains parse completion to produce nearly the right set of procedures. However, it has an ad hoc ring to it. It is conjectured that some kind of impasse-driven learning process would offer a better explanation of the data. Last, some problems arose because parse completion continues to generate tail recursive procedures even though the representation has an iteration construction in it. The FOREACH assumption fixes the problem by merely assuming that a FOREACH construction is preferred over an AND construction.

The version space algorithm overgenerates and requires severe constraints to produce only the patterns that actually appear in core procedures. This is the pattern bias issue shown in 8.4. The first and most severe constraint to be placed on the algorithm is the assumption that patterns contain only conjunctions of relations (the conjunctive patterns assumption). Patterns with disjunctions, implications, universal quantification, and other logical constructs are prohibited. This bias still leaves the algorithm overgenerating. The consideration of further biases is decomposed into two subissues: the bias on fetch patterns and the bias on test patterns. The bug evidence is clearly on the side of maximal specificity for the bias for fetch patterns (the fetch bias assumption). The bug evidence mostly supports the assumption of maximal specificity for test patterns (the test bias assumption), but there are some bugs that seem to require a different sort of bias, a bias toward overly general patterns. This issue can be resolved by assuming that some primitives, notably the mathematical predicts, are ambiguous in roughly the same way that natural language is ambiguous (the ambiguous primitives assumption). Because both types of patterns are biased toward maximal specificity, a last issue is raised: How much of the situation is encompassed by the patterns? This issue can be resolved by assuming that patterns were focused on the part-whole structure that is used by the arguments of the goals that they are a part of (the focus assumption).

8.2 Comments on the Argument Structure

Although it is fairly clear what competitive arguments and implications are, the overall support for the theory also rests on mysterious decompositions and raising dependencies. These deserve some discussion.

The dependencies called raisings are mostly due to a demand that the theory actually run on a computer. For instance, the whole local problem-solving story could have been left informal. It is only the desire to assess its computational sufficiency that requires a procedural representation to be used. In looking over the figures, it appears that all but three of the raisings therein are due to computational sufficiency of some sort. The three that seem out of place are those for which the bug evidence is contradicted by the assumptions. For instance, the examples assumption cannot generate the missing rule bugs. These instances of raising are driven by responsibility to the data.

Most of the decompositions are founded on the current understanding of computation, which is notoriously weak because computer science is such a young field. This forces one to decompose abstractions like "procedure" into "control structure" and "interface" without really understanding whether other decompositions are coherent or even what this decomposition really is. A whole new way of looking at computation could appear any day. In fact there seems to be one around the corner: situated action. The basic idea, being developed by Lucy Suchman and her colleagues (Suchman and Wynn 1984, Suchman 1987), seems to be that the situation does much more of the work than had previously been thought. Indeed procedures do not even have a control structure. Instead the long-term knowledge consists of a set of rules that interpret the current situation. In my formulation of the situation action approach (called the "annotated grammars hypothesis" in talks that I have been giving), these interpretation rules are like context-free grammar rules for parsing the current situation. These rules are just like grammar rules shown in 3.9, except that they bear annotations that describe what actions should be taken should one desire the parse situation to be changed in certain ways. Thus if one wants to fill in a blank in the situation, an annotation on the rule for parsing columns explains how to do that. It is not yet clear whether this new way of representing procedural knowledge works in general, or even for subtraction.

Clearly there are some procedures (for example, mental arithmetic) where the external situation does not change, and yet the procedure moves forward. Something is being reparsed, even though it is not the visible situation. To get the situated action theory to work for mental arithmetic, and perhaps even for written arithmetic as well, better theories of short-term memory than those we currently have are needed. This is one direction of my current research.

I should add that this research direction was prompted when I was trying to understand the argument structures of this theory well enough to draw the illustrations for this book. I was using a tool, the Notecards system, that makes it easy to display and modify the structure of arguments (VanLehn 1985). In the heat of modification I discovered the decomposition that is now labeled by the decomposition assumption and discovered that it was doing quite a bit of work in supporting the theory. I decided to try to justify it. Of course I used competitive argumentation. I tried to conjure up an alternative to the control structure versus interface distinction and shortly arrived at the annotated grammars hypothesis. The moral of this anecdote is that trying to uncover the dependencies among the hypotheses of a theory is a productive practice, particularly when combined with competitive argumentation.

Chapter 9
A Glossary of Bugs, Star Bugs, and Coercions

This appendix describes each bug, star bug, and coercion in Debuggy's data base in the following format: the name of the bug, a pair of numbers that indicates how many times the bug has occurred alone and as part of multibug diagnosis, a natural-language description of the bug, and one or more examples of the bug's work. If Sierra generates the bug, then a dollar sign ($) is appended to the pair of numbers. These data come from the reanalysis that was performed after the new bugs generated by Sierra were entered in the data base. There are 121 bugs (including Zero-Borrow-From-Zero, which is not really in Debuggy's data base), 7 star bugs, and 14 coercions in the data base. Of these, 75 bugs, no star bugs, and 5 coercions occurred at least once. Sierra generated 42 bugs, 7 star bugs, and 6 coercions.

Bugs

0 − N = 0-after-borrow   (2 3) When a column has a one that was changed to a zero by a previous borrow, the student writes zero as the answer to that column. $914 − 486 = 508$, $906 − 484 = 422$

0 − N = 0-except-after-borrow   (0 2) The student thinks $0 − N$ is zero except when the column has been borrowed from. $906 − 484 = 502$, $914 − 486 = 428$

0 − N = N-after-borrow   (1 6) When a column has a one that was changed to a zero by a previous borrow, the student writes the bottom digit as the answer to that column. $512 − 136 = 436$

0 − N = N-except-after-borrow   (4 7) The student thinks $0 − N$ is N except when the column has been borrowed from. $906 − 484 = 582$

1 − 1 = 0-after-borrow   (1 7) If a column starts with one in both top and bottom and is borrowed from, the student writes zero as the answer to that column. $812 − 518 = 304$

1 − 1 = 1-after-borrow   (0 2) If a column starts with one in both top and bottom and is borrowed from, the student writes one as the answer to that column. 812 − 518 = 314

add-borrow-decrement   (0 0) Instead of decrementing, the student adds one, carrying to the next column if necessary.

```
   8 6 3        8 9 3
 − 1 3 4      − 1 0 4
 ───────      ───────
   7 4 9        8 0 9
```

add-borrow-decrement-without-carry   (0 0) Instead of decrementing, the student adds one. If this addition results in ten, the student does not carry but simply writes both digits in the same space.

```
   8 6 3        8 9 3
 − 1 3 4      − 1 2 4
 ───────      ───────
   7 4 9        7 8 9
```

add-instead-of-sub   (1 0) The student adds instead of subtracts. 32 − 15 = 47

add-LR-decrement-answer-carry-to-right   (1 0) The student adds instead of subtracts columns from left to right. Before writing the column's answer, it is decremented and truncated to the units digit. A one is added into the next column to the right. 411 − 215 = 527

add-no-carry-instead-of-sub   (0 0) The student adds instead of subtracts. If carrying is required, he does not add the carried digit. 47 − 25 = 62

always-borrow   (0 0) The student borrows in every column regardless of whether it is necessary. 488 − 229 = 1159

always-borrow-left   (6 0 $) The student borrows from the leftmost digit instead of the digit immediately to the left. 733 − 216 = 427

blank-instead-of-borrow-from-zero   (0 0 $) When a column requires a borrow from zero, it is left blank instead. 3058 − 90 = 30 8

blank-instead-of-borrow   (0 1 $) When a borrow is needed, the student simply the skips the column and goes on to the next. 425 − 283 = 2 2

blank-instead-of-borrow-except-last   (0 0 $) If a column requires a borrow, and it is not the penultimate column in the problem, then its answer is left blank. 4238 − 444 = 38 4

blank-instead-of-borrow-unless-bottom-smaller   (0 0 $) If a column requires a borrow, and the left-adjacent column has $T \leq B$, then the column is left blank.

$$\begin{array}{r} 4\,4\,4\,4 \\ -\,1\,4\,5\,7 \\ \hline 3\,0 \end{array}$$

borrow-across-second-zero   (2 5 $) When borrowing across multiple zeros is required, the rightmost zero is changed to nine, but the second and following zeros are skipped over. $5003 - 3058 = 1045$

borrow-across-top-smaller-decrementing-to   (2 0) When decrementing a column in which the top is smaller than the bottom, the student adds ten to the top digit, decrements the column being borrowed into, and borrows from the next column to the left. Also the student skips any column that has a zero over a zero or blank in the borrowing process.

$$\begin{array}{r} 1\,8\,3 \\ -\ \ \,9\,5 \\ \hline 9\,7 \end{array} \qquad \begin{array}{r} 5\,1\,3 \\ -\,2\,6\,8 \\ \hline 2\,5\,4 \end{array}$$

borrow-across-zero   (13 29 $) When borrowing across a zero, the student skips over the zero to borrow from the next column. If this requires her to borrow twice, she decrements the same number both times.

$$\begin{array}{r} 9\,0\,4 \\ -\ \ \ \,7 \\ \hline 8\,0\,7 \end{array} \qquad \begin{array}{r} 9\,0\,4 \\ -\,2\,3\,7 \\ \hline 5\,7\,7 \end{array}$$

borrow-across-zero-over-blank   (0 9) When borrowing across a zero over a blank, the student skips to the next column to decrement. $402 - 6 = 306$

borrow-across-zero-over-zero   (1 13) Instead of borrowing across a zero that is over a zero, the student does not change the zero but decrements the next column to the left instead. $802 - 304 = 308$

borrow-add-decrement-instead-of-zero   (0 0 $) Instead of borrowing across a zero, the student changes the zero to one and does not decrement any column to the left. $307 - 108 = 219$

borrow-add-is-ten   (0 0) Instead of borrowing, the student merely changes the top digit in the column into a ten. $83 - 29 = 51$

borrow-decrementing-to-by-extras   (0 0) When there is a borrow across zeros, the student does not add ten to the borrow column's top digit but instead adds ten minus the number of zeros borrowed across.

```
   3 0 8        3 0 0 8
 − 1 3 9      − 1 3 5 9
 ─────────    ─────────
   1 6 8        1 6 4 7
```

borrow-don't-decrement-top-smaller   (2 1) The student does not decrement a column if $T < B$.

```
   7 3 2        7 3 2
 − 4 8 4      − 4 3 4
 ─────────    ─────────
   2 5 8        2 9 8
   Wrong       Correct
```

borrow-don't-decrement-unless-bottom-smaller   (2 2 $) The student does not decrement a column if $T \le B$.

```
   7 3 2        7 3 2
 − 4 8 4      − 4 3 4
 ─────────    ─────────
   2 5 8        3 0 8
```

borrow-from-all-zero   (1 0) When borrowing across one or more zeros, the student changes all the zeros to nines, but does not decrement the appropriate nonzero digit. $3006 − 1807 = 2199$

borrow-from-bottom   (0 0) The student borrows from the bottom instead of top row.

```
   8 7        8 2 7
 − 2 8      − 2 0 8
 ───────    ─────────
   7 9        8 3 9
```

borrow-from-bottom-instead-of-zero   (0 1) When borrowing from a column of the form $0 − N$, the student decrements the bottom number instead of the zero.

```
   6 0 8        1 0 8
 − 2 4 9      −   4 9
 ─────────    ─────────
   3 7 9          7 9
```

borrow-from-larger   (0 0) When borrowing, the student decrements the larger digit in the column regardless of whether it is on the top or the bottom. $872 − 294 = 598$

borrow-from-one-is-nine   (0 2 $) When borrowing from a one, the student changes it to a nine instead of a zero. $316 − 139 = 267$

borrow-from-one-is-ten   (0 1 $) When borrowing from a one, the student changes the one to ten instead of zero. $414 - 277 = 237$

borrow-from-zero   (10 4 $) Instead of borrowing across a zero, the student changes the zero to nine, but does not continue borrowing from the column to the left.

```
  3 0 6        3 0 0 6        1 0 3
- 1 8 7      - 1 8 0 7      -   4 5
-------      ---------      -------
  2 1 9        1 2 9 9        1 5 8
```

borrow-from-zero & left-ok   (1 1) Instead of borrowing across a zero, the student changes the zero to nine, but does not continue borrowing from the column to the left. However, if the digit to the left of the zero is over a blank, then the student does the correct thing.

```
  3 0 6        3 0 0 6        1 0 3        2 0 3
- 1 8 7      - 1 8 0 7      -   4 5      -   4 5
-------      ---------      -------      -------
  2 1 9        1 2 9 9          5 8        1 5 8
 Wrong         Wrong         Correct      Correct
```

borrow-from-zero-is-ten   (1 1 $) When borrowing across zero, the student changes the zero to ten and does not decrement any digit to the left. $604 - 235 = 479$

borrow-ignore-zero-over-blank   (0 0) If a column originally had a zero over a blank, and it was borrowed across, then the answer is left blank.

```
  5 0 5        5 0 8
-     7      -     7
-------      -------
  4   8        5 0 1
 Wrong        Correct
```

borrow-into-one = ten   (0 5) When a borrow is caused by a column of the form $1 - N$, the student changes the one to a ten instead of adding ten to it. $71 - 38 = 32$

borrow-no-decrement   (10 8 $) When borrowing, the student adds ten correctly, but does not change any column to the left. $62 - 44 = 28$

borrow-no-decrement-except-last   (4 2 $) The student omits decrementing unless the column to be decremented is the leftmost column in the problem. $6262 - 4444 = 1828$

borrow-once-then-smaller-from-larger   (0 12) The student borrows only once per exercise. From then on he subtracts the smaller from the larger digit in each column regardless of their positions. $7127 - 2389 = 5278$

borrow-once-without-recurse   (0 0) The student borrows only once per problem. After that if another borrow is required, the student adds the ten correctly, but does not decrement. If there is a borrow across a zero, the student changes the zero to nine, but does not decrement the digit to the left of the zero.

$$
\begin{array}{r}
5\;3\;2 \\
-\,2\;7\;5 \\
\hline
3\;5\;7
\end{array}
\qquad
\begin{array}{r}
4\;0\;8 \\
-\,2\;3\;9 \\
\hline
2\;6\;9
\end{array}
$$

borrow-only-from-top-smaller   (1 3) When borrowing, the student tries to find a column in which the top number is smaller than the bottom. If there is one, she decrements that, otherwise she borrows correctly. $9283 - 3566 = 5627$

borrow-only-once   (0 1) The student does the first borrow in a problem correctly. After that the student only does the adding of ten and omits the decrementing. $535 - 278 = 357$

borrow-skip-equal   (0 4) When decrementing, the student skips over columns in which the top digit and the bottom digit are the same. $923 - 427 = 406$

borrow-ten-plus-next-digit-into-zero   (0 0) When a borrow is caused by a zero, the student does not add ten correctly. What he does instead is add ten •plus the digit in the next column to the left. $50 - 38 = 17$

borrow-treat-one-as-zero   (0 1 $) When borrowing from one, the student treats the one as if it were zero; that is, she changes the one to nine and decrements the number to the left of the one. $313 - 159 = 144$

borrow-unit-diff   (0 1) The student borrows the difference between the top digit and the bottom digit of the current column. In other words he borrows just enough to do the subtraction, which then always results in zero. $86 - 29 = 30$

borrow-won't-recurse   (0 0 $) Instead of borrowing across a zero, the student stops doing the exercise. $8035 - 2662 = 3$

borrow-won't-recurse-twice   (0 0 $) If a column requires borrowing from multiple zeros, the student stops doing the exercise. $80045 - 66 = 9$

borrowed-from-don't-borrow   (0 0) When there are two borrows in a row, the student does the first borrow correctly, but with the second borrow she does not decrement (she does add ten correctly). $143 - 88 = 155$

can't-subtract   (1 0) The student skips the entire problem. $8 - 3 =$

copy-top-except-units   (0 0 $) The student does the units column correctly then copies the top digits into the answer for the remaining columns. $35 - 13 = 32$

copy-top-in-last-column-if-borrowed-from   (0 0) After borrowing from the last column, the student copies top digit as the answer. $80 - 34 = 76$

decrement-all-on-multiple-zero   (3 3) When borrowing across a zero, and the borrow is caused by zero, the student changes the right zero to nine instead of ten. $600 - 142 = 457$

decrement-by-one-plus-zeros   (0 0) When there is borrow across zero, the student decrements the number to the left of the zero(s) by an extra one for every zero borrowed across. $4005 - 6 = 1999$

decrement-by-two-over-two   (0 0) When borrowing from a column of the form $N - 2$, the student decrements the N by two instead of one. $83 - 29 = 44$

decrement-leftmost-zero-only   (1 0) When borrowing across two or more zeros, the student changes the leftmost of the zeros to nine, but changes the other zeros to tens. $1003 - 958 = 1055.$

decrement-multiple-zeros-by-number-to-left   (1 1) When borrowing across zeros, the student changes the leftmost zero to a nine, changes the next zero to eight, and so on. $8002 - 1714 = 6278$

decrement-multiple-zeros-by-number-to-right   (3 1) When borrowing across zeros, the student changes the rightmost zero to a nine, changes the next zero to eigth, and so on. $8002 - 1714 = 6188$

decrement-on-first-borrow   (0 0) The first column that requires a borrow is decremented before the column subtract is done. $832 - 265 = 576$

decrement-one-to-eleven   (0 1) Instead of decrementing a one, the student changes the one to an eleven. $314 - 6 = 2118$

decrement-top-leq-is-eight   (1 1) When borrowing from zero or one, the student changes the zero or one to eight and does not decrement digits to the left of the zero or one. $4013 - 995 = 3998$

diff-0 − N = 0   (0 13) When the student encounters a column of the form $0 - N$, she does not borrow but instead writes zero as the column answer. $40 - 21 = 20$

diff-0 − N = N   (1 42) When the student encounters a column of the form $0 - N$, he does not borrow but instead writes N as the answer. $80 - 27 = 67$

diff-0 − N = N-when-borrow-from-zero   (0 2)   When borrowing across a zero, and the borrow is caused by a zero, the student does not borrow. Instead she writes the bottom number as the column answer. She borrows correctly in the next column or in other circumstances.

$$\begin{array}{r} 1\,0\,0 \\ -\ \ 3\,2 \\ \hline 7\,2 \end{array} \qquad \begin{array}{r} 4\,0\,0 \\ -2\,4\,8 \\ \hline 1\,6\,8 \end{array}$$

diff-1 − N = 1   (0 0) When a column has the form 1 − N, the student writes one as the column answer. $51 - 27 = 31$

diff-N − 0 = 0   (0 6)   The student thinks that N − 0 is zero. $57 - 20 = 30$

diff-N − N = N   (0 1) Whenever there is a column that has the same number on the top and the bottom, the student writes that number as the answer. $83 - 13 = 73$

doesn't-borrow-except-last   (0 1 $) The student quits doing the exercise as soon as a borrow column is encountered, unless it is the penultimate column in the problem. $634 - 117 = \ , 346 - 171 = 171$

doesn't-borrow-unless-bottom-smaller   (0 0 $) The student quits doing the exercise when he encounters a borrow that requires decrementing a column that has $T \le B$. $634 - 177 = \ , 634 - 117 = 517$

doesn't-borrow   (0 0 $) The student stops doing the exercise when a borrow is required. $833 - 262 = 1$

don't-decrement-second-zero   (0 0) When borrowing across a zero, and the borrow is caused by a zero, the student changes the zero she is borrowing across into a ten instead of a nine. $700 - 258 = 452$

don't-decrement-zero   (3 4 $) When borrowing across a zero, the student changes the zero to ten instead of nine. $506 - 318 = 198$

don't-decrement-zero-over-blank   (4 2) The student does not borrow across a zero that is over a blank. $305 - 9 = 306$

don't-decrement-zero-over-zero   (0 0) The student does not borrow across a zero that is over a zero. $305 - 107 = 208$

don't-decrement-zero-until-bottom-blank   (0 1) When borrowing across a zero, the student changes the zero to a ten instead of a nine unless the zero is over a blank, in which case he does the correct thing.

```
  5 0 6        3 0 4
- 3 1 8      -     9
  ─────      ───────
  1 9 8        2 9 5
  Wrong       Correct
```

don't-write-zero   (1 3) The student doesn't write zeros in the answer. $442 - 141 = 3\ 1$

double-decrement-one   (1 2) When borrowing from a one, the student treats the one as a zero (that is, she changes the one to nine and continues borrowing to the left) unless the one is over a blank, in which case she does the correct thing. $813 - 515 = 288$

forget-borrow-over-blanks   (1 3 $) The student does not decrement a number that is over a blank. $347 - 9 = 348$

ignore-leftmost-one-over-blank   (0 6) When the left column of the exercise has a one that is over a blank, the student ignores that column. $143 - 22 = 21$

ignore-zero-over-blank   (0 0) Whenever there is a column that has a zero over a blank, the student ignores that column. $907 - 5 = 92$

increment-over-larger   (0 0) When borrowing from a column in which the top is smaller than the bottom, the student increments instead of decrements. $833 - 277 = 576$

increment-zero-over-blank   (0 0 $) When borrowing across a zero over a blank, the student increments instead of decrements the zero. $402 - 6 = 416$

N − 9 = N − 1-after-borrow   (0 0) If a column is of the form $N - 9$ and has been borrowed from, when the student does that column, he subtracts one instead of nine. $844 - 796 = 127$

N − N-after-borrow-causes-borrow   (0 2) The student borrows with columns of the form $N - N$ if the column has been borrowed from. $953 - 147 = 7106$

N − N-causes-borrow   (1 0 $) The student borrows with columns of the form $N - N$. $953 - 152 = 7101$

N − N = 1-after-borrow   (1 3) If a column had the form $N - N$ and was borrowed from, the student writes one as the answer to that column. $944 - 348 = 616$

N − N = 9-plus-decrement   (0 0) When a column has the same number on the top and the bottom, the student writes nine as the answer and decrements the next column to the left, even though borrowing is not necessary. $94 - 34 = 59$

ﬂ-borrow-always-borrow (0 0) Once a student has borrowed, he continues to borrow in every remaining column in the exercise. $488 - 229 = 1159$

only-do-units (0 1 $) The student does only the units column. $234 - 101 = 3$

quit-when-bottom-blank (0 5 $) When the bottom number has fewer digits than the top number, the student quits as soon as the bottom number runs out. $439 - 4 = 5$

simple-problem-stutter-subtract (1 0) When the bottom number is a single digit, and the top number has two or more digits, the student repeatedly subtracts the single bottom digit from each digit in the top number. $348 - 2 = 126$

smaller-from-larger (103 12 $) The student does not borrow, but in each column subtracts the smaller digit from the larger one. $81 - 38 = 57$

smaller-from-larger-except-last (0 3 $) The student answers all columns by taking the smaller digit from the larger one unless the column is second to the last, in which case the student borrows if necessary. $344 - 177 = 173$

smaller-from-larger-instead-of-borrow-from-zero (0 5 $) The student does not borrow across zero but instead subtracts the smaller from the larger digit.

$$
\begin{array}{r}
3\ 0\ 6 \\
-\quad\ \ 8 \\
\hline
3\ 0\ 2
\end{array}
\qquad
\begin{array}{r}
3\ 0\ 6 \\
-1\ 4\ 8 \\
\hline
1\ 6\ 2
\end{array}
$$

smaller-from-larger-instead-of-borrow-from-double-zero (0 0 $) If a column requires borrowing from multiple zeros, the student takes the absolute difference instead. $1005 - 9 = 1004$

smaller-from-larger-instead-of-borrow-unless-bottom-smaller (2 5 $) If a column requires borrowing from a column where $T \le B$, the student takes the absolute difference instead. $3434 - 1737 = 1703$

smaller-from-larger-when-borrowed-from (0 7) When there are two borrows in a row, the student does the first one correctly, but for the second one she does not borrow; instead she subtracts the smaller from the larger digit. $824 - 157 = 747$

smaller-from-larger-with-borrow (0 0 $) When borrowing, the student decrements correctly then subtracts the smaller digit from the larger as if he had not borrowed at all. $73 - 24 = 41$

stops-borrow-at-multiple-zero   (2 1 $) Instead of borrowing across several zeros, the student adds ten to the column she is doing, but does not change any column to the left. $4004 - 9 = 4005$

stops-borrow-at-second-zero   (0 0 $) When borrowing across several zeros, the student changes the rightmost zero to nine, but does not change other columns to the left. $4004 - 9 = 4095$

stops-borrow-at-zero   (34 30 $) Instead of borrowing across a zero, the student adds ten to the column he is doing, but does not change any column to the left. $404 - 187 = 227$

stutter-subtract   (2 0) When there are blanks in the bottom number, the student subtracts the leftmost digit of the bottom number in every column that has a blank. $4369 - 22 = 2147$

sub-bottom-from-top   (1 0) The student always subtracts the top digit from the bottom digit. If the bottom digit is smaller, he decrements the top digit and adds ten to the bottom before subtracting. If the bottom digit is zero, however, he writes the top digit in the answer. If the top digit is one greater than the bottom he writes nine. $4723 - 3065 = 9742$

sub-copy-least-bottom-most-top   (1 0) The student does not subtract. Instead she copies digits from the exercise to fill in the answer space. She copies the leftmost digit from the top number and the other digits from the bottom number. $648 - 231 = 631$

sub-one-over-blanks   (0 2) When there are blanks in the bottom number, the student subtracts one from the top digit. $548 - 2 = 436$

top-after-borrow   (0 0 $) After borrowing correctly, the student writes the top digit of the column in the answer instead of adding ten and subtracting. $34 - 17 = 14$

top-instead-of-borrow-from-zero   (0 1 $) If a column requires borrowing from a zero, the student merely writes the top digit in the answer instead. $305 - 177 = 135$

top-instead-of-borrow   (0 0) If a column requires borrowing, the student merely writes the top digit in the answer instead. $34 - 17 = 24$

top-instead-of-borrow-except-last   (0 0 $) If a column requires borrowing, and it is not the penultimate column, then the student merely writes the top digit in the answer instead. $348 - 179 = 178$

top-instead-of-borrow-from-double-zero   (0 0 $) If a column requires borrowing from multiple zeros, the student merely writes the top digit in the answer instead. $3004 - 7 = 3004$

top-instead-of-borrow-unless-bottom-smaller   (0 0 $) If a column requires borrowing from a column where $T \leq B$, the student merely writes the top digit in the answer instead. $345 - 177 = 175$

treat-top-zero-as-nine   (0 0) In a $0 - N$ column the student does not borrow but instead treats the zero as if it were a nine. $30 - 4 = 35$

treat-top-zero-as-ten   (0 1) In a $0 - N$ column the student adds ten to it correctly, but does not change any column to the left. $40 - 27 = 23$

X − N = 0-after-borrow   (0 1) If a column has been borrowed from, the student writes zero as its answer. $234 - 115 = 109$

X − N = N-after-borrow   (0 1) If a column has been borrowed from, the student writes the bottom digit as its answer. $234 - 165 = 169$

zero-after-borrow   (0 0) When a column requires a borrow, the student decrements correctly, but writes zero as the answer. $65 - 48 = 10$

zero-borrow-from-zero   (? ?) When borrowing from a zero, instead of changing the zero to nine and continuing, the student crosses out the zero and writes zero above it. This bug has exactly the same effects as Stops-Borrow-At-Zero, both in isolation and as a member of compound bugs. Hence it is in Debuggy's data base, but no objective statistics on its occurrence are available, although several cases of it have been found with hand analysis. Accordingly some fraction of Stops-Borrow-At-Zero's occurrences should actually be counted as occurrences of Zero-Borrow-From-Zero.

$$
\begin{array}{r}
0 \\
7\ \cancel{0}^1 2 \\
-\quad\ 8 \\
\hline
7\ 0\ 4
\end{array}
$$

zero-instead-of-borrow-from-zero   (0 0) If a column requires borrowing from a zero, the student writes zero as its answer instead.

$$
\begin{array}{r}
7\ 0\ 2 \\
-\quad\ 8 \\
\hline
7\ 0\ 0
\end{array}
\qquad
\begin{array}{r}
7\ 0\ 2 \\
-3\ 4\ 8 \\
\hline
3\ 6\ 0
\end{array}
$$

zero-instead-of-borrow   (1 4) If a column rquires borrowing, the student writes zero as its answer instead. $42 - 16 = 30$

Coercions

Debuggy's diagnosis sometimes contains coercions. A coercion is a modifier that Debuggy includes in a diagnosis to improve the fit of the bugs to the student's errors. Most often these slightly perturb the definitions of bugs. For example, certain bugs modify the procedure so that on occasion it writes column answers that are greater than 9. Some students who have these bugs apparently know from addition that there should be only one answer digit per column, so they only write the units digit. To capture this, the coercion !Write-Units-Digit-Only is added to the diagnoses of such students by Debuggy. Coercions can easily be picked out because their names have exclamation points as prefixes. For more on coercions, see Burton 1982.

!forget-to-write-units-digit   (0 0) The student solves the units column in his normal way, but forgets to write the answer down.

!last-column-special-sub   (0 0) The last column of the problem is not solved in the student's usual (buggy) way, but is solved correctly instead.

!last-full-column-special-sub   (0 0) The last column of the problem, provided its bottom is not blank, is not solved in the student's usual (buggy) way, but is solved correctly instead.

!N − 0 = N-always   (0 0) Columns with $N - 0$ are exceptions to whatever the student's usual (buggy) method is. They are always answered correctly.

!only-write-units-digit   (0 2) Some bugs, such as Don't-Decrement-Zero or N − N-Causes-Borrow, cause the student to generate two-digit numbers as the answer to some columns. This coercion modifies the bugs so that only the units digit is written down in such cases. Without the coercion both digits are written.

!sub-units-special   (0 1) The units columns is an exception to whatever the student usually does. It is answered correctly.

!write-left-ten   (0 3) If the top row has one and zero as the leftmost digits, they are treated as if there was a ten in the penultimate column. Thus bugs like diff-0 − N = N are not triggered by that column.

!zero-minus-blank-is-zero   (0 0) A column with a zero over a blank is answered correctly, regardless of what the student's bug is.

!touched-0 − N = 0   (0 0 $) If Borrow-Across-Zero skipped over a zero during borrowing, then the column containing that zero is answered by a zero.

!touched-0 − N = blank   (0 0 $) If Borrow-Across-Zero skipped over a zero during borrowing, then the column containing that zero is answered by a blank.

!touched-0 − N = N   (0 4 $) If Borrow-Across-Zero skipped over a zero during borrowing, then the column containing that zero is answered by writing the bottom digit in the answer.

!touched-0-is-ten   (0 6 $) If Borrow-Across-Zero skipped over a zero during borrowing, then the column containing that zero is answered as if it had a ten instead of a zero on top.

!touched-0-is-quit   (0 0 $) If borrow-across-zero skipped over a zero during borrowing, then the student quits working the exercise when she reaches the column containing that zero.

!touched-double-zero-is-quit   (0 0 $) If borrow-across-zero skips two or more zeros, then the student quits when he reaches the column containing the second zero.

Star Bugs

Sierra currrently generates seven star bugs. A star bug is an un-observed bug that is so unusual that the diagnosticians on the project believe that it will never be observed. Most of these bugs are caused by the lack of a FOREACH construct in Sierra's representation language.

*blank-instead-of-borrow-from-double-zero   (0 0 $) If a column requires a borrow from multiple zeros, then its answer is left blank. $30056 − 11191 = 289$ 5

*blank-with-borrow   (0 0 $) Borrows occur successfully, but the answers to columns requiring borrows are left blank anyway. $345 − 170 = 1$ 5

*only-do-first & last-columns   (0 0 $) The first and last columns of the problem are done correctly, but other columns are omitted. $345 − 111 = 2$ 4

*only-do-units & tens   (0 0 $) The student does only the first two columns of the problem then quits. $345 − 111 = 34$

*only-do-units-unless-two-columns   (0 0 $) The student solves two-column problems correctly, but does only the units columns of problems with three or more columns. $345 − 111 = 4, 34 − 23 = 11$

*quit-when-second-bottom-blank   (0 0 $) The student correctly solves columns with a blank in the bottom if the column is the left most column in the problem. If the column is not leftmost, then the student quits doing the exercise. $345 − 3 = 2, 345 − 22 = 323$

*skip-interior-bottom-blank   (0 0 $) The student correctly solves columns with a blank in the bottom if the column is the leftmost column in the problem. If the column is not leftmost, then the student leaves its answer blank. $345 - 3 = 3\ \ 2$

Chapter 10

Observed Bug Sets

Of the 1,147 students in the Southbay study, Debuggy analyzed 375 (33 percent) as having bugs. This appendix lists those 375 diagnoses, ordered by their frequency of occurrence. Diagnoses are shown in parentheses. There are 134 distinct diagnoses, or which only 35 occurred more than once. These 35 diagnoses, however, account for 276 of the 375 cases (74 percent).

103 occurrences
(Smaller-From-Larger)

34 occurrences
(Stops-Borrow-At-Zero)

13 occurrences
(Borrow-Across-Zero)

10 occurrences
(Borrow-From-Zero)
(Borrow-No-Decrement)

7 occurrences
(Stops-Borrow-At-Zero   Diff-0 − N = N)

6 occurrences
(Always-Borrow-Left)
(Borrow-Across-Zero   !Touched-0-Is-Ten)
(Borrow-Across-Zero   Diff-0 − N = N)
(Borrow-Across-Zero-Over-Zero   Borrow-Across-Zero-Over-Blank)
(Stops-Borrow-At-Zero   Borrow-Once-Then-Smaller-From-Larger
Diff-0 − N = N)

5 occurrences
(Borrow-No-Decrement   Diff-0 − N = N)

4 occurrences
(0 − N = N-Except-After-Borrow)
(Borrow-Across-Zero   Diff-0 − N = 0)

(Diff-0 − N = N   Zero-Instead-of-Borrow)
(Borrow-No-Decrement-Except-Last)
(Don't-Decrement-Zero-Over-Blank)
(Quit-When-Bottom-Blank   Smaller-From-Larger)

3 occurrences
(Borrow-into-One = Ten   Stops-Borrow-At-Zero)
(Decrement-All-On-Multiple-Zero)
(Decrement-Multiple-Zeros-By-Number-To-Right)
(Don't-Decrement-Zero)
(Smaller-From-Larger   Ignore-Leftmost-One-Over-Blank)

2 occurrences
(0 − N = 0-After-Borrow)
(Borrow-Across-Second-Zero)
(Borrow-Across-Top-Smaller-Decrementing-To)
(Borrow-Don't-Decrement-Top-Smaller)
(Borrow-Don't-Decrement-Unless-Bottom-Smaller)
(Borrow-Only-From-Top-Smaller   Borrow-Across-Zero-Over-Zero
Borrow-Across-Zero-Over-Blank)
(Smaller-From-Larger-Instead-of-Borrow-From-Zero
Borrow-Once-Then-Smaller-From-Larger   Diff-0 − N = N)
(Smaller-From-Larger-Instead-of-Borrow-Unless-Bottom-Smaller)
(Stops-Borrow-At-Multiple-Zero)
(Stops-Borrow-At-Zero   Small-From-Larger-When-Borrowed-From)
(Stops-Borrow-At-Zero   Diff-0 − N = N
Smaller-From-Larger-When-Borrowed-From)
(Stutter-Subtract)

1 occurrence
(!Only-Write-Units-Digit   N − N-After-Borrow-Causes-Borrow)
(!Only-Write-Units-Digit   Stops-Borrow-At-Multiple-Zero
N − N-After-Borrow-Causes-Borrow)
(!Sub-Units-Special   Borrow-Across-Zero   Smaller-From-Larger)
(!Write-Left-Ten   Smaller-From-Larger   Diff-0 − N = 0)
(!Write-Left-Ten   Borrow-Across-Second-Zero   Diff-0 − N = N)
(!Write-Left-Ten   Forget-Borrow-Over-Blanks   Diff-0 − N = N)
(!Touched-0 − N = N   Borrow-Across-Zero   Diff-N − 0 = 0)
(!Touched-0 − N = N   Borrow-Across-Zero
Borrow-Once-Then-Smaller-From-Larger)
(!Touched-0 − N = N   Borrow-Across-Zero
Borrow-Across-Second-Zero   Smaller-From-Larger-When-
Borrowed-From)
(0 − N = N-After-Borrow   Borrow-Across-Zero-Over-Zero
Borrow-Across-Zero-Over-Blank)

(0 − N = N-After-Borrow   N − N = 1-After-Borrow
Smaller-From-Larger-Instead-of-Borrow-From-Zero)
(0 − N = N-After-Borrow)
(0 − N = N-Except-After-Borrow   1 − 1 = 0-After-Borrow)
(0 − N = N-Except-After-Borrow   1 − 1 = 1-After-Borrow)
(1 − 1 = 0-After-Borrow)
(Add-Instead-of-Sub)
(Add-LR-Decrement-Answer-Carry-To-Right)
(Blank-Instead-of-Borrow   Diff-0 − N = N)
(Borrow-Across-Second-Zero   Don't-Write-Zero)
(Borrow-Across-Second-Zero   Borrow-Skip-Equal)
(Borrow-Across-Zero   0 − N = 0-Except-After-Borrow)
(Borrow-Across-Zero   1 − 1 = 0-After-Borrow)
(Borrow-Across-Zero   Borrow-Once-Then-Smaller-From-Larger
0 − N = N-Except-After-Borrow)
(Borrow-Across-Zero   Sub-One-Over-Blank
0 − N = N-After-Borrow   0 − N = N-Except-After-Borrow)
(Borrow-Across-Zero   Borrow-Skip-Equal)
(Borrow-Across-Zero   Quit-When-Bottom-Blank
0 − N = 0-After-Borrow)
(Borrow-Across-Zero   Forget-Borrow-Over-Blanks   Diff-0 − N = N)
(Borrow-Across-Zero   Ignore-Leftmost-One-Over-Blank
Borrow-Skip-Equal)
(Borrow-Across-Zero   !Touched-0 − N = N)
(Borrow-Across-Zero-Over-Zero   0 − N = N-Except-After-Borrow
1 − 1 = 0-After-Borrow)
(Borrow-Across-Zero-Over-Zero)
(Borrow-Don't-Decrement-Unless-Bottom-Smaller
X − N = 0-After-Borrow)
(Borrow-Don't-Decrement-Unless-Bottom-Smaller
Don't-Write-Zero)
(Borrow-From-All-Zero)
(Borrow-From-Bottom-Instead-of-Zero   Diff-0 − N = N)
(Borrow-From-One-Is-Nine   Borrow-From-Zero
Diff-0 − N = N-When-Borrow-From-Zero)
(Borrow-From-One-Is-Nine   Borrow-From-Zero
Don't-Decrement-Zero-Over-Blank)
(Borrow-From-One-Is-Ten   Borrow-From-Zero-Is-Ten
Borrow-Only-Once)
(Borrow-From-Zero   0 − N = 0-After-Borrow)
(Borrow-From-Zero   0 − N = N-After-Borrow)
(Borrow-From-Zero & Left-Ten-OK   0 − N = N-After-Borrow)
(Borrow-From-Zero & Left-Ten-OK)

(Borrow-From-Zero-Is-Ten)
(Borrow-Into-One = Ten   Decrement-Multiple-Zeros-By-Number-To-Left)
(Borrow-Into-One = Ten   Decrement-Multiple-Zeros-By-Number-To-Right   Borrow-Across-Zero-Over-Zero)
(Borrow-No-Decrement   Smaller-From-Larger-Except-Last
Smaller-From-Larger-Instead-of-Borrow-Unless-Bottom-Smaller
Diff-0 − N = N)
(Borrow-No-Decrement   Sub-One-Over-Blank)
(Borrow-No-Decrement-Except-Last   Treat-Top-Zero-As-Ten)
(Borrow-No-Decrement-Except-Last   Decrement-Top-Leq-Is-Eight
X − N = N-After-Borrow)
(Borrow-Only-From-Top-Smaller)
(Borrow-Only-From-Top-Smaller   0 − N = N-After-Borrow)
(Borrow-Treat-One-As-Zero   N − N = 1-After-Borrow
Don't-Decrement-Zero-Over-Blank)
(Borrow-Unit-Diff   Only-Do-Units)
(Can't-Subtract)
(Decrement-All-On-Multiple-Zero   Double-Decrement-One)
(Decrement-Leftmost-Zero-Only)
(Decrement-Multiple-Zeros-By-Number-To-Left)
(Decrement-Top-Leq-Is-Eight)
(Diff-0 − N = 0   Diff-N − 0 = 0   Stops-Borrow-At-Zero)
(Diff-0 − N = 0   Diff-N − 0 = 0   Doesn't-Borrow-Except-Last
Smaller-From-Larger-Instead-of-Borrow-Unless-Bottom-Smaller)
(Diff-0 − N = 0   Diff-N − 0 = 0   Smaller-From-Larger-Except-Last
Smaller-From-Larger-Instead-of-Borrow-Unless-Bottom-Smaller)
(Diff-0 − N = N)
(Diff-0 − N = N   Diff-N − 0 = 0)
(Diff-0 − N = N-When-Borrow-From-Zero   Don't-Decrement-Zero)
(Diff-N − 0 = 0   Smaller-From-Larger   Diff-0 − N = 0)
(Don't-Decrement-Zero   Borrow-Across-Second-Zero)
(Don't-Decrement-Zero   1 − 1 = 0-After-Borrow)
(Don't-Decrement-Zero   Decrement-One-To-Eleven)
(Don't-Decrement-Zero-Unit-Bottom-Blank
Borrow-Across-Zero-Over-Zero)
(Don't-Write-Zero)
(Double-Decrement-One)
(Double-Decrement-One   Smaller-From-Larger-When-Borrowed-From)
(Forget-Borrow-Over-Blanks)
(Forget-Borrow-Over-Blanks
Borrow-Don't-Decrement-Top-Smaller   Borrow-Skip-Equal)

(Ignore-Leftmost-One-Over-Blank
Decrement-All-On-Multiple-Zero)
(N − N-Causes-Borrow)
(N − N = 1-After-Borrow   0 − N = N-Except-After-Borrow)
(N − N = 1-After-Borrow)
(Simple-Problem-Stutter-Subtract)
(Smaller-From-Larger   Diff-N − N = N   Diff-0 − N = 0)
(Smaller-From-Larger   Diff-0 − N = 0)
(Smaller-From-Larger-Except-Last
Decrement-All-On-Multiple-Zero)
(Smaller-From-Larger-Instead-of-Borrow-From-Zero
Diff-0 − N = N   Smaller-From-Larger-When-Borrowed-From)
(Smaller-From-Larger-Instead-of-Borrow-From-Zero
Borrow-Once-Then-Smaller-From-Larger)
(Smaller-From-Larger-Instead-of-Borrow-Unless-Bottom-Smaller
0 − N = N-Except-After-Borrow)
(Smaller-From-Larger-Instead-of-Borrow-Unless-Bottom-Smaller
Top-Instead-of-Borrow-From-Zero   Diff-0 − N = N)
(Stops-Borrow-At-Zero   0 − N = 0-Except-After-Borrow
1 − 1 = 0-After-Borrow)
(Stops-Borrow-At-Zero   Borrow-Across-Zero-Over-Zero
1 − 1 = 0-After-Borrow)
(Stops-Borrow-At-Zero   1 − 1 = 1-After-Borrow)
(Stops-Borrow-At-Zero   Diff-0 − N = 0)
(Stops-Borrow-At-Zero   Ignore-Leftmost-One-Over-Blank)
(Stops-Borrow-At-Zero   0 − N = 0-After-Borrow)
(Stops-Borrow-At-Zero   Borrow-Once-Then-Smaller-From-Larger)
(Stops-Borrow-At-Zero   1 − 1 = 0-After-Borrow)
(Stops-Borrow-At-Zero   Diff-0 − N = N   Don't-Write-Zero)
(Sub-Bottom-From-Top)
(Sub-Copy-Least-Bottom-Most-Top)
(Zero-Instead-of-Borrow)

Notes

1. Following Newell and Simon (1972), I use "memorization" to stand for the processes of encoding, storage, and retrieval.
2. Indeed their existence was predicted by Brown and VanLehn (1980), but concrete evidence was not found until several years late (VanLehn 1982).
3. The basic idea would be to adopt Singley and Anderson's (1985) hypothesis that transfer consists of sharing productions between two procedures. This hypothesis makes specific prediction such as, for instance, that bugs in whole-number subtraction show up as bugs in fraction subtraction. But such a prediction is pretty mundane, and almost any theory would be consistent with such a finding. Because transfer data do not seem as likely as bug data to reveal inadequacies in this theory, no efforts have been made to apply the theory to them.
4. In the second column of 2.3, the frequencies for the No-op and Barge-on repairs are estimates. Because the bugs Stops-Borrow-At-Zero and Zero-Borrow-From-Zero generate exactly the same answers, Debuggy does not distinguish between them, so they must be distinguished by looking at the scratch marks. Of the 74 cases that Debuggy judged to be either Stops-Borrow-At-Zero or Zero-Borrow-From-Zero, I classified 37 (50 percent) as Zero-Borrow-From-Zero, 10 (13 percent) as Stops-Borrow-At-Zero, 15 (21 percent) as bug migrations between the two bugs, and 12 (16 percent) as unclear cases (often because the student did not use scratch marks). To make these estimates compatible with the figures used in the rest of 2.3, the $37:10$ ratio of clear cases of the two bugs was applied to the 74-bug figure, thus arriving at an estimate of 58 bugs worth of Zero-Borrow-From-Zero and 16 bugs worth of Stops-Borrow-At-Zero.
5. Grapes (Anderson, Farrell, and Saurers 1984) uses a tree of goals. However, when Grapes wants to find the currently active goal, the tree is always searched in depth-first, left-to-right order. This makes it equivalent to a stack, as far as controlling execution is concerned. The reason that Grapes keeps a whole tree of goals is that the tree is used to constrain production compounding, which is a form of automatic learning built into Grapes. Soar (Laird, Rosenbloom, and Newell 1986) has a goal stack, but it also has the ability to save that stack away when it takes an interrupt and start a new stack to handle the interrupt (J. Laird, personal communication, June 1987). Interrupt processing can in turn be interrupted, causing that stack to be saved away as well. The storage of saved stacks is itself a stack, so that when an interrupt's processing is finished, execution resumes with the most recently saved stack. As with Grapes this stack of stacks is meant not to increase the flexibility for controlling execution but rather to prohibit Soar's automatic learning mechanisms from learning things that people do not learn.
6. At the end of the preceding chapter, an anecdote was told about assembling a barbecue grill in which the repair to one impasse was to partially disassemble the

grill to recover some bolts that had been mistakenly used up. This certainly qual-
ifies as a type of backing up, but it is also neither chronological nor hierarchical. A
chronoglogical Back-up would undo *all* the actions back to a certain point, whereas
this type of backing up only undid the relevant actions, those involving particular
bolts. This type of backing up corresponds most closely to dependency-directed
Back-up (de Kleer 1986). Dependency-directed Back-up requires knowledge of the
dependencies among actions. It is plausible to assume that the person assembling
the grill had such knowledge and arithmetic students do not. Indeed lack of knowledge about the dependencies among arithmetic actions is implied by the ateleological assumption. So for arithmetic one would not expect to see dependency-direct
Back-up, although one might see it in more knowledge-rich domains. It is an open
question whether chronlogical Back-up occurs in knowledge-rich domains.

7. Grapes (Anderson, Farrel, and Saurers 1984) has a near equivalent to FOREACH in
its *MAPGOAL function.

8. There is a well-known trick for interpreting tail-recursions so that the stack depth
remains constant. OR goals are not pushed on the stack, and AND goals are only
pushed on the stack if they have subgoals left that have not yet been executed. This
trick could be applied here to block the star bugs, but unfortunately it also blocks
some good bugs, namely, those generated by returning to Sub1Col or Borrow.

9. These correspond, strangely enough, to the situational primitives Adjacent and
Ordered.

10. Explanation-based learning is another form of learning that takes in an example
and yields a generalization in return (Mitchell, Keller, and Kedar-Cabelli 1986).
However, this type of learning requires extensive background knowledge, enough
to be able to derive the example from first principles. If it is procedural knowledge
that is being learned, this type of knowledge would be the teleology (design) for
the procedures. However, we have already assumed that students in this domain
either do not possess or do not use appropriate teleological knowledge. So
explanation-based learning would not be a good model of the type of induction
found in this domain, at least not by those students who have bugs.

11. Forgetting the only rule that calls a subprocedure creates a procedure that is identical to a procedure that lacks the subprocedure altogether. Although forgetting is a
perfectly reasonable hypothesis for where the incomplete subprocedure bugs come
from, the intention is not to align psychological processes like forgetting with formal mechanisms like deletion.

12. Technically a context-free grammar with arguments is an affix grammar (Koster
1971) or an attribute grammar (Knuth 1968). The power of the grammar depends
on the power of the function vocabulary for computing arguments. Even the simple function vocabulary consisting of C and $C + 1$ makes the resulting affix grammar language able to express grammars that are higher in the Chomsky hierarchy
than context-free grammars. For instance, it is simple to write an affix grammar that
generates the language $a^n b^n c^n$.

13. Actually the derivational version space only contains grammars of a restricted
form, called *simple* grammars. The major restriction is that rules must have more
one member on their right sides. Given this restriction, the derivational version
space is finite. However, this restriction is violated by some of the procedures that
seem necessary for generating the bug data. For instance, the rule Sub1Col $\rightarrow$ Diff
violates the restriction, but it is necessary for generating many bugs (that is, bugs
with a decision impasse at Sub1Col or a Back-up to Sub1Col). So the theory cannot
assume that procedures are simple. Thus the derivational version space referred to

in the text is not exactly the same as the one for simple context-free grammars, although it has many of the same features.

14. Actually because simplicity of procedures has not been assumed, the set is even larger. Indeed it is infinite.

15. Sierra obtains instances by parsing a given example, then inferring from the parse tree what the pattern matches must have been. For instance, if an OR node has two rules, and only one appears in the parse tree at a certain point, then it can be inferred that the test pattern for the rule in the tree matched, whereas the other rule's test pattern did not match. Thus the situation at that point in the tree is a positive instance of one rule's test pattern and a negative instance of the other rule's test pattern.

16. For predicate calculus patterns A is a generalization of B if and only if B implies A. The ability to answer any question of the form "Is A a generalization of B?" is equivalent to the ability to prove theorems in predicate calculus. If calculation of S and G requires the ability to calcuate the answer to the question "Is A a generalization of B?" for any A or B, then S and G cannot be effectively computed, because there is no algorithm that effectively proves any theorem in the predicate calculus. It is not clear if requiring patterns to be reduced allows S and G ato be effectively computed (compare with VanLehn and Ball 1986).

17. To avoid the impasse, we must also assume that the test patern for the non borrow rule has $T > B$ rather than the correct predicate, $T \geq B$. Alternatively we could adopt a new assumption about the execution that handles cases of conflict resolution in a systematic way. For instance, it could be assumed that the first rule whose pattern matches is chosen, or the rule whose pattern is largest among the rules whose patterns match is chosen. Sierra uses the first conflict resolution strategy because it simplifies pattern acquisition (VanLehn 1983b).

18. The overly general test pattern bugs (except those whose derivation involves deletion) have the odd characteristic that they get the correct answer on all problems, provided that carrying is performed whenever a column's answer is greater than nine. Because one must look carefully at the scratch marks to detect these bugs, they might not even be detected by the teacher.

19. Diagnostic testing undoubtedly has some effect on a student's knowledge state. If the model were used to make predictions about students who are tested twice, it would be advisable to route the solver-modified Pi back up to the learner (see the discussion of the patch hypothesis in chapter 2). This is not done in the current version of Sierra because almost all of the data come from students who were tested just once. Some were tested twice, but without intervening instruction.

20. The observed bugs generated by HB alone are Borrow-Don't-Decrement-Zero-Unless-Bottom-Smaller, Borrow-Across-Second-Zero, Borrow-From-One-Is-Nine, Borrow-From-One-Is-Ten, Borrow-From-Zero, Borrow-from-Zero-Is-Ten, Stops-Borrow-At-Multiple-Zero, Forget-Borrow-Over-Blanks, and Smaller-From-Larger-Instead-of-Borrow-Unless-Bottom-Smaller.

21. This version of Sierra was based on the assumption that test patterns were members of the G set of the appropriate version space. Hence negative instances, such as those encountered in solving $34 - 13$ are crucial for learning when to borrow. If Sierra were revised to conform to the ambiguous primitives assumption, then this lesson would have to replace the negative examples with natural-language descriptions of when to borrow, so that "less than" could be interpreted ambiguously. Either way the output of L_4 would contain procedures with $T \leq B$ as the test pattern.

22. The observed bug Borrow-From-Bottom-Instead-of-Zero can be generated by modifying the grammar rule that defines COL. The bugs Zero-Instead-of-Borrow and Zero-Instead-of-Borrow-From-Zero can be generated by modifying the primitive SUB function so that it implements $max(0, x - y)$ instead of $|x - y|$. Zero-Instead-of-Borrow is an observed bug, but its partner is not. The bug Zero-Borrow-From-Zero, an observed bug, can be generated by modifying the SUB1 primitive so that it imlements $max(0, x - 1)$ instead of $|x - 1|$. Thus there are the four bugs (three of which are observed bugs) that are generated by a nonstandard P_0 and not by the standard P_0.

23. At the end of the Southbay experiment, the data base had grown to 103 bugs. The tests had been thoroughly examined by myself and two other analysts. We were confident that few bugs, if any, lurked undiscovered in the data. However, our confidence was misplaced. Sierra invented some bugs that we did not think of, and six of them turned out to be observed bugs!

24. The subset included all the core procedures from the H core procedure tree, except the P100 branch and the Blk branch. From the SF core procedure tree only the procedures that are in a direct line from the root to the "ok" procedure were run. From the HB core procedure tree only three procedures were run: 3c-1bor, 3c-1bfz, and 3c-1bfid. All the deletion-generated procedures from H and HB were run, except for those that are generated before three-column subtraction is taught. Because a FOREACH loop would change the early procedures' structures, the procedures that would be generated from them by deletion would be different as well.

25. The bugs are Borrow-Across-Second-Zero (7 occurrences), Doesn't-Borrow-Except-Last (1 occurrence), Only-Do-Units (1 occurrence), Smaller-From-Larger-Except-Last (3 occurrences), Smaller-From-Larger-Instead-of-Borrow-Unless-Bottom-Smaller (7 occurrences), and Top-Instead-of-Borrow-From-Zero (1 occurrence).

26. The bugs generated by the current version of the theory and not the old version are estimated to be Borrow-Across-Zero-Over-Blank, Borrow-Across-Zero-Over-Zero, Borrow-Don't-Decrement-Top-Smaller, Borrow-From-Bottom-Instead-of-Zero, Borrow-Once-Then-Smaller-From-Larger, Don't-Decrement-Zero-Over-Blank, Don't-Decrement-Zero-Over-Zero, N-N-After-Borrow-Causes-Borrow, N-N = 1-After-Borrow, Smaller-From-Larger-When-Borrowed-From, Top-Instead-of-Borrow, X-N = 0-After-Borrow, and X − N = N-After-Borrow. Of these 13 bugs, 11 are observed bugs.

References

Amarel, S. (1971). Representations and modelling in problems of program formation. In B. Meltzer and D. Michie, eds. *Machine Intelligence 6*. New York: Elsevier.

Anderson, J. R. (1982). Acquisition of cognitive skill. *Psychological Review* 89 : 369–406.

Anderson, J. R. (1983). *The Architecture of Cognition*. Cambridge, MA: Harvard University Press.

Anderson, J. R. (1987). Skill acquisition: Compilation of weak-method problem solutions. *Psychological Review* 94(2) : 192–210

Anderson, J. R. (1989). The analogical origins of errors in problem solving. In D. Klahr and K. Kotovosky, eds. *Complex Information Processing: The Impact of Herbert A. Simon*. Hillsdale, NJ: Erlbaum.

Anderson J. R. (1990). *The Adaptive Character of Thought*. Hillsdale, NJ: Erlbaum (in press).

Anderson, J. R., and Thompson, R. (1989). Use of analogy in a production system architecture. In S. Vosniadou and A. Ortory, eds. *Similarity and Analogical Reasoning*. New York: Cambridge.

Anderson, J. R., Farrell, R., and Saurers, R. (1984). Learning to program in LISP. *Cognitive Science* 8 : 87–129.

Anderson, J. R., Kline, P. J., and Beasley, C. M. (1979). A general learning theory and its application to schema abstraction. *The Psychology of Learning and Motivation* 13 : 277–318.

Anzai, Y., and Simon, H. A. (1979). The theory of learning by doing. *Psychological Review* 86 : 124–140.

Ashlock, R. B. (1976). *Error Patterns in Computation*. Columbus, OH: Bell and Howell.

Austin, J. L. (1962). *How to Do Things with Words*. New York, NY: Oxford University Press.

Badre, N. A. (1972). *Computer Learning from English Text*. Berkeley, CA: University of California at Berkeley, Electronic Research Laboratory.

Bauer, M. A. (1975). A basis for the acquisition of procedures from protocols. In *Proceedings of the Fourth IJCAI*. Los Altos, CA: Morgan Kaufmann.

Biermann, A. W. (1972). On the inference of Turing machines from sample computations. *Artificial Intelligence* 10 : 181–198.

Biermann, A. W. (1978). The inference of regular LISP programs from examples. *IEEE Transactions on Systems, Man, and Cybernetics* SMC-8(8) : 585–600.

Bloom, B. S. (1984). The two sigma effect: The search for methods of group instruction as effective as one-to-one tutoring. *Educational Researcher* 13 : 3–16.

Brown, J. S., and Burton, R. B. (1978). Diagnostic models for procedural bugs in basic mathematical skills. *Cognitive Science* 2 : 155–192.

Brown, J. S. & VanLehn, K. (1980). Repair theory: A generative theory of bugs in procedural skills. *Cognitive Science* 4 : 379–426.

Brownell, W. A. (1941). The evaluation of learning in arithmetic. In *Arithmetic in General Education*. Washington, DC: Council of Teachers of Mathematics.

Brueckner, L. J. (1930). *Diagnostic and Remedial Teaching in Arithmetic*. Philadelphia, PA: Winston.

Burton, R. B. (1982). Diagnosing bugs in a simple procedural skill. In D. H. Sleeman, and J. S. Brown, eds. *Intelligent Tutoring Systems*. New York: Academic, pp. 157–183.

Buswell, G. T. (1926). *Diagnostic Studies in Arithmetic*. Chicago, IL: University of Chicago Press.

Carbonell, J. G. (1986). Derivational analogy: A theory of reconstructive problem solving and expertise acquisition. In R. S. Michalski, J. G. Carbonell, and T. M. Mitchell, eds. *Machine Learning: An Artificial Intelligence Approach*. Vol. 2. Los Altos, CA: Morgan Kaufmann.

Chi, M. T. H., Bassok, M., Lewis, M., Reimann, P, and Glaser, R. (1989). Learning problem solving skills from studying examples. *Cognitive Science* 13 (2): 145–182.

Chomsky, N. (1965). *Aspects of Syntax*. Cambridge, MA: MIT Press.

Cox, L. S. (1975). Diagnosing and remediating systematic errors in addition and subtraction computation. *The Arithmetic Teacher* 22:151–157.

Davis, J. H., Carey, J. H., Foxman, P. N., and Tarr, D. B. (1968). Verbalization, experimenter presence, and problem solving. *Journal or Personality and Social Psychology* 8:299–302.

de Kleer, J. (1986). An assumption-based truth maintenance system. *Artificial Intelligence* 28:127–162.

Gagne, R. H. & Smith, E.C. (1962). A study of the effects of verbalization on problem solving. *Journal of Experimental Psychology* 63:12–18.

Greeno, J. G., Riley, M. S., and Gelman, R. (1984). Conceptual competence and children's counting. *Cognitive Psychology* 16:94–143.

Haugeland, J. (1978). The nature and plausibility of Cognitivism. *The Behavioral and Brain Sciences* 2: 215–260.

Hayes, J. R., and Simon, H. A. (1974). Understanding written problem instructions. In L. W. Gregg, ed. *Knowledge and Cognition*. Hillsdale, NJ: Erlbaum. Reprinted in H. A. Simon (1979). *Models of Thought*. New Haven, CT: Yale University Press.

Hempel, C. G. (1945). Studies in the logic of confirmation. *Mind* 54:1–26, 97–121.

Hempel, C. G. (1966). *Philosophy of Natural Science*. Englewood Cliffs, NJ: Prentice Hall.

Hiebert, J. (1986). *Conceptual and Procedural Knowledge: The Case of Mathematics*. Hillsdale, NJ: Erlbaum.

Hunt, E. B., Marin, J, and Stone, P. J. (1966). *Experiments in Induction*. New York: Academic.

Just, A. J.,and Carpenter, P. A. (1987). *The Psychology of Reading and Language Comprehensionl*. Boston, MA: Allyn and Bacon.

Klahr, D., Langley, P., and Neches, R. (1987). *Production System Models of Learning and Development*. Cambridge, MA: MIT Press.

Knuth, D. E. (1968). Semantics of context-free languages. *Mathematical Systems Theory* 2:127–145.

Koster, C. H. A. (1971). Affix grammars. In J. E. Peck, ed. *ALGOL 68 Implementation*. Amsterdam: North-Holland.

Laird, J. (1983). *Universal Subgoaling*. Carnegie-Mellon University Computer Science Department, Pittsburgh, PA.

Laird, J.E. (1986). *Soar User's Manual*. Tech. Rep. ISL-15. Xerox Palo Alto research Center.

Laird, J. E., Newell, A., and Rosenbloom, P. S. (1987). Soar: An architecture for general intelligence. *Artificial Intelligence* 33:1–64.

Laird, J. E., Rosenbloom, P. S., and Newell, A. (1986). Chunking in Soar: The anatomy of a general learning mechanism. *Machine Learning* 1(1):11–46.

Langley, P. (1982). Strategy acquisition governed by experimentation. In *Proceedings of the European Conference on Artificial Intelligence.*

Langley, P. (1987). A general theory of discrimination learning. In Klahr, D., Langley, P., and Neches, R., ed. *Production System Models of Learning and Development.* Cambridge, MA: MIT Press.

Langley, P., and Ohlsson, S. (1984). Automated cognitive modeling. In *Proceedings of AAAI-84.* Los Altos, CA: Morgan Kaufmann.

Lankford, F. G. (1972). *Some Computational Strategies of Seventh Grade Pupils.* University of Virginia, Charlottesville, VA.

LeFevre, J., and Dixon, P. (1986). Do written instructions need examples? *Cognition and Instruction* 3(1):1–30.

Leinhardt, G. (1987). Development of an expert explanation: An analysis of a sequence of subtraction lessons. *Cognition and Instruction* 4(4):225–282

Marr, D. (1977). Artificial Intelligence — a personal view. *Artificial Intelligence* 9:37–48.

Matz, M. (1982). Towards a process model for high school algebra errors. In D. Sleeman, and J. S. Brown, eds. *Intelligent Tutoring Systems.* New York, NY: Academic Press.

Mitchell, T. M. (1980). *The Need for Biases in Learning Generalizations.* Tech. Rep. CBM-TR-117. Rutgers University Computer Science Department, Rutgers, NJ.

Mitchell, T. M., Keller, R. M., and Kedar-Cabelli, S. T. (1986). Explanation-based generalization: A unifying view. *Machine Learning* 1(1):47–80.

Mitchell, T. M., Utgoff, P. E., and Banerji, R. B. (1983). Learning problem-solving heuristics by experimentation. In R. S. Michalski, T. M. Mitchell, and J. Carbonell, eds. *Machine Learning.* Palo (Alto, CA: Tioga Press.)

Neves, D. M. (1981). *Learning Procedures from Examples.* Doctoral dissertation. Department to Psychology, Carnegie-Mellon University, Pittsburgh, PA.

Newell, A. (1973). Production systems: Models of control structures. In W. C. Chase, ed. *Visual Information Processing.* New York: Academic.

Newell, A. (1978). Harpy, production systems and human cognition. In R. Cole ed. *Perception and Production of Fluent Speech.* New York: Erlbaum.

Newell, A. (1980). Reasoning, problem solving and decision processes: The problem space as a fundamental category. In R. Nickerson, ed. *Attention and Performance VIII* Hillsdale, NJ: Erlbaum.

Newell, A. (1987). Unified Theories of Cognition: The 1987 William James Lectures. On video tape, available from Harvard University, Department of Psychology. Cambridge, MA.

Newell, A. (1990). *Universal Theories of Cognition.* Cambridge, MA: Harvard University Press (in press.)

Newell, A. & Simon, H. A. (1972). *Human Problem Soving.* Englewood Cliffs, NJ: Prentice-Hall.

Norman, D. A. (1981). Categorization of action slips. *Psychological Review* 88:1–15.

Nowlan, S. (1987). *Parse Completion: A Study of an Inductive Domain.* Tech. Rep. PCG11. Department of Psychology, Carnegie-Mellon Univeersity, Pittsburgh, PA.

Ohlsson, S. (1980). *A Possible Path to Expertise in the Three-Term Series Problem.* Working paper. Cognitive Seminar, Department of Psychology, University of Stockholm.

Pirolli, P. L., and Anderson, J. R. (1985). The role of learning from examples in the acquisition of recursive programming skills. *Canadian Journal of Psychology* 39(2):240–272.

Pylyshyn, Z. (1973). The role of competence theories in cognitive psychology. *Journal of Psycholinguistics Research* 2:21–50.

Pylyshyn, Z. W. (1984). *Computation and Cognition.* Cambridge, MA: MIT Press.

Resnick, L. (1982). Syntax and semantics in learning to subtract. In T. Carpenter, J. Moser, and T. Romberg, eds. *A Cognitive Perspective.* Hillsdale, NJ: Erlbaum.

Rich, C. (1981). *Inspection Methods in Programming.* Tech. Rep. AI-TR-604. Massachusetts Institute of Technology, Artifical Intelligence Laboratory, Cambridge, MA.

Rivest, R., and Sloan, R. (1988). Learning complicated concepts reliably and usefully. *Proceedings of AAAI-88.* In Los Altos, CA: Morgan-Kanfmon.

Roberts, G. H. (1968). The failure strategies of third grade arithmetic pupils. *The Arithmetic Teacher* 15:442–446.

Rosenbloom, P., and Newell, A. (1981). Mechanisms of skill acquisition and the law of practice. In J. R. Anderson, ed. *Cognitive Skills and their Acquisition.* New York: Erlbaum.

Rumelhart, D. E., McClelland, J. L., and The PDP Research Group. (1986). *Parallel Distributed Processing: Explorations in the Microstructure of Cognition. Volume 1.* Cambridge, MA: MIT Press.

Rumelhart, D. E., and Norman, D. A. (1978). Accretion, Tuning and Restructuring: Three modes of learning. In J. W. Cotton, and R. Klatzky, eds. *Semantic Factors in Cognition.* Hillsdale, NJ: Erlbaum.

Shaw, D. J., Standiford, S. N., Klein, M. F., and Tatsuoka, K. K. (1982). *Error Analysis of Fraction Arithmetic–Selected Case Studies.* Tech. Report 82-2-NIE. Computer-based Education Research Laboratory, University of Illinois at Urbana-Champaign.

Shaw, D. E., Swartout, W. R., and Green, C. C. (1975). Inferring Lisp programs from examples. In *Proceedings of the Fourth IJCAI.* Los Altos, CA: William Kaufmann.

Siegler, R. S. (1987). Strategy choices in subtraction. In J. Sloboda, and D. Rogers, eds. *Cognitive Processes in Mathematics.* Oxford, UK: Oxford University Press, pp. 81–106.

Siegler, R. S. (1988). Strategy choice procedures and the development of multiplication skill. *Journal of Experimental Psychology: General* 117:258–275.

Siegler, R. S., and Shrager, J. (1984). Strategy choices in addition: How do children know what to do? In C. Sophian, ed. *Origins of Cognitive Skill.* Hillsdale, NJ: Erlbaum.

Siklossy, L., and Sykes, D. A. (1975). Automatic program synthesis from example problems. In *Proceedings of IJCAI-4 .* Los Altos, CA: William Kaufmann.

Silver, B. (1986). Precondition analysis: Learning control information. In Michalski, R. S., Carbonell, J. G., and Mitchell, T. M., eds. *Machine Learning: An Artificial Intelligence Approach.* Vol. 2. Los Altos, CA: Morgan Kaufmann.

Simon, H. A. (1975). The functional equivalence of problem solving skills. *Cognitive Psychology* 7:268–288. Reprinted in H. A. Simon (1979). *Models of Thought.* New Haven, CT: Yale University Press.

Singley, M. K., and Anderson J. R. (1985). The transfer of text-editing skill. *International Journal of Man-Machine Studies* 22:403–423

Sleeman, D. H. (1982). Assessing competence in basic algebra. In D. Sleeman, and J. S. Brown, eds. *Intelligent Tutoring Systems.* New York, NY: Academic. 186–199.

Sleeman, D. H. (1984a). Basic algebra revised: A study with 14-year olds. *International Journal of Man-Machine Studies* 22 (2):127–150.

Sleeman, D. (1984b). An attempt to understand students' understanding of basic algebra. *Cognitive Science* 8 : 387–412.

Suchman, L. A. (1987). *Plans and Situated Actions: The Problem of Human-Machine Communication*. New York: Cambridge University Press.

Suchman, L., and Wynn, E. (1984). Procedures and problesm in the office. *Office: Technology and People* 2 : 133–154.

Sussman, G. J. (1976). *A Computational Model of Skill Acquisition*. New York: Springer Verlag.

Sussman, G. J., Winograd, T., and Charniak, E. (1971). *Micro-Planner Reference Manual*. Tech. Rep. AIM-302A. Massachusetts Institute of Technology, Artificial Intelligence Laboratory, Cambridge, MA.

Tatsuoka, K. K. (1984). *Analysis of Errors in Fraction Addition and Subtraction Problems*. Tech. Rep. Computer-based Education Research Laboratory, University of Illinois at Urbana-Champaign.

Tatsuoka, K. K., and Baillie, R. (1982). *Rule Space, the Product Space of Two Score Components in Signed-Number Subtraction: An Approach to Dealing with Inconsistent Use of Erroneous Rules*. Tech. Rep. 82-3-ONR. Computer-based Education Research Laboratory, University of Illinois at Urbana-Champaign.

Valiant, L. G. (1984). A theory of the learnable. *Communications of the ACM* 27(11) : 1134–1142.

VanLehn, K. (1974). *The Sail User Manual*. Tech. Rep. AI Laboratory, Stanford University, Stanford, CA.

VanLehn, K. (1982). Bugs are not enough: Empirical studies of bugs, impasses and repairs in procedural skills. *The Journal of Mathematical Behavior* 3(2) : 3–71.

VanLehn, K. (1983a). Human skill acquisition: Theory, model and psychological validation. In *Proceedings of AAAI-83*. Los Altos, CA: Morgan Kaufmann.

VanLehn, K. (1983b). The representation of procedures in repair theory. In H. P. Ginsberg, ed. *The Development of Mathematical Thinking*. Hillsdale, NJ: Erlbaum.

VanLehn, K. (1983c). Felicity conditions for human skill acquisition: Validating an AI-bared theory. Tech. Rep. CIS-21, Xerox Palo Alto Research Center, Palo Alto, CA.

VanLehn, K. (1985). *Theory Reform Caused by an Argumentation Tool*. Tech. Rep. ISL-11. Xerox Palo Alto Research Center.

VanLehn, K. (1986). Arithmetic procedures are induced from examples. In J. Hiebert, ed. *Conceptual and Procedural Knowledge: The Case of Mathematics*. Hillsdale, NJ: Erlbaum.

VanLehn, K. (1987). Learning one subprocedure per lesson. *Artificial Intelligence* 31(1) : 1–40.

VanLehn, K. (1988). Toward a theory of impasse-driven learning. In H. Mandl, and A. Lesgold, eds. *Learning Issues for Intelligent Tutoring Systems*. New York, NY: Springer Verlag.

VanLehn, K. (1989). Efficient specialization of relational concepts. *Machine Learning* (in press).

VanLehn, K. (1990). *Architectures for Intelligence*. Hillsdale, NJ: Erlbaum (in press).

VanLehn, K., and Ball, W. (1987). A version space for context-free grammars. *Machine learning*. 2(1) : 39–74.

VanLehn, K., and Brown, J. S. (1980). Planning nets: A representation for formalizing analogies and semantic models of procedural skills. In R. E. Snow, P. A. Federico, and W. E. Montague, eds. *Aptitude, Learning and Instruction: Cognitive Process Analyses*. Hillsdale, NJ: Erlbaum.

VanLehn, K., Brown, J. S., and Greeno, J. G. (1984). Competitive argumentation in computational theories of cognition. In W. Kinsch, J. Miller, and P. Polson, eds. *Methods and Tactics in Cognitive Science*. Hillsdale, NJ: Erlbaum.

Waters, R. C. (1978). *Automatic analysis of the logical structure of programs*. Tech. Rep, 492. Massachusetts Institute of Technology, Artificial Intelligence Lab, Cambridge, MA.

Wilder, L., and Harvey, D. J. (1971). Overt and covert verbalization in problem solving. *Speech Monographs* 38 : 171–176.

Woods, W. A. Kaplan, R., Nash-Webber, B. (1972). *The Lunar Sciences Natural Language Information System*. BBN Rep. 2378. Cambridge, MA: Bolt, Beranek, and Newman.

Young, R. M., and O'Shea, T. (1981). Errors in children's subtraction.*Cognitive Science* 5 : 153–177.

Index